DISCORD AND DIRECTION

DISCORD AND DIRECTION

The Postmodern Writing Program Administrator

edited by

SHARON JAMES MCGEE
CAROLYN HANDA

UTAH STATE UNIVERSITY PRESS
Logan, Utah

Utah State University Press
Logan, Utah 84322–7800

Manufactured in the United States of America
Cover design by Barbara Yale Read

Library of Congress Cataloging-in-Publication Data

Discord and direction : the postmodern writing program administrator / edited by Sharon James McGee, Carolyn Handa.
p. cm.
Includes bibliographical references and index.
ISBN 0-87421-617-6
1. English language–Rhetoric–Study and teaching. 2. Report writing–Study and teaching (Higher)
3. Postmodernism and higher education.
4. Writing centers–Administration. I. McGee, Sharon James. II. Handa, Carolyn.
PE1404.D576 2005
808'.042'0711–dc22

2005014248

For DAVID *who did more of his fair share of household chores whenever a publication deadline approached and who is always my biggest supporter. And for* JOHN *and* SAMUEL *who are my life's true work.*

SJM

As always, for my mother, PATRICIA SAKON HANDA, *this one is also for* JOSEPHINE *and "the boys":* SHEA, EVAN, EVERETT, DONOVAN, *and* AARON. *May your young lives be Peppered by joyful success and cooling Shadows that protect you from life's most searing disappointments.*

CH

CONTENTS

ACKNOWLEDGMENTS

Like many good ideas, the one for this collection came during a conversation we had at a CCCC Convention a few years ago. By the following CCCC we brought our idea to the Utah State University Press booth and talked with Michael Spooner who expressed interest in our proposal. From that point forward, Michael has been an outstanding editor. We thank him for his vision, timely responses to even the most mundane questions, and patience when we felt as if we were herding bees rather than collecting and editing essays. To our contributors, each of whom brings a unique and thoughtful perspective to the work of WPAs: thank you for adding your voices to this collection. We also owe a special debt of gratitude to the two anonymous readers of this manuscript who provided us with detailed, useful guidance—and we might add did so very promptly—to shape this work further.

INTRODUCTION
Postmodernity and Writing Programs

Sharon James McGee and Carolyn Handa

> *At worst, postmodernism appears to be a mysterious, if ubiquitous, ingredient—like raspberry vinegar, which instantly turns any recipe into nouvelle cuisine.*
>
> —Ihab Hassan

CONTENDING WITH THE POSTMODERN

A cliché in academe generally and English departments particularly, postmodernism has come to characterize nearly every facet of contemporary life from Architecture, art, and film to feminism, music, lifestyles, photography, and popular culture. One day soon, we suspect, we might even find that someone has constructed a Zoo labeled "postmodern." Given such a ubiquitous term, we need to clarify exactly what parts of the term "postmodern" we focus on in this collection and explain why we use the term in conjunction with the work of Writing Program Administrators (WPAs) today.

Ihab Hassan jokes above about what overusing the term "postmodernism," at worst, can come to. Postmodernism, by its very nature, defies easy description. Hassan, however, tries to pin down some of its characteristics when he says that "postmodernism . . . remains, at best, an equivocal concept, a disjunctive category, doubly modified by the impetus of the phenomenon itself and by the shifting perceptions of its critics" (1987, 173). He constructs a two-column chart juxtaposing postmodernism and modernism, the movement it reacts against (see appendix). This schema has helped composition scholars like Lester Faigley to envision their field in relation to the two movements.[1] Faigley argues that composition studies itself sides more with modernism than postmodernism in the ways that most writing instructors have conceived of "good" student texts. He draws on Hassan's list of modern and postmodern oppositions to illustrate his point that modernist qualities such as "romanticism, form (conjunctive, closed), purpose, design, hierarchy, mastery/logos, and art object/finished work" have traditionally been rewarded by composition teachers (Faigley 1992, 14).

Postmodernism's elusiveness and its focus on cultural contexts has also provided the focus for an entire collection of essays (Harkin and Schilb 1991), each exploring or problematizing different aspects of postmodern thought such as feminism, Marxism, dialogism, and ideology in relation to composition studies as a field.

On the whole, however, postmodernism's questioning of hierarchy, its recognition of paratactic associations, and its rejection of grand narratives, among other characteristics, has yet to be explored in depth in relation to the work of Writing Program Administrators. Their work places WPAs in spaces outside of the microcosmic individual classroom where they must assume overarching responsibility for a program, a curriculum, a group of instructors with varying pedagogies and technological expertise, the program in relation to a university with its own particular mission, and to a state with its view of accountability and assessment. If we shift our focus from the field of composition studies as a whole to the typical writing program, then, we actually find that the other column of Hassan's list, the one itemizing postmodern qualities, aptly characterizes the world in which WPAs must function everyday: "antiform (disjunctive, open), chance, anarchy, exhaustion/silence, process, participation, dispersal, rhetoric, parataxis, metonymy, antinarrative" (Hassan 1987, 91). One problem of being a WPA might be exactly this disjunction between modernism and postmodernism: while composition studies still might side more with modernism, the WPA's job in reality must grapple with postmodern habits of thought and ways of being. This struggle may or may not mean that WPAs adopt a postmodern stance; it does mean, however, that the being a WPA requires dealing with postmodern fallout. Discord, anyone?

The argument behind this collection of essays is that the cultural and intellectual legacies of postmodernism affect the world of WPAs daily as they work to direct their composition programs and tackle the unending numbers of problems that invariably arise. Postmodernism, furthermore, offers a useful lens through which to view the work of WPAs and to examine those various cultural and institutional issues that shape their work. As Stuart Sim posits:

> In a general sense . . . postmodernism is to be regarded as a rejection of many, if not most, of the cultural certainties on which life in the West has been structured over the last couple of centuries. . . . [P]ostmodernists are invariably

> critical of universalizing theories, . . . as well as being anti-authoritarian in their outlook. To move from the modern to the postmodern is to embrace scepticism about what our culture stands for and strives for. (Sim 2001, vii)

For the individual WPA, Sim's particular notion of postmodernism is useful. Because WPA scholarship has begun to theorize what it means to *be* a WPA and work as a WPA, we can see postmodernity in action: the tensions of bureaucratic power wielding and the deconstruction of that notion, and the WPA as a collaborative, decentered facilitator depending on participatory processes that make writing programs open, fluid associations rather than closed, rigid hierarchies (see for example Dickson 1993; Gunner 1994; Goodburn and Leverenz 1998; Mirtz and Cullen 2002; Gunner 2002). WPAs are, as Sim suggests, criticizing universalizing theories, examining alternatives to authoritative positions, and doing so with savvy coupled with constructive skepticism.

WPAs, then, may assume a postmodern stance in relation to hierarchies surrounding their programs. But they may also be the targets of postmodern skepticism themselves as they attempt to direct university programs that are some of the most complex of all on campus. In fact, few university programs see the entire (or almost entire) entering and transfer-student population during the year, yet writing programs are expected to hone these students' academic literacy, polish their grammar and syntax problems, and send them off into their "real" courses free of comma splices. WPAs often find themselves negotiating with local hierarchies—that is, university administrators—as they develop, change, enhance, and staff their writing programs. All WPAs, likewise, are trying to create or struggling to maintain a writing program that is a site of plenty—plenty of resources, staff, and budgets—where robust, well-developed, and innovative writing courses thrive to meet the needs of students, the academy, the workplace, and society, a site where student learning and literacy occupy the core of all decision making.

Considering the postmodern legacy in relation to WPA work can help us understand our situations so that we may then act, fully realizing that any act will always be fraught with discord; while grand writing program narratives are no longer possible in our time, reflections within the context of specific programs can help us all understand the multiple philosophical and ideological forces that constantly press on any WPA. Like Weiser and Rose, we take issue with Stanley Fish's dismissal of post-structural theory as it relates to administration, or at least, writing program administration.

> According to Fish, theory, or at least poststructural theory, "can't tell you what to do or what not to do" (Fish 2000, 16); so it's of no consequence to an administrator whose job it is to act—or to decide not to act. We want to argue that theory should not be judged by whether it tells us how to solve our administrative problems; instead, we should look to theory for its explanatory power—its power to help us understand the problem, situations, and contexts of our work, thus positioning us to make decisions and take actions based on a richer understanding of their implications. (Weiser and Rose 2002, 189)

Postmodern theory can move us from discord to direction, if even (and always) only momentarily.

"POSTMODERNISM ONCE MORE—THAT BREACH HAS BEGUN TO YAWN!" —IHAB HASSAN

As we mentioned above, Faigley refers to select characteristics of modernism as schematized by Hassan. We are using the antitheses of these terms plus a few others to explore how postmodernism affects the WPA. Hassan is useful because in developing his schema, he "draws on ideas in many fields—rhetoric, linguistics, literary theory, philosophy, anthropology, psychoanalysis, political science, even theology—and draws on many authors—European and American—aligned with diverse movements, groups, and views" (Hassan 1987, 92). The chart, then (see p. 17), represents the essence of many thinkers' ideas about postmodernism—not just one's or not just Hassan's.

Antiform (disjunctive/open)

The writing programs that WPAs guide are much farther from being reified structures than we might like to think, much closer instead to the disjunctive, open antiform that Hassan posits as a postmodern quality. The comings and goings of part-timers, faculty, students, and staff all mark a writing program as porous on at least the level of personnel. On the level of placement, curricula, and pedagogy as well, a writing program bears disjunctive and open characteristics. Many placement procedures may not measure what writing faculty want to know before placing students in different writing classes; placement tests used may be antiquated or adopted for financial reasons, and university administrators may even have decided on placement procedures without consulting the WPA. Students in various classes come to the university with different skills and training from various high schools and colleges.

Some are basic writers; some are honors students. Some may never even have written expository essays, attaining their placement in first-semester composition merely by taking the requisite number of literature and speech classes before arriving on the university campus. We can never count on a given level of knowledge when we begin teaching any class. So a writing program's curriculum must be open enough to account for all this variance.

Chance

Along with being structurally open, a writing program is subject to chance as far as its teaching personnel and the administrators to whom a WPA must report. WPAs must often rely in large part on graduate teaching assistants and part-time faculty, getting to choose only among students who apply for particular programs and part-time faculty who live in the immediate area. These teaching assistants may or may not arrive with prior teaching experience; part-timers may or may not be familiar with a program's goals and outcomes. Sometimes in emergencies, teaching assistants (TAs) or part-timers may even be hired without input from the WPA, yet the WPA must work with these teaching staff members.

The administrators with whom WPAs work are also left to chance, at least as far as input from WPAs is concerned when these administrators are hired, promoted, or elected. Occasionally we do have sympathetic provosts or deans who support our programs and understand the myriad pressures competing for a WPA's attention. We can never be certain, however, when these supportive administrators will move on to other positions, especially in today's economy, and those administrators' exact opposites will take over. Department heads also rotate, and may or may not be sympathetic to writing studies, may or may not have even taught composition, may or may not consider the WPA's work legitimate and administrative.

And again, WPAs are left open to legislative chance, state budgets, and the ways higher education and accreditation are viewed by elected officials and their appointed boards, who also go and come and go, usually misapprehending the implications of their acts and the effects of these acts as they work their ways through university systems. As Stanley Fish so cheerfully and bluntly puts it:

> In the past few months I have been saying nasty things . . . about members of Congress, Illinois state representatives and senators, the governor of Illinois, the governor's budget director, and the governor-appointed Illinois Board of

> Higher Education (IBHE). I have called these people ignorant, misinformed, demagogic, dishonest, slipshod, and have repeatedly suggested that when it comes to colleges and universities either they don't know what they're talking about or (and this is worse) they do know and are deliberately setting out to destroy public higher education. (Fish 2004, C1)

If WPAs' programs exist in anything but a vacuum, well, then, we are subject to some board somewhere, and we definitely occupy prime real estate at the foot of Chance, aka the goddess Fortuna.

Anarchy

While Hassan offers the term "anarchy" as a condition of postmodernism, we prefer the less warlike term "resistance" to articulate the tensions that exist throughout writing programs. From the students in our classes to our TAs, our instructors, and even ourselves, the potential for resistance exists throughout a writing program. Students in our first- and second-semester classes often question their need to take them since they have already had four years of high school English. The lack of student motivation to write or participate in writing classes is the least confrontational form of resistance. Resistance, then, can show up in a variety of actions—from passive lack of participation to outright hostility. And students, of course, are not the only ones who can balk. TAs, part-timers, and tenured faculty can resist changes to the writing curriculum or not buy into the pedagogy and theory behind a writing program. The tension between academic freedom and program continuity, outcomes, and the mission statements of both the university and program may be the source of outright refusal to teach classes within the program's broad outlines. TAs may have had different pedagogical experiences, causing a disjunction between what they've experienced and what they are learning about teaching writing. Or resistance may come from meager working conditions often faced by adjunct faculty: no office + no benefits = no cooperation. Whatever the reasons, postmodern WPAs realize that because resistance can often be fruitful instead of destructive, they seek to engage it.

Even WPAs themselves are sometimes the source of resistance. For example, we may often tend to come into a program and make what we think are much-needed changes to that program. Such a well-intentioned effort, however, invariably causes an upheaval—a type of anarchy—because few people, particularly academics, embrace sweeping reform. Rather, these changes may cause hurt feelings, resistance, and isolation. In addition to being the source of discomfort, furthermore, WPAs may be *seen* by others as anarchists if they try to break down or gain access to institutional hierarchies that do not recognize their positions as legitimate administrators.

Exhaustion/silence

Exhaustion and silence can often overcome anyone running a writing program. In February 2000, a post entitled "Thinkin' about quittin'" on the WPA listserv resulted in a lengthy and impassioned thread in which WPAs across the country reflected on the toll exhaustion and silence can take on them.[2]

Sometimes exhaustion and silence go hand in hand, but not necessarily. Exhaustion may begin with the investment that directors make in their own writing programs: having seen what works in other programs and being theoretically and pedagogically grounded, WPAs want their writing programs to be strong, vibrant sites of student and faculty engagement with writing. Sometimes a department or university, however, understands neither the WPA's professionalization nor investment in the program. Directors may have attended the WPA workshop, taken a graduate course in writing program administration, or served as an assistant WPA during graduate school. They are likely members of the Council of Writing Program Administrators and its listserv, and attend WPA sessions at the Conference on College Composition and Communication or the annual WPA conference. Unfortunately a collective departmental attitude that "any warm body can teach composition," and more so that "any warm body can serve as a WPA," wears on those possessing the skills and qualifications needed for running a writing program.

A WPA's exhaustion can be both mental and physical, and it can be triggered from both inside and outside the department. A few representative types of scenarios that cause exhaustion:

- WPAs without tenure invest half of their time administering a writing program, and the other half performing the activities acceptable for tenure. These activities would normally constitute a faculty member's full responsibility, but untenured WPAs often find themselves acting as two—both the administrator and the tenure-seeking assistant professor.
- A postmodern WPA may also feel the tension caused by an administrator's typical position at the top of a hierarchy and a postmodernist's resistance to this position while simultaneously trying to foster a collaborative program.

- A WPA's exhaustion can also arise from trying to meet the expectations that stakeholders across and outside of the university have about student writing ability and program consistency across multiple sections of first-year writing classes.
- A WPA's routine can cause physical exhaustion: listening to student complaints and problems, facilitating solutions between multiple parties, mentoring adjunct faculty and TAs, and completing bureaucratic paperwork. The physical exhaustion can vary depending upon how much (if any) help the WPA receives from a sympathetic administration and any funding available for an associate director, assistant director, secretary, and student workers.

WPAs without tenure or job security often work to the point of exhaustion while their precarious positions may also force them into silence either to keep their jobs or receive tenure. In addition, silence can affect WPAs when they feel as if their expert opinions are undervalued by the department or unit or when upper administrators make budget, curricular, or class-load decisions without WPA input. Finally, students themselves may in effect silence a WPA when they assume that the director, by virtue of being part of a hierarchy, will automatically overlook their concerns.

Process

A writing program always exists in process, never achieving the finished state of a final product. A writing program is always in the middle of staffing courses, revising curriculum, and meeting departmental, university, or even legislative mandates, so no part of it can ever be complete. For the WPA, a job that is never finished and always in flux can be incredibly frustrating. On the other hand, by recognizing that we are not striving for the "well-wrought urn," as formalist literary theorists would call it, can be liberating. A writing program, unlike a piece of art, cannot exist apart from its historical, social, and political contexts. Even conditions far removed from its local contexts can affect the writing program, necessitating changes in curriculum. For example, political upheaval in eastern Europe during the past decade caused many to flee and immigrate to the United States. Suddenly, colleges and universities on the West Coast faced an influx of entirely new students in writing classes; to meet these students' needs, changes in writing programs were necessary—both in training faculty how to teach this unfamiliar, non-native, English-speaking population and in revising curriculum.

Participation

Modernist notions of administration rely on hierarchical structures. Postmodern notions of administration, on the other hand, deconstruct hierarchies, opening spaces for alternative visions of administration built on collaboration and community. Quite a few writing programs fit a modernist scenario so those that do could benefit from a postmodern examination, especially in regard to participation. Fostering participation among faculty, administration, and graduate students keeps the WPA from being an administrator in the modernist sense—a hierarchical dogmatist—instead becoming a postmodern facilitator who clears space for and values the input of others. Having other perspectives involved in shaping a writing program gives rise to ideas and perspectives that no one person could have thought about alone. Furthermore, participation allows people to claim ownership of or investment in the program. Rather than having decisions made unilaterally for them, they make decisions collaboratively.[3]

Dispersal

In Hassan's schema, centering lies in opposition to dispersal; the notion of centering that we are working with is embodied in the phrase "the ivory tower." Some years ago, and perhaps still even today, many writing programs viewed expository writing classes from the perspective of English studies or as a way to prepare students to become English majors—very much an ivory tower approach to composition. Viewed through a postmodern lens, however, first-year composition should not strictly fall under the purview of the English department or the writing program; it is an investment made by the university to hone students' writing abilities so that—regardless of their majors—they can move through the academy as well as into the workplace and the community. Postmodern theories of composition deconstruct the notion that the only way to write is to write like English professors. Students who come through the writing program are literally dispersed throughout the university, so the job of the writing program is not to indoctrinate or conscript them into one notion of writing. Our job is to provide them with the heuristics needed to meet the demanding writing challenges they face as students, workers, and citizens.

Rhetoric

As Ed White says, rhetoric lies at the heart of writing programs (1995, 133). While this may not be the case for all writing programs, for postmodernists it should be. In Hassan's schema, rhetoric sits across from semantics. As opposed concepts, rhetoric suggests contextualized meanings full of possibilities while semantics suggests decontextualized meanings that bring closure. In "Argument as Emergence, Rhetoric as Love," Jim Corder argues "Language is closure, but the generative ethos I am trying to identify uses language to shove back the restraints of closure, to make a commodious universe, to stretch words out beyond our private universe" (1985, 31). The rhetorical form of language then embodies postmodernism's workings: rhetoric strives to include, defying the modernist tendency to exclude. Being rhetorical means that we consider audience, even though this consideration can bring about either harmony or discord.

WPAs are in some ways preoccupied with questions of audience, or if not, they should be. James Porter argues that audience is a complex consideration for the rhetorician: "The question rhetoric theory asks is, Where is the audience located? In the text? Outside the text? Or somewhere in between? The answer is all of the above and, at the same time, none of the above" (1992, x). Not caring about who your audience is (at one extreme) or misjudging your audience (at the other)—there's the conflict.[4] Direction can take place when WPAs rethink their audiences.

Parataxis

While parataxis may initially seem an odd way to characterize writing programs, it does describe, structurally, how parts of a writing program relate to each other and how a WPA relates to the university community. Rhetorically, parataxis is the technique of placing clauses one after the other without using transitions to indicate whether the clauses relate to each other as coordinates or whether clauses occupy subordinate positions in relation to one main clause. Thinking of parataxis as a federation or association of clauses or ideas (or in the case of a writing program and its university, as a multi-vocal or collaborative venture) might help to visualize the more horizontal grouping implied by paratactic junctions. Writing programs, indeed, work best when many voices work together rather than following one giving orders at the top of a hierarchy.[5] Multiple-author papers and coedited collections, another way to view parataxis, also characterize the scholarly work of composition studies as a discipline.

Parts of a writing program such as the first-year writing component, advanced composition, technical and business writing, and writing across the curriculum may all exist within the writing program without any one part taking precedence. And the WPA, too, must view the job of WPA as one devoted to forming alliances with other departments and with administrators, rather than considering the writing program superior to other disciplines on the subject of expertise in writing. In order to accomplish the task of making good writing a priority on campus, a WPA must think paratactically, that is, associatively.

Metonymy

Like parataxis, metonymy as a figure of speech is associative. It refers to using an object closely related to another as a stand-in or substitute for that other. Metonymy functions by contiguity; close proximity or association triggers the replacement. Understanding a metonymic figure thus entails grasping the association between the two objects in order to understand how and why the substitution was made. The standard example of metonymy given in poetry and grammar handbooks is something like "The White House decided to raise taxes." We understand the association between the president, the Senate, the Congress, *and* the White House and thus accept the contiguous relationship as the reason for substituting the house for the people who occupy it.

WPAs and their writing programs also work metonymically. The WPA comes, in the mind of some, to stand for the writing program and vice versa. The WPA also becomes a substitute for the curriculum and the pedagogy of that program.

Anti-narrative

And so, as we have worked our way through these notions of postmodernism, we can see that writing programs have no grand narratives, no monolithic construction. Each writing program, situated within its unique historical, social, and political frame, faces its own distinct set of circumstances, discord, and direction. There are no generalizations, only petite narratives specific to each locale.

DISCORD TO DIRECTION OR DIRECTION TO DISCORD

> *[P]ostmodernism is useful precisely because it breaks down given relationships and hierarchies. But just as importantly . . . that breakdown in itself is always undertaken (or ought to be undertaken) as part of a continual process of rebuilding.*
>
> —Johndan Johnson-Eilola

Administering a writing program, then, in this time of postmodern influences, might seem to range in description from discordant at the best to absurd at the worst, from barely controlled chaos at one moment to utter pandemonium if we stopped to list each and every aspect of our work that can never be absolutely controlled. But the breakdowns we experience are, as Johndan Johnson-Eilola says above, "part of a continual process of rebuilding" (2002, 434). Each chapter in this collection tackles a problem local to its author's writing program or experience as a WPA, and each responds to existing discord in creative ways that move toward rebuilding and redirection. The first four, while sometimes drawing on specific programs for illustrative points, are more global in their approaches.

Opening the discussion is Deborah Holdstein, who addresses the hopelessness and powerlessness that inevitably occur for WPAs at some point. To help them overcome these debilitating inevitabilities and think in terms of possibilities, she argues that outside evaluations can provide leverage and assist the WPA in moving beyond discord on the departmental, collegiate, and university levels. Holdstein notes that because discord usually prompts consultant-evaluator visits it can be productive, rather than paralyzing, thus leading to rebuilding. Consultant-evaluator visits help break down the modernist hierarchy and give WPAs access to external leverage that may lead to productive action.

For Jeanne Gunner, postmodern discord arises when a writing program's narrative ossifies and smothers any dialectic. At this point, a writing program sees itself, like the pastoral genre, as being untroubled, isolated from the cultural milieu and its conflicts. Drawing upon pastoral theory, Gunner shows how change to the writing program is seen not only as disruptive but morally transgressive. She uses this theory to urge WPAs to avoid metonymizing pragmatic local changes as shifts in larger ideological systems, perpetuating the writing program as an untroubled, pastoral product.

Using metaphors drawn from judicial relations work to counteract the "religious" orientation governing the training of writing teachers in this country, Christy Desmet sees judicial notions of equity, as developed in critical legal studies and feminist jurisprudence, as an *institutional* way of negotiating the tension between sameness and difference that defines any community of teachers. She argues that the concept of equivalence—an alternative to both the fetishization of individuality and the insistence on legislated "community"—is key to negotiating that postmodern tension on a programmatic level. Desmet further describes transitions from one teaching culture to another in order to offer a theoretical description of the ways in which judicial principles might guide a composition curriculum and teacher training program based on a commitment to equity and equivalence and remain perpetually *in medias res.*

Especially when they conceive of the university as a hierarchy, WPAs can often feel that disappointment and dissatisfaction permeate their identities: to view the institution as such a vertical structure allows for only one point of access—the bottom. Sharon James McGee uses postmodern mapping to help WPAs visualize both the role of the writing program and the WPA's situation within an institutional structure that is more like a web with multiple points of access. By examining the loci of power within an institution, WPAs can both forge strategic alliances within what they can now recognize as a webbed confederation as well as engage in institutional critique. As a tool that breaks down the notion of hierarchy, a postmodern map predicated on process and change offers a more fluid than static representation of institutions at particular moments and from particular angles, rather than depicting them as reified, oppressive monoliths.

The next two chapters examine basic writing as a part of university writing programs. Anthony Edgington, Marcy Tucker, Karen Ware, and Brian Huot discuss the discord that arises when a WPA misjudges an audience and the motivation of different levels of administration. For these coauthors, mainstreaming within the field of composition studies connotes attention to political, pedagogical, and theoretical concerns about labeling students, teaching them differently, keeping class size small, and providing basic writing students with equal access to the university. For the dean and provost, however, leaving basic writing in place was costly in terms of economics and prestige, and to this audience accepting mainstreaming meant finances rather than ethics: their priority was "the bottom line" and their motivation was eventually to "get out of the remedial business." Although no redirection can take place for these coauthors, they offer their cautionary tale to help us realize that the concept of mainstreaming for a WPA must transcend semantics and include contextualized implications.

As Edgington et al. point out, basic writing is one of the few courses in the university in which so many people believe that they have a stake and that they can decide what is best for the students, the course, and the university. Keith Rhodes sees pragmaticism as an alternative way for WPAs to view writing program administration, in particular directing basic writing programs. To embrace pragmaticist thinking helps WPAs see choices that can move a program closer to what it would choose ethically, realizing that to evolve means to relinquish a rigid notion of commitment to a singular ideal. Pragmaticist administrators find value in a variety of possibilities and choose the option that comes closest to bettering the program.

In the twenty-first century WPAs must consider technology's place and power within their programs, and the next two chapters focus on the possibility of technology improving pedagogy. Mike Palmquist discusses the dissonance that he feels as both a scholar of computers and writing and a former WPA: the superficiality of using computers as an application to composition rather than having technology interwoven inextricably into the pedagogy. This felt difficulty leads him to critique the tendency to keep technology on the surface of our pedagogy rather than making it deeply rooted in our practice.

Fred Kemp's chapter is one possible resolution to the felt difficulty of technology's still superficial place in many writing programs' praxis, but more importantly to the disjunction between composition theory, teaching practices, and administrative accountability we find in large writing programs staffed primarily by graduate students and part-timers. Kemp argues for a paradigm shift in the way that technology is integrated into the writing classroom and the opportunities for alternative pedagogy that result. This shift, pregnant with possibilities for radically changing the way that writing is taught, learned, and administered, decenters the teacher's identity by proposing a split between a teacher in the classroom and a teacher to provide feedback on writing. A romantic notion of teaching identity thus becomes replaced by a postmodern solution separating the roles into the advocate for students and the commentator on and grader of students' papers. This split is founded on students' using technology to submit papers and receive anonymous comments. Further, Kemp challenges the grand notion of what a writing classroom should be like, one teacher and twenty-plus students who learn at the feet of the master—even if the teacher subscribes to a student-centered classroom—without trying to create an alternative grand narrative. Perhaps many WPAs will find this piece aggravating because it calls for such a disjunction between theory and lived reality, between classroom performance and assessing student work, and gives the illusion that instructors lose personal control of their classrooms and that the curriculum becomes systematized.

The next three chapters analyze how local problems have been addressed in creative ways at particular institutions, and while the solutions remain site-specific the way of solving these problems gives us pause for reflection. Like Fred Kemp, Richard Miller and Michael Cripps are questioning long-held beliefs about teaching writing, but in their case they ask whether it belongs only to those in English departments. A confluence of events—enrollment growth, union stipulations about faculty teaching loads, and the university's wise decision to reduce TA loads from three courses a year to two—precipitated a need for creative problem solving in order to staff over 150 sections of first-year writing. "The Rutgers Solution" was a postmodern one, breaking the traditional disciplinary boundaries to train and mentor TAs both in and outside of English. As a result of this solution, the teaching of writing is now dispersed throughout the university community and its graduate students rather than being centered in the English department or the writing program.

Although program assessment is becoming more important in academia, many academics resist or at least dislike it because internal administrators and external agencies usually mandate it. Academics sometimes consider assessment as an anti-intellectual waste of their energy, believing that it forces labeling and pigeonholing. Susanmarie Harrington discusses the notion of communal assessment where value is constructed by the community—in other words, what do we value, why do we value it, and what can we learn from it? She argues that reconceptualizing program assessment can change the way WPAs do their jobs for the better. Using her campus's recent experience with the Consultant-Evaluator Service of the Council of Writing Program Administrators as a touchstone, Harrington develops principles to guide administrative efforts with program assessment into the daily work of a program by seeing assessment as constructed within the community and as a source for reflection rather than an imposition from higher-level administrators.

Andrew Billings, Teddi Fishman, Morgan Gresham, Angie Justice, Michael Neal, Barbara Ramirez, Summer Smith Taylor, Melissa Tidwell Powell, Donna Winchell, Kathleen Blake Yancey, and Art Young describe the struggles and successes of one project in Clemson University's Communication Across the Curriculum (CAC) effort: Poetry Across the Curriculum (PAC). This project's paratactic activities constitute one way to address the problem of "follow up" after faculty development workshops. Instead of attending isolated workshops on various topics, faculty now meet regularly as teachers to share experiences using this teaching strategy, to generate collaborative scholarship on teaching and learning, to become sustaining members of an interdisciplinary academic community, and to open up themselves and their students to "thinking outside the box." The CAC effort emphasizes multiple modes and media, partners with a wide variety of groups, embodies the postmodern concept of physical and virtual space, and embraces an open and malleable philosophy for sustainable program development.

The final chapter uses a local problem of metonymic reduction and resistance to analyze the effects of visual misperception on a writing program's instructors. Carolyn Handa asks what happens when power and language come together in the space of an online document attempting to convey a sense of identity. She answers this question by arguing that when the visual portrayal of identity comes to be misperceived as an exercise of one person's power rather than an interactive construction of programmatic strengths, discord results. She argues that a collaboratively constructed group identity may be nearly impossible to convey in a social context where members, unaccustomed to positive characterization and a democratic construction process, have been constantly faced with an organizational emphasis on hierarchy and a culture of pointing out faults.

A POSTMODERN ENDING

> *The fate of an epoch that has eaten of the tree of knowledge is that it must . . . recognize that general views of life and the universe can never be the products of increasing empirical knowledge, and that the highest ideals, which move us most forcefully, are always formed only in the struggle with other ideals which are just as sacred to others as ours are to us.*
>
> —Max Weber (quoted by Giddens)

Appendix

SCHEMATIC DIFFERENCES BETWEEN MODERNISM AND POSTMODERNISM

 **Modernism**	 **Postmodernism**
Romanticism/Symbolism	Pataphysics/Dadaism
Form (conjunctive, closed)	Antiform (disjunctive, open)
Purpose	Play
Design	Chance
Hierarchy	Anarchy
Mastery/Logos	Exhaustion/Silence
Art Object/Finished Work	Process/Performance/Happening
Distance	Participation
Creation/Totalization	Decreation/Deconstruction
Synthesis	Antithesis
Presence	Absence
Centering	Dispersal
Genre/Boundary	Text/Intertext
Semantics	Rhetoric
Paradigm	Syntagm
Hypotaxis	Parataxis
Metaphor	Metonymy
Selection	Combination
Root/Depth	Rhizome/Surface
Interpretation/Reading	Against Interpretation/Misreading
Signified	Signifier
Lisible (Readerly)	*Scriptible* (Writerly)
Narrative/*Grande Histoire*	Anti-narrative/*Petite Histoire*
Master Code	Idiolect
Symptom	Desire
Type	Mutant
Genital/Phallic	Polymorphous/Androgynous
Paranoia	Schizophrenia
Origin/Cause	Difference-Differance/Trace
God the Father	The Holy Ghost
Metaphysics	Irony
Determinacy	Indeterminacy
Transcendence	Immanence

—Ihab Hassan 1987, 91–92

1

WHERE DISCORD MEETS DIRECTION

The Role of Consultant Evaluation in Writing Program Administration

Deborah H. Holdstein

Over the last fifteen years there have been numerous, often successful, attempts to define and theorize the role of the WPA and the place of writing programs, Writing Across the Curriculum, and the like on campus. For instance, in "Ideology, Theory, and the Genre of Writing Programs," Jeanne Gunner writes,

> Examining writing programs as a genre, a social and institutional genre, yields some fairly familiar answers to questions about program purpose. In their social and institutional setting, writing programs as a genre serve both an ideological and hence also epistemological function; they help structure a relation of language and culture. (2002, 11)

Further, Gunner elaborates, writing programs "help establish the cultural rules for language use, what its cultural work is: how we are to form categories of language users; how we are to hierarchize discourses; how we are to correlate specific discourses with ability and social worth; how we are to validate the differences produced" (11).

The same can be said, however, for the larger institutional context in which the WPA and the writing program do their work: the administration of an institution is local, influenced by its own, larger context of often vexing state mandates, accreditation bodies, and boards of trustees. A given institution, too, has its cultural rules for language work, its sense of what the important cultural work of the institution is and how (in the best circumstances) it is to be carried out. It, too, correlates specific discourses with ability and social/hierarchical worth.

Within this complex and often conflicting set of contexts and interactions is the legion of work regarding the relative powerlessness of most WPAs. Gary Olson and Joseph Moxley's "Directing Freshman Composition and the Limits of Authority" (1989) articulates the negligible value of WPAs to the English department. But as Edward White puts it, department chairs "appreciate us principally for our accessibility and ability to communicate, that is, for our ability to keep things nicely under control without exerting any real authority" (2002, 108). As White notes, he had been a "statewide administrator in halls where nobody pretended (as they do on campus) that everyone is powerless" (106). Indeed, White

> absorbed from the atmosphere certain lessons: recognize the fact that all administration deals in power; power games demand aggressive players; assert that you have power (even if you don't) and you can often wield it. (106)

All this is well and good. However, as Richard Miller posits, "[I]nstitutional life gives rise to a *general* feeling of hopelessness and powerlessness" (1999, 8; my emphasis). Miller's is an important point: that these feelings are pervasive throughout the academy, which

> guarantees that anyone involved in this business can easily be prodded into sharing his or her vision of some better world where the work wouldn't be so alienating, the bureaucratic structure so enfeebled, the administration so indifferent. (8)

Therefore, the pervasive rhetoric of WPAs that often describes the work as "eating our livers in anger and frustration" (Malenczyk 2002, 80) can be transformed, in the words of Jim Corder, through an "emergence towards the other" (1985, 26), a move from internalized tension to outside support. As Rita Malenczyk writes, this tendency toward self-reliance (or mutilation?) coupled with the daily variety of administrative work indicates the "physical and too-often-abused self as an inescapable component of WPA life" (2002, 80). While we do not forget the working conditions of many writing faculty and WPAs—the reason for many a consultant-evaluator (C-E) visit, by the way—we must as WPAs concurrently turn our attention elsewhere.

As WPAs, we often embody a postmodern condition: we work as individual persons but must function within part of an institution. We attempt to navigate and thereby enact on campus the near-universal truths of the discipline and profession in contrast to what campus administrators will allow and what they promote, most often than not, for economic reasons. We operate in a discipline and academic context that reveal the incongruities of postmodernism and writing programs: we want to operate in ways that defy hierarchies, but in the interest of our students and programs we must work productively and well within those hierarchies.

If we are ready to accept that many aspects of a WPA's plight reflect similar administrative or quasi-administrative struggles throughout the academy—as I'm certain our Director of Student Development, for instance, would attest—where, then, do we go from here? Recognizing and enacting our roles through the structures of our institutions (and the structures outside the institution that, in turn, structure us) provide the strongest opportunity for WPAs to effect change (or, if you prefer White's take, wield power).

Unlike programs in nursing and education, for instance, that garner the leverage and benefits provided by outside program accreditation (this in addition to the foundation of larger, institutional accreditation), we in composition and rhetoric (and our usual departmental home, English) have no such leverage. While program accreditation might seem to be a nuisance, it does get programs what they need: for instance, if the university values physical therapy and the outfit that accredits physical therapy has determined that doctoral level will be the entry point for the physical therapist by 2008, then the program will get the faculty, equipment, and other resources to make that possible.

Consequently, WPAs and their administrative and faculty allies must tap into this system, pure and simple. Most institutions will allow for, if not demand, outside consultant evaluations toward program review, particularly in the absence of formal program accreditation. In English, having a secondary teacher-education program helps: National Council for Accreditation of Teacher Education (NCATE) accreditation of education programs can have a beneficial trickle-over effect for the English major. However, such benefits often barely touch the concerns of writing and rhetoric programs.

IS THERE A MISSION IN THIS UNIVERSITY?

One of the central ways to indicate a writing program's centrality to the institution is to prove its congruence with the university's mission statement, out of which has most likely grown the institution's strategic plan. Usually, language in these documents is critical for determining an institution's priorities—and out of priorities, naturally, come budgeting priorities. Rarely, if ever, has there been a mission statement or strategic plan that does not at minimum imply the importance of thinking, critical analysis, and communication or writing. Can an outside program evaluation assist WPAs and their colleagues as they argue for resources and curricula for their programs? Most emphatically, yes. An outside evaluation can assist WPAs who attempt to move beyond departmental, college, or university-wide discord—and the rhetorical discord that often pervades our own stories—into constructive and (it is hoped) ultimately productive action, taming to a great extent the postmodern indeterminancies of writing programs. At their best, these visits foster collaboration and participation, reconciling forms of difference and academic policies toward a multivalent yet constructive path for WPAs, their programs, and (most importantly) for their students.

THE CONSULTANT-EVALUATOR SERVICE OF THE COUNCIL OF WRITING PROGRAM ADMINISTRATORS: SOME BACKGROUND

Since the early 1980s when it was initiated with a grant from the Exxon Foundation, the Consultant-Evaluator Service of the Council of Writing Program Administrators has sent teams consisting of two highly experienced and well-published (often well-known) former or current WPAs to evaluate writing programs within their own, indigenous institutional contexts.[1] A capstone experience for all those who do the work, the consultant-evaluator (C-E) team is charged with expertise and circumspection regarding the issues and concerns of the particular campus they are visiting. The C-Es must attend a workshop every year at CCCC. Here campus reports are discussed and evaluated; each C-E, in roundtable format, leads the group in a brief discussion centered on a particular topic related to writing program administration and evaluation (program and curriculum assessment, technology, English as a Second Language, and the like). Despite each person's area of interest—or set of interests—the members of a given team must to a great extent be generalists in composition and rhetoric. They must also have expertise in and familiarity with English departments in general (where most programs are housed), administrative systems and idiosyncrasies, issues related to contingent faculty, tenure and promotion decisions, budgeting processes, various state mandates, higher levels of administration, and so forth. C-Es must be comfortable talking with (and, as is appropriate, educating) students, faculty, and administrators—whether adjuncts or, for that matter, the college president.

The C-E service is modeled after the procedures of regional accreditation agencies. The codirector of the C-E service sends, after an initial inquiry, a packet with the following documents: a general information sheet regarding the service, its usefulness and purpose, and its fees; the "Guidelines for Self-Study to Precede a WPA Visit"; and three articles—Peter Beidler's "The WPA Evaluation: A Recent Case History" (1991); Susan McLeod's "Requesting a Consultant-Evaluation Visit" (1991);

and, in manuscript form, Laura Brady's "A Case for Writing Program Evaluation" (2004).

After the campus representative has received the materials, he or she discusses with the codirector the other parameters for the visit, realizing that the original impetus for the visit ("We want to look at the writing center") inevitably leads to investigations and discussions about first-year writing, WAC, assessment, and other related areas. After the dates and team are set, the codirector forwards a "Sample Schedule for a WPA Team Visit" to help the campus as it arranges the two-and-a-half-day schedule so it is as productive (and exhausting) as possible. The C-Es will spend considerable time after the visit preparing the report, which is due to the campus within six or seven weeks after the visit itself.

A C-E visit heightens the importance not only of decisive leadership in writing program administration, but also of the highly collaborative, institutionally complex nature of successful writing programs. The WPA at a given institution, having consulted with the C-E codirector, will have first determined who the "key players" are in the fate of writing on campus. This type of buy-in (or, to use the more overwrought term, "sense of ownership") is crucial to the success of the evaluation and to the hope that the campus will eventually implement the recommendations in the final report.

A broad-based sense of ownership also helps tremendously as those on campus begin to prepare the self-study—ideally, another collaborative affair—which is based on a set of questions sent by the co-director to the contact person on campus after discussion (or extensive e-mailing). However, the overwhelming impetus for many ultimately successful campus visits has been less than desirable circumstances and vexing (or unclear) relationships among programs and administrative roles; even then, campus contacts are encouraged to include what I like to call "naysayers" and other skeptics in the schedule. Clearly, most situations on campus are problematic, sparking the need for a visit to begin with.

As would be the case with other consultants brought to a given campus (and we see all the time consultants for enrollment management, the registrar's office, and so forth), the usefulness of this consultancy cannot be overemphasized. It can bring issues and possible resolutions to the attention of those too overwhelmed within their own spheres to remind themselves of the centrality of writing to the educational goals of their students. While no visit is perfect—nor can outcomes be guaranteed—it is one of the ways to tackle discord.

CONSULTANT-EVALUATOR VISITS AND SUCCESSFUL OUTCOMES

While the C-E service does not promise miracles it has, more often than not, improved conditions for writing programs and administrators—and more importantly, for students. It's important to note, again, that not all visits stem from negative circumstances, but that ultimately the goal is constructive validation, accountability and process, initiative, and change. As Susan McLeod delineates, the reasons for requesting a visit at Washington State University involved her new position as WPA and helped her to take stock of what had come before and what was hoped would come in the future. In McLeod's case, the goals included these:

> To highlight the strengths of the existing program
> To give external sanction to planned changes
> To learn a new job as quickly as possible
> To document how things worked—or didn't
> To start a faculty conversation that went beyond matters of procedure
> To matters of curriculum and articulation of courses. (1991, 74–75)

At West Virginia University, Laura Brady made sure to "give as clear a sense of our local context as possible" by concentrating on "broad categories" and formulating "three key questions":

> What are the most important points/purposes that we want to convey about our program?
> What specific details will help readers understand our particular writing program?
> How might headings and tables help us organize information and highlight key points? (2004, 84)

Note that Brady also "followed Peter G. Beidler's advice in 'The WPA Evaluation: A Recent Case History' and consulted broadly as we wrote our self-study and enlisted our administrators as allies" (Beidler 1991; Brady, 2004). A significant piece of advice given to all campuses is to take the guidelines and articles as starting points, not as documents with biblical-weight inerrancy. Brady and colleagues did just that. Since a successful C-E visit represents the collaboration of the local, the national, and the institutional, she writes,

> [W]e chose to add a final step that was not included in the guidelines for self-study: a reflective cover letter. The purpose of this letter was three-fold: It let us reflect on what we learned about our program in the process of the self-study; it provided an executive summary in less than two pages and drew

> our readers' attention to our original goals and questions; it introduced us to the consultant-evaluators by locating the self-study and the supporting documents within the unique context of our institution. (2004)

Keep in mind that West Virginia University's visit was not prompted by particular sets of discord or problems; direction is possible without the precondition of discord. Rather, as Brady notes, "I hope our experience with the WPA consultant-evaluator service will illustrate why a national perspective on a writing program's local context can be valuable, and how the processes of self-study and evaluation can foster conversation, collaboration, and change" (2004, 80). Note, too, how evaluation visits can fit into an institution's all-important investigation of program outcomes, often encouraging campus support for adjustments where the institutional outcomes are negligible at best.

Laura Brady's article concerning the C-E visit at West Virginia University also provides a local answer to an important question: what are the short- and long-term effects of an evaluation? Brady's documentation of the evaluation's outcomes are encouraging: the writing program colleagues have "acted on every recommendation [made by the team in its final report] in some way, have achieved most of our initial goals, and we continue to develop two remaining areas [in Professional Writing and Editing and a writing tutorial center]." Most significantly, "We've even made some progress in additional areas now that we have a well-articulated and collaboratively structured program to improve conversation among the current writing faculty and various stakeholders in the Center's projects" (2004, 87). The C-Es were able to add a national perspective to the faculty's own arguments, thereby boosting the greater likelihood of revised curricula and training, new hires, and new programs.

Other visits are as idiosyncratic as one might imagine. On one campus visit, the C-Es were highly uncertain until they arrived on campus that administrators would even be receptive to the goals and purposes of the visit and any potential recommendations that might come from it. Attempting to bolster the beleaguered and committed WPA, the C-Es nonetheless offered constructive commentary while on campus, actually meeting with the provost. Among the surprising, constructive results was the agreement by the provost while the C-Es were still on campus to change a WPA line designated as staff to a tenure-line position instead. In yet another visit one year before the arrival of the current WPA (who has now been at her institution for five years), the C-Es recommended that a professional WPA be hired—"not just literature faculty slumming, people who can't wait to get back to their 'usual' jobs."[2] As this WPA recalls, "Administration and faculty complained a bit about the recommendations, but agreed to just about all of them and implemented them, to boot" (2003).

In recent memory, only one visit seemed less successful than most, one in which there was only lip service on the part of the campus, its administration, and faculty to begin with concerning the fate of writing. It is almost impossible to determine these conditions before an actual visit. Given the C-E's customary, near missionary intent, difficult campus conditions will not in and of themselves prevent the visit from taking place, and, in fact, usually provide the impetus for validation, discussion, collaboration, debate, and eventual change. Where these types of conversations and collaboration do not already occur, the C-E visit can, quite often, transform "vexing" and "debate" into acceptable concepts for productive discussion.

WHAT THE CONSULTANT-EVALUATORS MIGHT FIND

The WPA C-E service protects the privacy of institutions requesting visits and the contents of the reports written by C-Es. As a result, these examples (and any others mentioned throughout this article) are of necessity anonymous, except where they represent quotations from publications written by faculty or administrators for a given institution.

For instance, at one institution the C-E's recommendations included suggestions about placement assessment, suggesting abandonment of the ACT as a placement device in favor of a written test. The recommendations were geared specifically for first-year writing and toward the goals for outcomes assessment mandated by the university. Furthermore, the C-Es recommended how the load on TAs could be reduced, again, within realistic university constraints. In another visit, an institution was persuaded—using terms that stemmed from the institution's own, particular context—to transform adjunct positions to full-time lectureships. While some might argue that these positions—temporary as they are—are not ideal, these full-time, renewable lines were far preferable to the previous part-time, semester-to-semester hiring practice. Each of these examples indicates the importance of a C-E's balancing disciplinary knowledge and expertise with national trends and local conditions. There is no "one size fits all" approach, and it is the proverbial kiss of death for a C-E to say "This is how we do it on my campus, so that's what you should do here." While the work of a WPA represents the postmodern, disjunctive nature of writing programs and the incongruities of their departmental contexts, the work of a C-E is, even in these contexts, to determine *sets* of local (if often complex) universal truths for a particular campus.

Most visits also address writing-intensive or writing-across-the-disciplines initiatives on campus—or such initiatives are often recommended where they do not exist. At one institution, however, the history department seemed far better prepared and committed to the teaching of writing than did other departments; they took the lead in WAC initiatives, essentially bringing the English department and writing program faculty along with them.

In another report, the C-Es quote the self-study, in which colleagues wonder "what form a WAC program might take on a campus such as ours." The C-Es then outline three possible models for WAC development, beginning with a faculty development model of reasonable, manageable scale for that particular institution. Furthermore, this particular institutional and programmatic context permitted reassigning some faculty members to enable development in the area of WAC, something highlighted in the report and its recommendations. And although it was not delineated as an initial reason for the visit, conditions in the Writing Center came into play through the inevitable, complex interrelationships of writing programs and their campus constituents. As a result, the report recommends additional support for the center, thereby freeing the director to work with students and faculty development. (And I've presented just a brief sample of the recommendations.) To date, most of the recommendations have been implemented, owing to the C-E's targeting their advice to the particular conditions and strengths of a particular campus.

FINAL THOUGHTS

C-Es can help WPAs become aware of the true scope of their work and the different, complex audiences they must address. Where this awareness exists, the C-Es can reaffirm or redirect the alternating strengths, discordant processes and policies, or other vexations inherent in a writing program—which, even with only first-year writing, is inevitably campus-wide. As Susan McLeod writes,

> Often, program directors see an outside evaluation as a threat—something like being graded when you are not sure exactly what the grading system is or what decisions will be made about you based on those grades. On the

> contrary, program review is an essential part of any university's ongoing self-assessment; it should be treated not as a threat, but as a process we should learn about and then learn from. (1991, 77)

And again, as McLeod implies, self-assessment and the ensuing evaluations can at many campuses provide the leverage usually reserved for programs with external, formal assessment processes, such as nursing, physical therapy, and elementary education.

Much has been made of the WPA and the relative presence or lack of power inherent in that position. As Edward White has written, "Power is in some ways like money or sex; it is only of pressing importance if you have none. . . . Administrators, including WPAs, cannot afford the luxury of powerlessness" (2002, 113). In the words of Doug Hesse, and in an alternative view of WPAs and relative power, "WPAs cannot afford to act like composition studies centers in the academic galaxy, let alone the social, political, and economic universe in which that galaxy exists. They should not be surprised when matters of curriculum, policy, or assessment that strike them as self-evident do not strike others the same way" (2002, 299). C-E visits can help bring this level of awareness—and to some extent, a renewed sense of "power"—to campus writing programs and the myriad persons across faculty and administrative lines who might influence them.

Indeed, leverage and self-knowledge are power, particularly when accompanied by the potential for long-term collaboration and ongoing, evaluative processes and sets of accountability across these often-troubled and hierarchical "lines" of administration, faculty, and students. In fact, a successful C-E visit is not entirely about the empowerment of a single WPA or easy, predictable remedy to the postmodern condition of the WPA. Rather, it's most appropriately about using, in White's words, "the considerable power we have for the good of our program" (2002, 113) and, I would emphasize, to reconcile the necessarily contradictory nature of our work wherever possible for the good of our students.

2
COLD PASTORAL
The Moral Order of an Idealized Form

Jeanne Gunner

> *. . . the Golden Age, a myth functioning as a memory.*
>
> —Raymond Williams

Approaching the topic of WPAs and change from a pastoral perspective might strike readers as a bit far-fetched; the writing program is hardly known as a bucolic landscape. And yet WPAs are usually quite experienced with *paraklausithyron*—a song sung before a closed door; well versed in amoebean song—a contest of alternating strains in an argument batted back and forth, without clear resolution; and prone to extolling friendship as an absolute value springing from a need for help. These familiar moves are part of the pastoral form—a form that, over time, came to operate by conventions that displaced real social tensions with an ideal not only of order, but order of a certain kind as an unquestionable moral good. By virtue of his or her relation to an institutionally sponsored writing program, the WPA inhabits a version of the pastoral: housed within the writing program, the WPA directs a set of formal practices that are intended to rehearse and refine dominant cultural values that subvert material change. The work we do as WPAs can thus become surprisingly controversial, unintentionally contestatory, and (in some cases) the justification for vehement personal rebuke. By examining our pastoral functions, we might more easily come to see how proposing program changes based on the logic of research and theory can be institutionally recoded as the moral transgressions of a bad shepherd who betrays the kindly master and puts the flock at risk.

THE PROBLEMATIC NATURE OF WRITING PROGRAM CHANGE

The WPA is the physical emblem of the writing program, and that emblematic status can open us to often extremely painful attack when we assume that a primary function of the job is to be an agent of change. Thus the conventional piece of advice in WPA circles that we should carefully choose our battles. Enacting such wisdom is problematic, however, since it is so difficult to know in advance when a given program decision will elicit a hostile response. The WPA who attempts to introduce changes in a writing program—be they curricular, pedagogic, evaluation-based, or otherwise administratively grounded—therefore faces what might be called a problem of perspective: as WPAs, we would do well to understand the place of the writing program not only in its local conditions but in larger systems of institutional and cultural power, since even apparently minor program changes can be interpreted as threatening challenges to dominant values. Such awareness might mean we are less likely to be blindsided by unexpectedly hostile resistance, and less likely to be immobilized by it when it occurs. It might also enable us to choose battles that can produce the foundation for substantive change—for what might be systemic change, as opposed to the "small victories" of administrative existence.

We logically look to the literature on writing program administration and politics to inform and guide our choices about instituting change and managing resistance. But we face a problem of perspective and hence methodology: if general rules apply only weakly to varying local conditions (a WPA truism), then the common situational approaches—the case studies of the Council of Writing Program Administrator's Intellectual Work document, for instance (1998), or the descriptive problem-solution scenarios of texts such as Myers-Breslin's edited collection, *Administrative Problem Solving for Writing Programs and Writing Centers* (1999)—necessarily require us to think about local conditions in ways that distort local realities, sometimes opening up fresh perspectives on them, certainly, but often providing riskily and unpredictably contingent acontextual frames for action at the local level. And so the WPA leadership role becomes even more bewildering by the apparently unstable conditions of reception we face, for what might count as a significant victory in one context is not even the source of a problem in another; what seems a modest programmatic change here is an almost unthinkable act in some programmatic elsewhere. Further complicating the mix, as we try to measure the impact of program changes, we necessarily circumscribe the object of study, for tracking its full effects even in a local situation is beyond our capability, and attempting to do so almost certainly reduces the significance of whatever we can claim.

An appealing metaphor to capture the complexity of the WPA's relation to change might be a WPA ecology. But such a metaphor suggests a holistic system that, if it does not exclude, then certainly de-emphasizes the powerful role dominant ideologies play in affecting our position as potential agents of change. Instead, as a way of understanding why introducing change in the writing program is often so unpredictable and resisted, I use Raymond Williams's study of the pastoral as a genre that evolved into a calcified form reproducing a hegemonic moral order, in order to understand the writing program less as an academic unit and more as a social genre, a conventionalized form in service of a cultural function. I move among the realms of our WPA conditions—the local, historical, theoretical, and individual—because the changes we have worked for or been forced to confront operate among them.

For new WPAs, this approach may seem far removed from more explicitly "applied" discussions of WPA work. It may also seem perversely pessimistic for an essay in a volume on change in the writing program. But I'm unwilling to celebrate those small victories that are the typical results of pragmatic approaches to WPA work without also recognizing their insufficiency and typical inability to produce systemic change. The celebration of small victories can reinforce a reluctance to seek change in the form of the writing program as an institutional structure. I'm equally unwilling to be blithely optimistic about WPA work in the face of the powerful cultural forces we must challenge for significant change to be possible. I acknowledge my own bias here: I believe that the writing program has a more powerful cultural than academic agenda, that the WPA is as much directed by this agenda as he or she is the director of it, and that real change can follow only if we recognize that the form of the writing program is conservative and inherently hostile to systemic change. How-to approaches to writing program administration can have (intentionally or not) a historically sanitizing effect, erasing the cultural critiques that should inform writing program work. The historical and theoretical critiques of composition practices that scholars such as James Berlin, Susan Miller, Sharon Crowley, and Donna Strickland have produced form necessary contexts for otherwise strictly administrative strategies for change.

At the same time, some WPA-led program changes have rich potential for transforming conventional writing program practices. I do not intend a binary of minor/major changes, but a sense (for new WPAs especially) of a Geertz-like "thick" context for battle-choosing, one that includes a sense of ideological along with pragmatic effects. Like the pastoral itself, the writing program has become a commonly practiced form, with defining figures and motifs, providing an apparent connection between high culture and the lower orders. Williams's study of the pastoral form deconstructs this connection, and it is this aspect of his literary analysis that might help inform a "thick" reading of our own programs.

THE FUNCTIONS OF PASTORAL FORM

An early chapter in Williams's *The Country and the City* is, coincidentally, entitled "A Problem of Perspective." In it he examines the pastoral, the literary form constructed to represent the virtues of rural life, derived from Hesiod's *Works and Days*, a kind of agricultural calendar, and formalized by Theocritus in Hellenic Greece of the third century BCE. Williams attempts to locate in historical time this pastoral "way of life" handed down over the centuries, a "country life" (1973, 9) of rural virtues lost through the changes wrought by modern practices. As he moves backward in time in search of sources he discovers, of course, that this golden age recedes with him, that its values "mean different things at different times" (12); as Derrida has put it, there is no plenitude of "before." Poetic characteristics may shift with the tastes of the time period: the shepherd becomes Wordsworth's highland lass or Arnold's scholar gypsy. But the function of the pastoral form does not change: it remains as the embodiment of a cultural argument that an ideal order once existed, one that rightly ordered human relations and protected natural goodness against forces of destructive change. The form supports any dominant ideology that grounds its authority in a fictional, idealized past.

Williams shows the pastoral form is not a historically locatable natural phenomenon but an invention of the "city," the site of cultural production and, in later centuries, the center of economic production as well. Williams argues that while Theocritean idylls and later Virgilian eclogues (two of the earliest pastoral forms) offered significantly idealized and distorted representations of actual country life (shifting the metaphoric landscape from farming to shepherds and their flocks, for example), both Theocritean and Virgilian pastoral nonetheless includes representations of economic, cultural, and political tensions of the poets' times, and both retain a materially recognizable representation of the rural. These early pastoral forms, he argues, served as a vehicle for imagining a future different from the present condition (even as they led, in Virgil's case, to the creation of the trope of Arcadia, "a magical invocation of a land which needs no farming" [17]). But later pastoral forms elided even a reductive material connection to country life and its tensions, privileging instead the vision of a future that would "restore" the "golden age" of a lost past:

> [E]ven in these [Greco-Roman] developments . . . which inaugurate tones and images of an ideal kind, there is almost invariably a tension with other kinds of experience. . . . The achievement, if it can be called that, of the Renaissance adaptation of just these classical modes is that, step by step, these living tensions are excised, until there is nothing countervailing, and selected images stand as themselves: not in a living but in an enamelled world. (18)

Losing their dialectical element, later forms of pastoral erase political tension and material realities, depicting instead "untroubled rural delight and peace." The voice that represents the "country"—those outside the sphere of cultural power—gradually gives way to the voice of the "city," the cultural center. Not surprisingly, the voice of the country soon speaks only in ways that serve the cultural center's values.

Tying the eradication of social tension to the pastoral genre's use in a culture whose "city" center has shifted to capitalist and colonialist enterprise, Williams demonstrates how its form, with its now state-apparatus function, allows some changes, resists others, and ultimately calcifies in relation to one dominant ideological system. In his history of pastoral, we arrive, in the seventeenth and eighteenth centuries, "at the decisive transition when [the generic conventions] have been relocated, in a new ideology, in the country-house." (22) We see, in other words, a form that assimilates difference and tension by invoking a mythical golden age and set of virtues, subsequently colonizing this redefined country for its own purposes and reproduction.

Like the prototypical writing program, the early pastoral consisted of a real world and an imaginary ideal, with a myth of return as its warrant. Here I think of Mina Shaughnessy's *Errors and Expectations* (1977) as one statement of early writing program practices in service of a return to mythologized standards; or many of the documents John Brereton has collected in *The Origin of Composition Studies in the American College* (1995) in which composition courses are premised on a recapturing of prelapsarian linguistic excellence; or the more overtly nationalist rhetoric of the state-sponsored Indian schools (see Enoch 2002) of the nineteenth century (which are, or ought to be, equally a part of writing program history as Harvard's Subject A is). These program narratives capture the real cultural conflict of class, race, and linguistic backgrounds; we see and hear the struggling open-admissions students in Shaughnessy's text and the resistant voice of Indian school critics such as Zitkala Sa. But in both the literary genre and the writing program as a social genre, this connection to material conditions loses over time its former dialectical character, and both become a form overdetermined by the self-interests of a particular ideology. We see the form of the writing program come to speak for and of students, to commodify them via conventional program practices, and to reconstruct their needs and values to be more in line with the cultural authority. The institutional writing program is the "country-house" next step, transforming earlier writing program versions that distorted but nonetheless included student voices and difference.

Williams's painstaking analysis of the pastoral genre thus offers us a useful interpretive model for exploring how the genre of the writing program can be used to suppress tension and contain actual change, even as program form seems to evolve. By creating and maintaining as its referent a "golden age" to be reclaimed, the writing program as a social genre ultimately allies itself with a mythically traditional moral order. Like the pastoral, the writing program points to an idealized social realm that validates not the tension of competing linguistic and cultural communities but a golden age of past and potential linguistic purity, where language and culture were and will once again be natural and simple, in a seamlessly pristine interrelationship. Modern writing programs evoke this Arcadian landscape through their generic operations, testing and placing students in courses that will cleanse them of difference, as Miller (1991) has argued; schooling and evaluating them in relation to the mythical past which their essays—their written and corrected productions—then help to memorialize, charging them with its (re)propagation.

TRANSGRESSIONS OF A MORAL ORDER

The ideological functions of writing program practices seem especially important to recognize in this time of increased attention to diversity in higher education. Difference and tension are what the genre disallows; the former must remain at the thematic level, in order to contain the latter. This process of assimilating difference is akin to Williams's notion of the "charity of consumption, not of production." The writing program promises access to cultural capital, the country house of the mainstream, but transforms resistance and so avoids systemic change. In its charitable provision of access, it consumes difference and reproduces the cultural values of the institution that houses and contains it. Change in theory, curriculum, or pedagogy is assimilated into the traditional form of the writing program. The individual writing program may evolve, but its generic activities continue to reproduce traditional values, and the future they point to inevitably references a mythical past. The five-paragraph theme may be nearly universally disdained, for instance, but the epistemology that produced it remains powerfully present. Writing process pedagogy can be championed, but its social-epistemic theory becomes reduced to prescriptive steps in an arhetorical conventionalizing formula, the mimetic mode displacing the rhetorical. Multiculturalism can be embraced, but it takes its place as a thematic addition to a canonical curriculum, a mythical notion of cultural unity, or simply a theatrical representation of cultural difference (the guest speaker, or attendance at a campus "cultural" event). This same hegemonic imperative to consume difference shapes the WPA's landscape, and it accounts for much of the tension that is (dis)placed onto the position. From this perspective, change—minor as it may seem out of a given context—becomes an enormous and usually self-consuming achievement, an evisceration of dialectical elements resulting in an enameling of curriculum, pedagogy, and politics.

Jane Hindman, in an essay on liberatory teaching and assessment, has examined how one common writing program practice has helped ensure the status quo of program effects. In liberatory teaching, the pedagogical goals are at odds with the institutional means of measuring instructional success, she argues. In liberatory pedagogy classrooms, students may feel threatened, resentful, uncertain, *untaught*; often, students come to value the critical methods they have encountered only after the course has ended, as this knowledge begins to intersect with their experience, as bell hooks has claimed. The liberatory teacher can logically expect negative response to her and her course, but institutional practices convert such response into negative instructor evaluations—a finger-wagging *bad teacher, bad teacher* moral judgment. Hindman argues "that distress [over negative response] is precisely what some of our professional practices perpetuate: composition studies inculcates student-centered and/or liberatory pedagogies in its literature as well as in most teacher-training programs; meanwhile, institutional reliance on conventional, performance-model teaching evaluation methods countermand that scholarship and training" (2000, 15). The system reflexively consumes the practices that threaten its privileging of instructional power.

And so we arrive at a WPA dilemma. As Hindman argues, "No matter what we may profess . . . our practices prove what we are for or against in the long run. We must recognize the habits and values we indoctrinate in our practices" (25). But working to change indoctrinating practices means sponsoring practices that (re)introduce into the writing program tensions of a social and political order, and we cannot be sure how change will be received. We can see an example of unpredictable response to change in a conventional writing program practice—placement—in the smooth implementation of directed self-placement (DSP) in one location but resistance when the same program was introduced in a different set of local conditions. What emerges from the two cases is that, while friendly subversion can in certain circumstances be possible and practical, a dominant ideology of the student as object of institutional consumption reasserts itself when the same practice is exported to a different location.

DSP, as theorized and implemented by Daniel J. Royar and Roger Gilles (1998) at Grand Valley State University, is a major subversion of conventional placement practice in that students have the authority to place themselves into what they decide is the appropriate writing course at their institution. This significant change in practice—one with great potential for weakening the ideological formation of students as incapable, unknowing objects of program processes—happened quite smoothly in Royar and Gilles's program, as they report it. In their account, the program's description is cloaked, in a sense, in the rhetoric of pragmatism and use of the familiar WPA rhetoric of efficiency:

> [A]dministrators are . . . pleased with DSP. Admission directors don't have to help organize placement exams or explain to students why they need to begin their college career with a not-for-college-credit course. They are pleased to invite potential students to compare the way we and other schools treat their incoming students: we provide options, while other schools take them away. And of course, unlike placement exams, DSP costs nothing. . . . (67)

As presented, this break with conventional practice and also its ideological framing offers almost a consumerist argument for DSP: admission administrators "invite potential [student-customers] to "compar[ison shop]" in order to see which "options" they can get for the same sticker price. This promotional practice is strictly value-added—it "costs nothing." With its potential to undermine a foundational ideology of students as objects of direction, DSP is a satisfying reversal in which the buyer should but does not beware, and instead accepts a writing program innovation that dislodges the familiar as natural and necessary. DSP empowers students, at least potentially, to avoid a class- and race-based gatekeeping system. In an admittedly small part of the larger hegemonic structure, this gatekeeping function has been dismantled, apparently without significant resistance.

Interestingly, however, the site of resistance can travel: the apparently minor change that successfully takes form in one program may, if enacted elsewhere, lead to direct or indirect countersubversion. David Blakesley offers a brilliant analysis of this traveling resistance in his *WPA: Writing Program Administration* essay, "Directed Self-Placement in the University." Because placement is a "process of socialization," he argues, "WPAs may have greatly underestimated the ethical and moral complexity of writing placement" (2002, 10). WPAs who have found themselves in battle, chosen or not, with institutional values might see their situation clearly described in Blakesley's account of his efforts as WPA to introduce DSP on his former campus. If our disciplinary authority is tied to ethos, as he argues—"[T]o those who don't share our disciplinary history, discipline-specific knowledge functions ethically rather than logically, establishing the intellectual integrity of the WPA more than it might rationalize or justify specific programmatic change" (13)—the attacks we experience are indeed personal; what we see as reasonable and supported claims only serve to give us credibility as speakers, not agents with disciplinary authority. In the cold pastoral of the writing program, our authority is of a moral order. Our authority is based in the community's consideration of us. When changes we have initiated or supported threaten the moral order, the charity of consumption that is the writing program's moral agenda in the institution is upended; as Blakesley's analysis of resistance in one campus entity (the Center for Basic Skills) so clearly shows, we have produced instead of consumed students. We have empowered them, ceded authority to them, and allowed them to participate in formerly privileged practices—whereas earlier models of placement would have consumed them, transformed them into basic writers, English as a Second Language (ESL) students, or other commodified bodies to be shipped to established program niches. When changes we have promoted strike others outside of the discipline as dangerous, threatening, or inappropriate, then we are seen to have personally transgressed, and so to have ceded our moral right to influence policy. Donna Strickland's historical study of composition work and writing programs (2001) shows them to be institutionally allied with the labor of correctness rather than intellectual labor, the outcome of the historical pattern of developing writing programs separate from the "head" work of literature. WPA-led change can thus itself strike those outside the program as incorrect, arrogant, transgressive, even insulting in its violation of conventional boundaries, justifying rebuke and requiring active realignment in the proper order of the hierarchy in the name of standards, common sense, prudence, or some other naturalized "truth" or moral virtue.

New WPAs, entering the field or moving to new programs, may blunder into discovering this ethos- rather than discipline-based authority. Several years ago, as the newly appointed WPA in my former institution, I met with a group of faculty in other disciplines who were eager to expand a writing component model for their courses, to be taught by writing program faculty. When I voiced my concern that the writing component and faculty member can easily become secondary appendages in such a model, a professor of history gasped, then screamed out, "*What* am I *hearing*?" What she was hearing, obviously, was an ideological position that broke with the epistemological order of disciplines and authority, knowledge and rank, and the status quo of the writing program genre. She grasped immediately the logic of my response, and equally quickly and automatically translated it into a moral challenge, one that sincerely and deeply offended her. My goal had been to participate in establishing a sense of shared community with colleagues interested in writing instruction (although as a kind of day labor, as I later realized). After this "casual" lunch, I saw entrance to this community, for the exposed ideological reasons, neither likely nor clearly desirable. In retrospect this blunder helped avoid an apparent coalition that would, I believe, have worked against the program's later self-directed redefinition of its courses as rhetorically based (a "minor victory"), but which also made for real difficulties in advancing writing across the curriculum. Threatening program changes were effectively contained.

Like choosing one's battles, the kind of coalition-building WPAs are advised to do in any attempted program innovation is a much more formidable task than it first appears to be. As we see in Blakesley's discussion of his attempts to include stakeholders in the DSP program planning, the WPA is enmeshed in a process of gaining the assent of others to dislodge the status quo and implement a moral reordering, even if neither WPA nor stakeholder fully recognizes the task as such. While the usual diction of "stakeholders," "community," and the WPA's "people skills" are part of such an engagement, these local behaviors connect to much less well-defined, less-easily locatable, and much more culturally important practices and ideological imperatives. Blakesley writes, "[W]ho would imagine that writing placement itself could carry with it such wide-ranging questions about identity, the role of the individual in society, or the function of institutions?" (10). He acknowledges that as he sought to implement the DSP program, he "underestimated the degree to which placement itself (and thus any changes [he] might instigate) functioned in the wider institutional context as the expression of power and a symptom of the institution's normalizing desire" (12).

WPAS AS DIALECTICAL CHANGE AGENTS

Sharon Crowley has written a powerful polemic toward ending the universal composition requirement (1998). Hers is a proposal that, if promoted by a WPA as an actual program revision, would clearly be in many departments a chosen battle of a spectacular order (which is not a criticism but an acknowledgment of the deeply entrenched nature of the writing program's ideological functions as she analyzes them), one that would almost certainly disrupt the writing program as a conservative genre by fundamentally altering its institutional functions.

Clearly, less obviously spectacular but nonetheless potentially foundational innovations such as DSP have the potential to undermine the writing program's ideological functions because they assist in abolishing the program structures and practices that perform conservative, repressive work. The agenda of a WPA change agent might be to support program changes that are potentially structural and systemic rather than static—changes in which the program form is filled with shifting content, but its ideological function remains intact. If we can help deconstruct common program practices that form the elements of writing programs generically, we can undertake program changes that reintroduce difference and tension as dialectical elements. Crowley's suggestion that the usual first-year course sequencing be abolished and replaced with survey, genre, and theory courses in rhetoric-composition is one such curricular innovation that can possibly take place over time, reordering the work of the program in relation to ideological functions. Incorporating alternative discourses, including the retheorized notions of personal writing that Hindman and others have advocated, into a program's curricular learning outcomes has a potentially dialectical effect, influencing pedagogical approaches and instructor-student relations. We might see the task of WPA leadership as a matter of identifying such moments of the potential interpellation of difference; as Cain and Kalamaras put it,

> [T]he site where the work of all WPAs begins [is] in the improvisatory and conditional nature of [WPA] decision-making and action. Improvisation is a matter of drawing upon as many pre-existing forms as possible in order to create, within a particular moment in time, a new form that reflects as well as responds to conditions that do not easily fit within conventional categories.

> But in order for the improvisation to work, one must first have access to many different, even competing forms of thought from which to draw upon. (1999, 56)

Their words suggest that we inhabit the writing program not as a country house, but as a contact zone.

In her June 29, 2002, contribution to Duane Roen and Joseph Janangelo's WPA "signature project" presented at the 2002 Conference of the Council of Writing Program Administrators (for which WPAs on the WPA listserv were invited to submit a brief description of the program features or projects they felt most significantly identified their work in the WPA position) Rebecca Moore Howard wrote,

> My signature project is to establish our introductory curriculum as a dialectic between disciplinary and public desires for writing instruction. Not as a place for nor a result of dialectic, but as itself a dialectic. The curriculum necessarily has fixed perimeters (grading guidelines, course requirements, etc.), but if it is itself a stable product, it does a disservice to the discipline of composition and rhetoric or to the public (academic or larger public) that endorses and sponsors its work. The desires of those two constituencies are often conflicting and irreconcilable; no fixed compromise between them is satisfactory. Hence the need for dialectic—not the product of nor place for dialectic, but dialectic itself, in the curriculum.

Howard's response embodies writing program administration as a contact zone whose purpose is to foreground competing ideologies and to place in creative tension the writing values of the program, institution, and larger public realms, reactivating the writing program genre's capacity to connect practices to real social conflicts.

Successful WPA-led innovations such as Howard's dialectical curriculum or Royar and Gilles's DSP are evidence that such changes can happen—sometimes smoothly, sometimes with but despite resistance. Without the WPA's critical questioning of common practices in the status quo writing program, we direct an endless pursuit of a mythical Golden Age and endorse an epistemology that, like Keats's Grecian urn, a "Cold Pastoral," utters the decree that "'Beauty is truth, truth beauty'—that is all / Ye know on earth, and all ye need to know." Unless WPAs become change agents, we valorize the assimilation of difference in a charity of consumption, and we serve the idealized order of a calcified hegemonic form.

3
BEYOND ACCOMMODATION
Individual and Collective in a Large Writing Program

Christy Desmet

REJECTING RELIGION, RESISTING DISCIPLINE

In the 1993 volume of *College English*, former TA Nancy Welch chronicled the disheartening story of her move from a process-based writing program (Program A) to one centered around cultural studies (Program B). Welch's narrative details an inexorable process by which teachers who resisted the group ethos of their new employer/community were isolated and even driven away. She herself, as the story goes, withdrew and returned to her original institution, where she completed a Ph.D. and went on to compose her indictment of teacher training in U.S. composition programs.

Welch's description of her transfer from the warm, nurturing environment of a writing program that embraced process pedagogy to one that aggressively promoted a cultural studies agenda frames its critique in terms of religious rhetoric. Listening to veterans profess their allegiance to the goals and practices of Program B, Welch identifies their talk as a form of conversion narrative. The majority of TAs embraced the pedagogical faith, while Welch and her fellow dissidents were isolated and even "excommunicated."[1] Readers of Foucault will recognize the notion that discipline is an inevitable counterpart of religion, employing the techniques of confession to "school" its already interpellated subjects. John Trimbur identifies Foucauldian discipline as an inevitable byproduct of the "politics of professionalization" in rhetoric and composition: "By a Foucauldian account of professionalization, WPAs, precisely because of their professional knowledges, are invariably implicated in acts of surveillance that constitute both staff and students as 'docile bodies'" (1996, 142).[2] Whether or not the politics of professionalization should take sole blame for the problem, I do believe that writing programs (like most educational institutions) are sites of discipline—if not actual punishment—a fact that raises the question of how both teachers and students should respond: With resistance or accommodation? Or something else altogether?

In composition studies, "resistance" to dominant ideologies has been examined from different theoretical perspectives, both as a positive pedagogical goal for writing teachers and as an institutional problem for teacher-trainers and administrators. Henry Giroux, most notably, sees resistance as a (political) weapon against a stultifying "tradition" of education and as a real alternative to an "accommodating" attitude that really is a capitulation to the system (Giroux 1983). Geoffrey Chase, applying Giroux's taxonomy of attitudes specifically to composition pedagogy, sees the teacher's role as helping students to "problematize" their existence by making them question the logic of moral and political structures. The teacher provides an environment in which "students are encouraged to see themselves as human actors who can make a difference in the world." Within this environment, for both teacher and student "writing needs to be seen as an ideological process whose aims should include teaching students to write as part of a larger project in which they can affirm their own voices, learn to exercise the skills of critical interrogation, and, finally, exercise the courage to act in the interests of improving the quality of human life" (Chase 1988, 21). Constructive resistance need not be confined to the individual classroom, of course; Giroux imagines a reform of teacher education in which teachers "function professionally as intellectuals" and argues that "teacher education should be inextricably linked to transforming the school setting, and, by extension, the wider social setting" (1988, 73). But for Giroux, as for some other liberatory pedagogues, the center of democratic educational reform remains the student-teacher nexus.

When looked at from the administrator's or teacher-trainer's perspective, "resistance" is more typically classified as a particular problem of individuals that is subject to psychological or social analysis. In a recent article, Sally Barr Ebest (2002) analyzes resistance to composition theory in general as a disabling characteristic of some new teachers who either lack a sense of their own efficacy in the classroom or, after years of successful practice as writers, have developed a modus operandi that works for them but is insulated from critique and not necessarily responsive to the needs of student writers. Within the world of teacher education, as well, resistance is often addressed as an individual problem, requiring timely intervention and a redirection of pedagogical energies.[3]

From both sides of the ideological spectrum, then, resistance is seen as a struggle, whether between teachers/students and consumer culture or between instructors and higher administration. As either hero or goat, the teacher-as-individual figures prominently not only in liberatory pedagogy and teacher education, but also in the epic tale of conversion and persecution with which this essay began. From the WPA's perspective, however, such events do not fit nicely into a folktale pattern. At the most concrete level, for the WPA resistance remains, first and foremost, a fact of life. Teachers who cannot or will not adapt to the basic policies and orientations of the program in which they work inevitably become the source of long, earnest conferences, student complaints, and (eventually) phone calls from the dean's office. But the ideological component of any writing program is at once more complex and less coherent than is often acknowledged. Composition pedagogy, within a programmatic and institutional setting, is and must be ideological; but when realized in, incorporated into, or represented by a writing program, the ideological bent of the dominant pedagogy is diluted, contradicted, qualified, and undermined by any number of extraneous factors ranging from system policies to staffing procedures. Thus, the range of instructor response—from accommodation to resistance—occurs within an ideological constellation that itself is conditioned by a bricolage of institutional policies and unspoken beliefs, departmental attitudes, and the perspectives of both the WPA who begins or manages the program and the WPA's predecessors—traces of whose decisions and beliefs a program's curriculum always bears.[4] The WPA, as hybrid administrator/teacher, exists in a particularly uneasy relationship to the affective dimension of the program she belongs to precisely because developing a program ethos necessarily cloaks the hidden fist of institutional discipline with the open hand of a quasi-religious community. And by virtue of her double position the WPA, perhaps more than any other member of a writing program, remains aware of the tension between individual and collective.

Nancy Welch's narrative of her unhappy translation from one kind of large writing program to another has haunted me ever since its publication, but most especially through the five years that I have served as the Director of First-Year Composition at the University of Georgia. What matters far more than the story's truth status—indeed, the story is framed as a parable—is its admonitory punch. Who wants to find herself in such an untenable position? Who wants to inflict such pain on others? Certainly not me. These questions pass through my mind most frequently during that crucial week of new TA and lecturer orientation, in which newly hired teachers from all over are introduced to our program, department, and administrators. Much of the week is taken up with "essential information." We meet and greet representatives from

Learning Disabilities, Disability Services, the Athletic Department, the Academic Honesty Office, and many other university constituencies. At this moment, our new teachers are experiencing the university as Althusser's "repressive state apparatus," in which teachers are legally bound by the terms of their syllabi and are subject to punishment for violations of department and university policy.

The mood lightens once this crash course in rules and regulations ends, but the new teachers and their supervisors also confront the reality of ideology during a more free-ranging discussion of pedagogy, grading, textbooks, and the use of technology in writing instruction. These are subjects that command the remainder of our attention during the weeklong orientation and during the semester-long practicum that follows and will be attended by most, although not all, of our new teachers. Recently, the group of new teachers has included a rather large body of second-year MA students who have finished a teaching apprenticeship but will be tackling their own classes for the first time. Members of this group have experienced the theory and practice of teaching only within their current environment; many were undergraduates at our institution, and so this group shows relatively little puzzlement or resistance to its policies and pedagogies. Others, however, are veteran teachers who have gravitated to our town and program from elsewhere. They ask concrete questions about pedagogy: "Is it OK if we write with our students?" asks a woman of about forty who first taught in a West Coast program. "In my former school, we taught some collaborative papers; can I substitute a collaborative paper for paper number four?" another queries. "Do you mind if I teach classical argument rather than Toulmin's model?" says a third. But our happy band of pedagogical brothers and sisters also contains newcomers like Welch who were reared, nurtured, and trained in one program and who, having left their first homes, find themselves in uncomfortably alien territory when dropped—like Dorothy from the tornado—at our door. Both anarchy and exhaustion/silence, two qualities that Ihab Hassan ascribes to postmodernism, are real and not particularly attractive possibilities.

I used to think that such teachers were a special case, but now have come to see their situation as representing, in hyperbolic fashion, that of all writing instructors who work not as itinerant sophists, but as members of a contemporary composition *program.* The inevitable tension between accommodation and resistance to programmatic imperatives informs, to some degree, the experience of us all. To purloin a phrase from Bruno Latour (1993), we have never been modern. But to theorize this dialectic between engagement and estrangement, we need to get beyond the heroic narrative that pits individuals against a faceless collective, a narrative that unhelpfully constructs any given writing program as a monolith rather than a bricolage of attitudes and practices that enjoys a long and rich—if often obscure—history. The remainder of this chapter examines first how composition theory has paradoxically exacerbated, rather than put to rest, the myth of the composition teacher as "heroic individual." This chapter then offers a "judicial" perspective on the relationship between individual and collective as one way of getting around the "conversion-excommunication" binary that informs the anecdote with which this chapter begins and a comparable "accommodation-resistance" binary that conditions current discussions of ideology and practice within writing programs.

THE WRITING PROGRAM AS CLASSROOM WRIT LARGE

Sharon Crowley's brief polemical history of university writing instruction in *Composition in the University* serves nicely as a prequel to Welch's story. Long ago, as Crowley and other historians have chronicled, composition classrooms were ruled by literary studies but staffed by full-time faculty. Then Arnoldian humanism reigned supreme and the universal freshman writing requirement justified itself in terms of vague notions of human cultivation and improvement. Material conditions for teachers degenerated as permanent faculty fled composition classrooms for literary study, a trend that poses a particular institutional problem for composition—namely, that over the years "first year composition has been remarkably vulnerable to ideologies and practices that originate elsewhere than its classrooms" (Crowley 1998, 6). Composition then becomes the colony of whatever disciplinary and institutional body acquires the right to "speak for" composition and so "dictate to teachers and students the goals they were expected to pursue as well as the texts they were to study and the curricula and pedagogical strategies they were to employ" (7). As Crowley writes,

> University and college faculty imagine composition as the institutional site wherein student subjectivity is to be monitored and disciplined. The continuing function of the required composition course has been to insure the academic community that its entering members are taught the discursive behaviors and traits of character that qualify them to join the community. The course is meant to shape students to behave, think, write, and speak as students rather than as the people they are, people who have differing histories and traditions and languages and ideologies. (8–9)

For Crowley, writing pedagogy is complicit with this agenda; she sees an enduring "current-traditional rhetoric," the disseminated remnant of a nineteenth-century pedagogy originally put in place to produce "Harvard men," as the prime obstacle to curricular and workplace reform in composition programs. In local academic communities, she argues, the machinery of current-traditional pedagogy is compounded by the accumulated "lore" that distinguishes insiders from outsiders.

Crowley's incisive, and admittedly polemical, account of first-year writing finds some confirmation in the testimonial with which this essay began. Welch's narrative alludes to both the global mechanics of rhetorical discipline and the local dynamics of academic communities. But her account also suggests, pace Crowley, that not an old-fashioned current-traditional rhetoric—but the very theories designed to supplant it—can lay at the root of the teacher's alienation. The more subtle barrier to institutional community within writing programs, she implies, is neither the provost's office nor the department elders but the ethos of composition studies itself. To a large extent this assessment is correct, although a number of additional factors—ranging from local politics to lack of local program histories—further complicate the picture. The end result, however, is an elision between the concept of a writing program and a writing class. The writing class becomes a synecdoche for the program as a whole, while the standardized syllabus models program coherence.

To some extent, any academic program is no more and no less than a bureaucratic unit organized around common goals, a set of bylaws, and policies governing both faculty and students. Within composition studies, however, "programs" have been increasingly defined as theory-driven, innovative, and standing in opposition to conservative teachers and sinister bureaucratic forces that seek always to economize at the expense of both teachers and students. Exemplary programs that spring to mind readily are identified with a particular person—Peter Elbow, Richard Lanham, Ross Winterowd, Andrea Lunsford—and therefore with a set of books, articles, and pedagogical applications associated with that leader's attempts to persuade others to accept his or her view of writing. A second elision, then, occurs between composition programs and composition theories.[5]

Our field often defines the evolution of writing instruction as a battle between programs, pedagogies, and political positions. Histories of rhetoric and composition tend to focus on "schools of thought," their chronology, their ideological status within the field(s) of writing instruction, and their inevitable demise. A number of important essays and books attempting to chart the territory have appeared steadily since the 1970s, but none perhaps has been more influential than James Berlin's "Rhetoric and Ideology in the Writing Class," brilliant in its own right and disseminated widely through its inclusion in Victor Villaneuva's influential anthology *Cross-Talk* and the Tate and Corbett *Writing Teacher's Sourcebook.* Every beginning teacher in our program who reads "Rhetoric and Ideology in the Writing Class" either identifies with, or feels vaguely guilty for not identifying with, "social-epistemic rhetoric." Most certainly, their instructor feels the unwelcome stirrings of guilt about her many ideological compromises in the name of program consistency or institutional reality.

Who, after all, would want to "refuse" "the ideological question altogether" and claim a highly unfashionable "transparent neutrality," as "the rhetoric of cognitive psychology" does? Better, perhaps, to align oneself with expressivism, a rhetoric that "has always openly admitted its ideological predilections." But expressivism is unfortunately "easily co-opted by the very capitalist forces it opposes," and who wants that? Better by far to join the "social-epistemic" cause, make ideology the center of classroom activity, and enjoy the privilege of self-consciousness that is denied to all other schools of thought (Berlin 1988, 487).

For Berlin, admittedly, the stakes of ideological self-definition are high: "To teach writing is to argue for a version of reality, and the best way of knowing and communicating it" (Berlin 1982, 234). Composition pedagogy is not just driven by theory, but a lived practice that amounts to a highly self-conscious merger of theory and ethics. For this reason if for no other, Berlin pulls no punches. He admits up front that he finds social-epistemic rhetoric to be "the alternative most worthy of emulation in the classroom, all the while admitting that it is the least formulaic and the most difficult to carry out" (Berlin 1988, 82). Yet because a fine line separates political from religious rhetoric, "Rhetoric and Ideology" can also seem evangelical. For while some might balk at the difficult task posed by epistemic rhetoric, according to Berlin, "[A] rhetoric cannot escape the ideological question, and to ignore this is to fail our responsibilities as teachers and as citizens" (698). Even those academics willing to avoid the "hard work" that social-epistemic pedagogy requires would feel hard-pressed to deny this final call to duty. The rhetoric of ideological critique itself "hails" teacher-subjects with the promise of a self-conscious, civic-minded community of teachers dedicated to students and to the needs of the polis.

Berlin's influential rhetoric of historiography has been succeeded by vigorous debate about the history of writing instruction;[6] and his more lengthy history of the field in *Rhetoric and Reality* (1987), to be fair, describes the intersection of different attitudes toward writing not only as a chronological fact, but also as a dynamic process throughout the decades he considers. Nevertheless, the tale of our discipline's history from "Rhetoric and Ideology" highlights with hyperbolic clarity a tacit consensus that in the history of rhetoric and composition a new school of thought—identified with a powerful and usually male figure and with certain pedagogical exercises and "tricks"—will inevitably overtake and supplant its predecessor. This foundational story may appeal to composition teachers for several reasons.

Defenses of rhetoric and composition as a discipline often have modeled themselves on literary theory and history, which also focuses on "schools of thought" and exemplary figures (Crowley 1994, 7). John Schilb derides this method as "taxonomania," a pseudoscientific effort to establish theoretical hierarchies by charting the terrain of rhetoric and composition (1994, 129). The master narrative in which important schools of thought inevitably succeed one another has also gained legitimacy from its (questionable) association with Thomas Kuhn's notion of a "paradigm shift," which has been evoked to elevate the vagaries of fashion in writing instruction to a higher status as quasi-scientific, and more loftily theoretical, revolutions of thought (see Hairston 1982).[7] Stephen North (1996) and others have argued, however, that our field's tendency toward "paradigm hope" is both illegitimate and disabling.[8] John Schilb agrees, cautioning that under the influence of "paradigm hope," "[T]he act of classifying might come to *appear* an end in itself, seeming to offer other scholars the convenient labels they are shopping for in their effort to establish rhetoric as a simple quasi science," but instead regulating the field it purports to describe (Schilb 1994, 130). In this way, the translation of theory into programmatic practice imposes a Foucauldian discipline on teachers and students. From Schilb's perspective, taxonomia can also lead to "canononia," an impulse to "boil rhetorical history down to a particular set of cherished texts, an official heritage" (131). Schilb's critique of the way in which theory regulates practice in composition programs confirms Welch's representation of how institutional discipline finds expression in a quasi-religious pedagogical "faith."

A less well-documented but equally important influence on our understanding of what constitutes a writing program is the frequent paucity of local history for most programs.[9] Lester Faigley (1992), albeit without bibliographical support, claims that the average life of a writing program is five years. My suspicion is that this definition relies on an equation between program and director. A new WPA is not only a new broom, but a source of new "god terms," in the vocabulary of Kenneth Burke (1961). With a new director often come new ideas, new textbooks, departmental syllabi, grading rubrics, assessment procedures, and new sets of commandments. These documents persist; what frequently is lost are the traces of conversations, committee meetings, and bitter struggles that prevent any one person from achieving the modernist gesture of "making new" a writing program. The equation between program and director, figured as a kind of monarchic succession, is reinforced by peripheral factors, such as the profession's definition of success as movement from one job to another, one cause of turnover in WPAs; the length of administrative appointments in any given department (ours offers three-year contracts, with the possibility of renewal for an additional term); and others that I, from my limited local perspective, cannot even identify.

What artifacts persist in a writing program record the force of individual personalities on the writing curriculum but are silent on the collaborative, combative, and negotiated processes that inform the underlife of academic institutions. I have worked at the same university now for almost twenty years. Although I became First-year Composition Director only in 1998, I had served loyally on the Freshman English Committee since 1984. No matter that within the last week I have discovered an undocumented change in placement policy that has no resonance with my memory of the committee's machinations during the year in which the change occurred and no discernible paper trail. I do remember, however, a meeting around 1991 when the then new director proposed that we replace the ten fifty-minute, in-class essays that teachers had been assigning with a smaller number of out-of-class essays, whose quality would benefit from drafting, revision, and peer editing. Despite this infusion of process pedagogy into the curriculum, the final exam continued to count for one-third of the students' final grade, and does so to this day. The reason? According to my memory, this was a concession to the elders who feared a plague of plagiarism if students produced papers away from the watchful eyes of their teachers. Whether or not my personal memory of the meeting is accurate, no trace of that discussion can be found in our evolving departmental syllabus, grading sheet, the finely honed handbook of policies and processes—or even, if I could lay hands on them, the circumspect minutes of that meeting. What we lack is, in the vocabulary of Shirley K Rose and Irwin Weiser, "an understanding of document-event relations" (2002, 280).[10] Without these connections, no one can satisfactorily discuss whether or not the final exam should continue to carry such weight, given the fact that the elders who defended its utility have long since retired.

Throw into the mix one final ingredient, the particular experiences of novice teachers, for whose benefit most standardized features of any curriculum are concocted. Novice teachers, according to Christine Farris's research, tend to relate their teaching to their own educational experience and disciplinary expertise; to identify with certain labels, approaches, and theorists; to focus closely on the textbook chosen by or assigned to them; and to feel ambivalent about their relation to programmatic discipline and their role as evaluators of students (Farris 1996). (In my experience, modeling on a current or favorite teacher from the past can also play a central role in the new teacher's construction of his or her ethos.) In a second phase, new teachers tend to focus more on consolidating authority and fine-tuning classroom discipline. In most cases, as Farris shows, the teachers emerge from their first year in the classroom with a stronger sense of ownership and more nuanced understanding of their pedagogical ethos in its relation to that put forth by the assigned textbook. Nevertheless, the perception of writing instruction as a dialectic involving lore, disciplinary theory, and specific textbooks—a perception common to first-year instructors and often to recent arrivals from other pedagogical cultures—exerts a strong influence on local concepts of what constitutes a writing program.

All of these factors, I would suggest, conspire to erase the distinction between a writing program and a composition classroom. The writing program is nothing more, and nothing less, than the writing class writ large. As Farris's study shows, such a conflation can be liberating for instructors, confirming William Irmscher's belief that teacher-student relationships have the single greatest effect on the quality of composition teaching (Irmscher 1987, 49; cited by Farris 1996, 107). But the substitution of classroom for program can also alienate teachers by obscuring their potential agency in both arenas, the classroom *and* the program.

ADJUDICATING DIFFERENCE: EQUIVALENCE AND HORIZONTAL RELATIONS IN A LARGE WRITING PROGRAM

The problem remains of how to imagine a writing program that invites individual teachers (and students) to exercise agency without deconstructing altogether the program itself. While most current debate about writing instruction concerns itself with deliberative rhetoric—

the relation of the classroom to civic duty and the public sphere—the untapped field of judicial rhetoric offers an equally useful model for defining writing programs as institutions *sui generis*. First of all, the judicial model addresses head-on what is, to me, the most trenchant criticism of contemporary writing instruction: its continuing connection with institutional discipline in the most austerely Foucauldian sense of that term. Judicial rhetoric concerns itself with laws and trespasses, crimes and punishments, and so helps us to confront the rule-bound and consequence-driven dimension of writing program administration that most of us glance away from in embarrassment. Second, the metaphor of "writing program-as-judicial-system" tacitly acknowledges both the individual WPA's power in relation to the teachers she supervises and her imbrication in a larger web of formal and informal power relationships within departmental, college, and university units. Finally, and most important to me, a judicial model for writing program administration acknowledges that "law" and judgments based on it necessarily commit violence against individuals' desires and beliefs (on both sides of the teacher's desk); judicial acts must inevitably involve violence as a product of power. As I hope to show, however, acknowledging the law's inevitable violence can suggest a more holistic approach to defining rights and responsibilities for both WPAs and teachers.

For the remainder of this chapter, I will sketch out a rhetorical perspective on the conflict between individual and collective in writing program administration through the metaphor of "writing program-as-judicial-system." I refer generally to some issues in contemporary jurisprudence, but will evoke more specifically useful lines of argument that have been developed in the work of Drucilla Cornell. Cornell's work is grounded in feminism, literary theory, and psychoanalysis, but also offers concrete applications to particular case law on social issues ranging from abortion and pornography to employment law.[11] For this reason her work, and jurisprudence in general, is congenial to the mix of theory and practicality that also characterizes writing program administration. Furthermore, Cornell's response to what Joan Scott calls the "equality versus difference dilemma" (Scott 1990) is useful for steering an administrative path between the idea that the collective trumps individual desires and beliefs (which, in programmatic terms, means an inflexible syllabus and assigned textbook) and the valorization of individual agency (which, at its extreme, means academic freedom at the expense of programmatic coherence).

Judicial rhetoric begins with the fact of power and its effects on individuals within institutions. In a recent essay, Louise Wetherbee Phelps makes a strong argument for the WPA's possession of and right to exercise power. Phelps rehabilitates power by redefining it as "leadership," an attitude that foregrounds moral agency. Although she grants that to a large degree the WPA is identified with an "institution, its enterprises, and more broadly, the ideologies that underlie them" (2002, 20), Phelps also believes that power is always negotiated and that hierarchy itself is at bottom a "collaborative" construction (27). Nevertheless, in recommending the "vigorous virtues" appropriate to leadership, Phelps merely reverses the parable with which we began; now, instead of the intrepid TA resisting heretical pressures, we have the noble WPA who forges a virtuous path between the needs of individuals and institutional mandates. The effect, in this second case, is to downplay the violence that underlies institutional discipline and lies at the heart of my judicial metaphor.

Violence is a logically inevitable counterpart to the power invested in law, Drucilla Cornell suggests, in a line of argument that is indebted to Jacques Derrida, Michel Foucault, and feminist legal thinkers. Writers within legal studies have responded to this stark view of legal institutions in different ways. Some stress the community established by shared stories; others discern the need for individuals to open themselves up to "otherness."[12] Derrida, most radically, follows the logic of the law's violence to a deconstructive conclusion; he argues that each case remakes the law anew, so that any attempt at equity—the adjustment of general laws to specific cases—is doomed to failure and therefore demonstrates the impossibility of justice and illegitimacy of the law. His conclusion is not nihilistic, however. Derrida responds to this dilemma with an ethical gesture, concluding that "we"—a rhetorically constructed collective based on ethical solidarity or friendship—have an unlimited and inescapable responsibility for the law's violence.

Cornell takes the pronouncement of law's violence in a slightly different direction. She argues that "equity" should not be defined in terms of either "sameness" or "difference" among individuals under the law and offers instead a politics of "equivalence." For Cornell, a concept of "equivalent" rights respects the "lived individuality" of subjects under the law (1993, 154). Such an attitude recognizes that insisting on "equality-as-sameness" constitutes sex discrimination, for instance, when a woman's leave for pregnancy is defined exactly as leave for a man's medical disability (such as a heart attack). While the logic of "equality-as-sameness" leads to inequity under the law, paradoxically so does rigid commitment to a monolithic concept of difference; one example would be when difference is evoked to justify committing childbearing women to an inferior "mommy track" in their professions. A theory of equivalent rights, according to Cornell, differs from "equal rights" in that parties in a position of less power do not have to define their situation in terms of the cultural construction of groups who already enjoy particular rights and power. For example, "homosexuals should be given the *equivalent right* to be left alone in their intimate associations, whether or not they choose to mimic the life pattern of traditional heterosexuals" (153; original emphasis). To enjoy privacy, therefore, homosexuals do not have to show that their intimate lives are the same as, equal to, or even different from those of other groups whose intimacy is recognized and protected by law. They can define their own right in terms of "lived individuality."

In Cornell's later work, we can see more clearly how the notion of "lived individuality," which might seem peculiarly essentialist coming from a Lacanian deconstructionist, helps to link both the narrower concerns of case law and Cornell's very broad essays into theory with the everyday politics of public life. In analyses of such topics as pornography, abortion, and employment law, Cornell's notion of lived individuality evolves into a fully fledged idea of personhood that elevates the politics of equivalence into a theory of equality. Without the minimum conditions for individuation, Cornell argues, "we cannot effectively engage in the project of becoming a person" (2000, 17). Personhood is not a given, she posits, but a process. Just as the noun "individuality" cannot exist without the verbal adjective "lived"—making the individual-as-essence dependent on the action of living—so too must the "person" be "personated" through public action or drama. In a clever inversion of the idea that a persona is a mask, Cornell resorts to etymology to define the (whole) persona as that which "shines through" the public mask: "[F]or a person to be able to shine through she must imagine herself as whole, or conceptually differentiate between the mask and the self. A person, in other words, is an aspiration because it is a project that can never be fulfilled, once and for all." Thus a person enters "an endless process of working through personae" (2000, 19).

"Worker's Rights and the Defense of Just-Cause Statutes" (Chapter Six in Cornell 2000) offers a concrete application of Cornell's understanding of equality based on the individual's inalienable right to develop as a person. In this essay, Cornell argues against the position that if employers must give "just cause" for terminating employees, by a reciprocal logic employees would have to justify leaving their current employment for another job. Cornell's critique of this position relies on her insistence that freedom, which guarantees the possibility of personhood and therefore of individuality, depends not on abstract reciprocity in workplace relations, but on concrete "horizontal" relations. An insistence on hierarchy gives all power to the boss and none to the workers. But an insistence on reciprocity, or contractual mutuality, between employer and employee glosses over the real differences in power between the two. In other words, "just cause" statutes that impose legal restraints on employers recognize that employers and workers are not "equal," but neither are they irrevocably "different." Because powerful employers and less powerful workers exist in a "horizontal" as well as a hierarchical relationship, the state can step in to regulate workplace relations in order to emphasize the horizontal relations between them as persons. While the law stabilizes these horizontal relations by passing judgment on who has the most power and who the most to lose when employment is terminated, that determination is not fixed in stone. In other words, what is law and what is up for negotiation is itself always in motion. Thus, exercising judgment remains a process, one whose conclusion is, of course, eternally deferred.

Finally, Cornell emphasizes that all members of a legal community—the metaphorical "plaintiffs" and "defendants"—have a responsibility first, to be active in "shining" through their masks toward a future anterior self rather than merely resting on the merits of pre-established identities; and second, to exercise freedom and seek equivalent rights within a communal context. The state guarantees "conditions of horizontality" (2000, 187), which is the precondition for equivalent rights and personhood, but does not etch in stone what constitutes a person. Thus, the "plaintiff" has the right but also the responsibility to move forward in aspiration and not fall back on past stereotypes, just as the "defendant" must. Individuality has, paradoxically enough, a communal basis within a constellation of "law" that by nature does violence to (present) individuality but holds forth a promise of (future) personhood.

BEYOND ACCOMMODATION

Cornell's explanation of the communal basis for individuality within a context of "law-as-violence" provides a starting point for working through the relation of individual and collective within a writing program, at the same time suggesting a model for understanding the WPA's role within that dynamic. I began by suggesting that the WPA has a hybrid role, not only as teacher/administrator, but as Phelps suggests, as an individual positioned between instructors and the upper levels of administration. So although she often "lays down the law" to those she supervises, she is not the law itself. Nevertheless, Cornell's model for employee relations, grounded as it is in a notion of equivalent rights, can help to define the WPA's adjudication between the curriculum she stands for (which might be considered "law") and the teachers with whom she enjoys a "horizontal" relationship.

What would a concept of writing program administration grounded in equivalent rights look like? Although other institutions of different sizes, shapes, and constituencies might identify "law" differently, I would say that for my program—housed in a large state school with over one hundred instructors and about six thousand students per year—the underlying "laws" of our program are defined not ideologically, but bureaucratically. If not exactly etched in stone, the basic requirements for any first-year composition class are set out clearly in the *First-Year Composition Handbook.* The requirements that guarantee some consistency across sections of the course are the number of papers assigned (five); the length of papers (1,000 to 1,500 words); a standardized grading rubric; and the amount of weight assigned to the program-wide final exam (30 percent). Not surprisingly, consistency in the amount of work assigned and in grading standards across sections are the most frequent causes of student litigiousness; length of papers is also one important criteria for determining whether a composition course from another institution counts for transfer credit. Because these factors are frequent targets of anger and pain on both sides, they might be considered the curricular violence for which the WPA must take responsibility.

Etched less firmly in stone are features of the program that bear on teaching philosophy and disciplinary interest. The first half of first-year composition is taught as an argument course, the second as writing about literature. While these curricular orientations have now been defined by the Regents as gospel throughout the University of Georgia system, there is latitude for improvisation within these boundaries. A number of experimental courses, some sponsored by the writing program and some proposed by individual teachers, have been introduced over the years. Although the first-year composition program has a consensus textbook and sample syllabus, only those individuals hired at the last minute (for practical reasons) and first-time teachers in our program, especially those who are participating in the Composition Pedagogy Practicum, are *required* to use it. (And yes, to some extent this requirement extends to those who have taught previously in other programs. Being on the same page throughout the semester helps the practicum's ethos a great deal.) Other instructors are not required to use either syllabus or textbook, although for some reason many continue to do so, even when they complain about its ideology, politics, or general infringement on their academic freedom.

I dwell on these mundane details not so much as an apologia for the state of the curriculum at the University of Georgia, but to suggest that what is "law" for one time and place may well not apply to others; more important, perhaps, within a concept of equivalence based on horizontal relationships, what is law and what is open for negotiation is always contingent. For these reasons, a curricular commitment to "equivalent rights" within the culture of a writing program is quite useful.

What remains is the even more vexing question of how to carry out a commitment to equivalent rights on a daily basis. Just to offer one example, once our program began to emphasize technology, teachers who wanted to substitute a collaborative Web project for one traditional paper have generally met with much more administrative enthusiasm than do those teachers who want to assign only in-class essays simply because they had assigned such essays in the past. An instructor who wants to collapse two papers into a lengthier one because of a well-defended proposal for teaching writing in the public sphere will have an easier time than one who just wants to concentrate on her own classes or upcoming oral exams. The examples I have given here may seem self-evident. Appeals based on curricular innovation are always more . . . well, appealing than excuses based on need or practicality. Within a dynamic of equivalent rights, however, the court is always in session. A teacher's relation to programmatic "law" depends on the process of personation, the "shining through" of a credible and appealing ethos through a succession of professional masks.

I have been asked, "How might a commitment to equivalency under the law empower instructors, or at least invite them to share power?" Such a goal, of course, is central to many important pedagogies, from Freire to feminism. But from the perspective I take here, it is the wrong question—or, at least, not the final question. To evoke again Hassan's charting of modernism against postmodernism, a commitment to writing program administration as a system of equivalent rights under the institutional law involves relinquishing the dream of modernism. Respect for "lived individuality" and belief in the process of personation both belong to petite histories, not to master narratives. Working on horizontal relations, another postmodern directive, means at once a willingness to wear a mask and a recognition of the power of chance. As I have suggested above, for the most part, writing programs under institutional law are always and already in process. So what a respect for lived individuality and the pursuit of horizontal relations probably entails on a daily basis is committee work, meetings, repeated conversations, political organization, and lots of storytelling. Being "beyond accommodation" finally means constructing an institutional autobiography that acknowledges the impossibility of epic endings.

"JUDICIOUS" CONCLUSION

Would the fictional "Nancy Welch" have fared any better under the writing program that I have described here? I can only offer a counter-parable that is "answerable," in the Bakhtinian sense, to the narrative published in the 1993 issue of *College English.* Let us call our antiheroine N. Under a system of "equivalent rights," during their orientation and first-semester practicum, N. and her compatriots (together with their WPA and other administrators) would have sorted out the "law" (program procedures and guidelines) from pedagogical philosophy and theory. They would have made their way through "Rhetoric and Ideology in the Writing Class," discussing not only the ins and outs of competing composition theories, but evaluating their own relationships to those pedagogies. Presentations by more advanced TAs, selected to represent a range of pedagogical philosophies and styles, assure the new teachers that there is more than one way to teach writing effectively.

As the semester progresses, the teachers begin to negotiate the boundaries of various policies. N. learns that although many of her peers use their required class time in the computer lab to explore issues on the Internet—reinforcing the textbook's emphasis on current events and popular culture—she can develop a useful set of prewriting and revision exercises related to upcoming papers for her days in the computer lab. N. also learns to adjust her classroom practice to a departmental grading rubric that, in her expressivist judgment, puts far too much emphasis on grammar and correctness. She makes this adjustment by constructing a series of process-oriented rubrics for drafts, using the departmental rubric only for the final product, and developing a sensible but liberal policy that encourages students to rewrite unsatisfactory papers. (And, of course, to satisfy the demands of law she adds a crystal-clear statement about drafting and rewrites in her course syllabus, then explains the rationale behind her pedagogical choices to her class!)

After the first paper, a student comes in to complain. In N.'s class he must produce three drafts for each and every paper while his roommate, who is in another class with a different teacher, has to write only one draft. This student never revised in high school and does not want to do so now. As N.'s choices have been arrived at by negotiation, the WPA recognizes the integrity of the teacher's "lived individuality." Nicely but firmly, she tells the student that his TA is not "required" to limit her number of drafts. Indeed, she has discussed this issue with the teacher, and together they have decided that in order to honor N.'s belief in the efficacy of drafting, she will require one less essay from her students than is called for by the *Handbook*. These decisions are explained to the student, and the WPA offers to move him to another section. Satisfied that his workload is equitable, if different from, that of students in other classes, the young man decides that he likes N. as a teacher and elects to remain in the class.

N. continues on in the Ph.D. program. After taking a course in composition theory and a seminar on service learning at the Institute of Higher Education, N. decides that expressivist pedagogy can be enriched by providing students with real-world imperatives for writing. She is chosen to participate in a campus-wide Learning Community Program that is grounded in social issues and involves a service-learning component at the local homeless shelter. For this class, N. is able to jettison altogether the departmental grading sheet and to construct a series of rubrics designed to reflect the processes of investigation and writing that are unique to this teaching situation. The WPA asks that N., in turn, stick to the departmental grading scale for the sake of program consistency, even though it differs from that used by other professors in the Learning Community. Her students, after all, will have roommates who are taking "regular" English 1101. This time there are no complaints. In fact, N.'s class is a real success. She receives a teaching honor and gives a paper on her experience at the CCCC. Back at home, the WPA invites N. to mentor several other interested TAs for the service-learning composition class. The service learning version of English 1101 is incorporated finally into the curriculum as an alternative route to satisfy the composition requirement. N. has fulfilled her right and responsibility to develop into a person whose identity continues to "shine through" her evolving teaching personae. She is rewarded with a tenure-track position at another university in the region.

The portrait I have painted here is transparently utopian, but N.'s experience is a collage drawn from real events and people. In imagining her trajectory for this essay, I have acquired a clearer sense of the benefits and drawbacks of a writing program based on a judicial model. In the ongoing negotiation of "horizontal relations" between teacher and WPA, the TA must surrender some autonomy and personal ideology, while the WPA gives up the right to mold the program in her own image. On the other hand, the WPA achieves a better working relationship with her teachers and N. claims her right to a "lived individuality" that, although falling short of complete autonomy, gives her a voice in the program's evolution. Most problematic but perhaps most exciting of all, the program itself grows and changes with time.

From this perspective as well, the TA who passes through our first-year composition program en route from one professional place to another becomes not an anomaly, but the epitome of a composition instructor. For if personhood is an aspiration whose end is always ahead, then who better epitomizes the personhood of a writing teacher under curricular law than the liminal subject, the instructor newly arrived from parts and pedagogies unknown and thrust into a new culture of composition? The TA in transit may feel like she is required either to profess the faith or risk excommunication, but neither the fact of pedagogical violence nor the imposition of disciplinary limits prohibits the construction of any given writing program as a public community in which teaching-persons negotiate with structures, and indeed, with the WPA as the law's representative. For me, such a construct offers an alternative to the widespread belief that accommodation to or resistance against writing program and institutional demands constitute a teacher's only choices.

In *Beyond Accommodation*, Cornell notes that revisionary metaphors are by necessity utopian: "[W]e are never simply working within what 'is,' because what is, is only reachable in metaphor, and therefore, in the traditional sense, not reachable at all" (1999, 168). In other words, to be "beyond accommodation" means simply understanding that you are *not yet* beyond accommodation. In my scenario, the heroic story of individual resistance and triumph with which this essay began would yield to another kind of epic, in which teachers, WPAs, students—and epic narratives themselves—are always *in medias res*. For me, that's a good place to be.

4

OVERCOMING DISAPPOINTMENT

Constructing Writing Program Identity through Postmodern Mapping

Sharon James McGee

Can the truth really be so hard to find? It all depends upon where you're standing.

—Denis Wood

Frustration. Disappointment. Anger. Exhaustion. Silence. WPAs often experience these emotions as part of their work as evidenced by frequent discussions on the WPA listserv and at conferences.[1] These negative feelings have even caused a backlash among some WPAs, who prefer only to talk about the "happy times" of being a WPA. Certainly, positive emotions are not antithetical to postmodernity; however, as Ihab Hassan (1987) notes, exhaustion and silence are conditions of the postmodern experience. Understanding potential causes of frustration, disappointment, anger, exhaustion, and silence can help us as WPAs find solutions to overcoming these feelings that creep into our jobs and identities.

In her March 2002 article in *College English*, Laura Micciche eloquently discusses the ways in which disappointment permeates the identities and work of WPAs. Central causes of disappointment, as Micciche and others have noted, is the devalued status of composition within English departments specifically and their institutions generally; the continued reliance upon exploitative labor practices in order to staff service courses; the constricted academic job market in other areas of English studies, which as a result inflames the disciplinary binaries and egos that already exist within many departments; and more recently the strained budgets, caused or exacerbated by the United States' recent economic downturn, resulting in WPAs waging bigger battles to secure fewer available financial resources. Certainly these factors affect our colleagues in other areas of the humanities as well; however, let us not belittle the fact that all of these conditions increase the pressures and disappointment felt by WPAs who must build or maintain writing programs. One way to combat the feeling of disappointment, Micciche posits, is for WPAs to educate themselves "about the way work is organized in the university" (435).

Over the past few years I have been thinking both about the process of work in the university and how that cycle of work affects administrating a writing program. Pragmatically, I come to this topic through what I've learned in my academic service opportunities at two universities where I have been in tenure-track positions. A colleague calls me "The Queen of All Things Service," and while arguably service responsibilities may divert my time away from other academic foci, my service responsibilities have also afforded me the opportunity to view the workings of the university through a scholarly lens. Three important service responsibilities have shaped my understanding of how work gets done in the university: serving as a faculty senator at two universities, being a member of one university's general education committee, and participating in a very small role in my current institution's Academic Quality Improvement Project (AQIP) accreditation process. What I have learned from these experiences continues to shape my thinking about politics, institutions, and getting the job done.

Several interpretative frameworks—postmodern critical theory, rhetorical theory, and the body of writing program administration theory—shape my analysis of the process of work in the academy. In this essay, I will map the way that WPA work proceeds at my current institution and discuss what this implies for the work of WPAs in general and the identities that they forge at their respective institutions.

THE ORGANIZATION OF ACADEMIC INSTITUTIONS

Academic institutions are social and organizational places, and as such they rely on mechanisms of operation by which information, ideas, people, and work flow. Without thinking, we often say that these mechanisms "help work get done" in the university (when, in fact, that point is arguable). As a social and organizational space, the academy relies on power to control, direct, enhance, or limit the work. In other words, the amount and type of work that flows through the channels is determined by those in power. Turning to Foucault, we understand that power formations seek to fulfill three criteria:

> [F]irst to obtain power at the lowest possible cost . . . ; second to bring the effects of this social power to their maximum intensity and to extend them as far as possible, without either interval or failure, and third, to link this

> "economic" growth of power with the output of the apparatuses [in our case educational] within which it is exercised. (1984, 207)

Within the academy, power must occur economically, certainly in monetary terms. For example, while a department has many faculty members, it has one chair; while an academic unit has several chairs, it has one dean; while a university has several deans, it has one provost, and one president or chancellor. Paying the salaries for a few deans is less expensive than paying the salaries of many deans. Further, power is interwoven into the fabric of the organization and because we wear clothes cut from this cloth, power then is somewhat invisible. To explain this point, consider an ethnographer who locates her research in a site with which she is very familiar—her own hometown, for example. Because she has been acculturated in this community, she may not notice patterns of behavior since she does not see them as unique or different. So it is with power: because power is interwoven into the system, it becomes unnoticeable. Spending years within the academy as undergraduate students, then graduate students, then as faculty, we have become acclimated to the loci of power. Because we become acclimated and power becomes transparent, that power then maintains the organization.

Before continuing I want to make clear that power is not necessarily malevolent, though the word's connotation often leads us to think of power negatively, as something that one person has and another doesn't.[2] Certainly in the academy, as in other places such as the business world, this notion of power holds true: some faculty have tenure-track positions and benefits while others do not. Some administrators use power to dictate courses of action. However, power is not always, nor even usually, malevolent. Consider the marathon runner who daily trains body and mind for the twenty-six-mile race; without powerful leg muscles, lungs, and mental focus, she could not complete the run. She does not harness her power to beat the other runners—for many marathon runners, success is not in beating others but in finishing the race—she harnesses it to endure.

For WPAs, understanding the way in which power is constructed and channeled within universities is important; however, it is often not something that WPAs are trained in or have time for, and they may forget about it because of its invisibility (as several of the essays in this collection attest). Too often WPAs cannot think much beyond the local—the operation of their own programs and departments—to the broader issues of the way in which power is situated and dispersed within our institutions because WPAs have multiple identities and responsibilities within a department. First, WPAs are administrators who deal with programmatic issues such as building or rebuilding a writing program or who are brought on board to maintain the status quo—even if that status quo is not theoretically grounded. Further, WPAs maintain the daily operation of a writing program, a job that is often part firefighter—putting out the small brush fires that spark up in a writing program's day-to-day existence—and counselor. WPAs are also faculty members who often teach classes, mentor graduate students, participate in departmental service, and engage in their own scholarship. So it's understandable why WPAs become mired in the daily grind of administering a writing program, why ennui takes hold, and why in spite of all the great teaching and learning that takes place within writing programs, WPAs often find themselves beating their heads against walls of one kind or another. However, by thinking beyond the local writing program, we can become aware of the way that the university forms and organizes power both locally and institutionally. By doing so, we can begin to uncover ways to deal with the kinds of problems that often confront a writing program.

While Foucault and other theorists such as Bourdieu, Marx, and Althusser provide useful lenses through which we can explore the overarching concerns of monoliths and their power formation, realizing that Western universities are also modeled on the democratic process is also constructive; this recognition offers another way to view the process through which work gets done in the university. Democratic principles are exercised in faculty governance and its fraternal twin: shared governance. Faculty or shared governance structures the university so that faculty and often staff have voices in the decision-making processes of each institution, advising the administration about or creating academic policy within the institution. Faculty governance works much like the legislative and executive branches of our country. Certainly, faculty governance has its problems, especially within the last decade, causing the Association of American Colleges and Universities to devote the spring 2001 issue of its journal, *Peer Review*, to the problems facing faculty governance. Faculty governance, if working, is a way to oversee all aspects of academic decision making—budgeting and allocating fiscal resources, planning for facility and technological needs, overseeing academic and student affairs, and even managing public relations. Whatever weaknesses faculty governance may have, it *is* a primary way of managing work within the university. By recognizing faculty governance as a way of managing work within the university, a WPA can begin to see ways in which work can be done—as well as understand how issues that affect the writing program may happen without much consideration of the WPA.

POSTMODERN MAPPING

Postmodern mapping is a strategy to view organizational space. The activity of mapping is making its way from geography and cartography into other disciplines, including composition and professional writing studies, and is essential to the act of institutional critique (Porter et al. 2000). Recently, Tim Peeples made a case for using postmodern mapping as a way to "enable WPAs to investigate their own positioning in an institution as well as to investigate and analyze a variety of relationships among various institutional spaces within and outside the writing program" (1999, 154). Postmodern mapping, as Peeples posits, has two distinct uses: First, it allows representation of the "unsettled subject"—one whose identity, values, ideology, and perceptions are in flux. Second, postmodern mapping seeks to "unsettle static, structural conceptions of space and to represent its dynamic, socially constructed characteristics" (1999, 154). When using postmodern mapping to examine WPA work, Peeples argues that multiple, competing maps should be constructed within each case and then, once maps are constructed, those maps can be examined across cases in order to understand the complex endeavor that is WPA work. For Peeples, postmodern mapping allows the WPA to become an organizational planner.

Like Peeples, postmodern cartographer Denis Wood claims that multiple maps illustrate more than just a guide to get from one location to another or to locate particular points within a geographical plane. In his book, *The Power of Maps*, Wood (1992) argues that maps display for us representations of society and culture in terms of leisure (the map of a shopping mall), economics (the location of desirable real estate), values (the size of parks or green space), and more. When viewed together, multiple maps show us the best and worst of our culture; furthermore, maps display for us relationships. Importantly, maps do not show reified representations or relationships: they show only the geographic points or cultural ideas that the cartographer (whether professional or novice—Wood argues that we all draw maps) places on them. Wood states

> Maps are about relationships. In even the least ambitious maps, simple presences are absorbed in multilayered relationships integrating and

> disintegrating sign functions, packaging and repackaging meanings. The map is a highly complex supersign, a sign composed of lesser signs, or more accurately, a synthesis of signs; and these are supersigns in their own right, systems of signs of more specific or individual function. It's not so much that a map conveys meanings so much as *unfolds* them through *a cycle of interpretation* in which it is continually torn down and rebuilt; and, to be truthful, this is not really the map's work but that of the user, who creates a wealth of meaning. (132; original emphasis)

Because maps are supersign structures with which users interpret meaning, they are rhetorical, both discursive and persuasive. Wood writes

> In presentation, the map attains . . . the level of discourse. Its discursive form may be as simple as a single map image rendered comprehensible by the presence of a title, legend, and scale; or as complex as those in *The New State of the World Atlas,* hurling multiple images, diagrams, graphs, tables, and texts at their audience in a ranging polemic. (140)[3]

Taking both Peeples's and Wood's views into account, we can see that the act of mapping makes WPAs active as planners; the maps themselves become powerful rhetorical tools.

I turn now to discussing several alternative ways of mapping the WPA's position at Southern Illinois University Edwardsville. I should add that I am only going to discuss a few of the possible maps that can be drawn to depict this situation. One of the valuable uses of postmodern mapping is that by drawing the map in different ways, the mapper can identify particular trends and alliances; of course, not everyone needs to know about all of these maps. Although this example is unique to one institution, I suspect that with a few slight modifications, these maps would detail the work of other WPAs at similarly sized public institutions.

Because I am taking this example from a specific institution that has a specific WPA, it would be easy to conflate the WPA position with the person who holds that position; however, I think it is useful to separate the two—the position from the person—in order to gain a fuller picture of the identity issues that arise.

Locating the Writing Program and WPA in the Organization

Figure 1 depicts one representation of the WPA's position within the university. The WPA is situated within an English Department whose Full Time Equivalent (FTE) is almost as large as some entire college's FTE

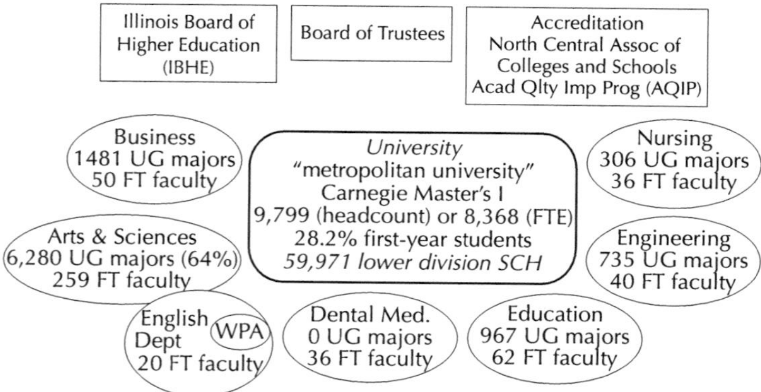

Figure 1

appointments. The department is housed in the largest college on campus. While the WPA is just one appointment within the department, the WPA is responsible for overseeing approximately two hundred sections of first-year writing each year through which nearly every first-year student passes. Therefore, the WPA and the writing program have contact with every student in every college within the university, even though the position is localized within one department.

At first glance, this map appears to show a static representation of the university and the WPA's position within it; however, as a map of an organization, nothing is in fact static—what happens in the first-year composition sequence and what students learn (or do not learn) in it have an impact on almost every unit on the map. (These units are represented by circles on the map to suggest interconnection and motion.) Collectively the students who pass through first-year composition take what they learned about writing to subsequent courses in the university.

Furthermore, the writing program is not just part of this map, but of other maps. As noted in figure 1, there are other bodies to which the university is responsible (and even others such as legislators that aren't mapped); these stakeholders are represented by boxes on the map. These bodies include the Illinois Board of Higher Education (IBHE), which oversees all public colleges and universities in the state and serves as a conduit to the governor and legislature, the Board of Trustees, and accreditation boards. Although the WPA does not have regular contact with these bodies—in fact may never have direct contact—typically the WPA must address issues or implement changes as directed by these agencies. One of the problems faced by the WPA in this map is that some units within the university, let alone some outside stakeholders, do not in fact realize that the position even exists.[4]

This map is *my* rendering of the organization where I have been able to locate the WPA as part of the institution. By positioning the WPA on the map, I have made a significant change from a map that others within the organization might draw. In fact the WPA, who is a program director, is not recognized as a program director in the same way that, for example, the director of the women's studies program is. The women's studies program is an interdisciplinary program not housed in any one department; however, the director's position would likely appear on a map of our college's organization: the director is invited to the Chairs and Program Directors meeting with the dean of Arts and Sciences while the WPA is not. Why the WPA is not represented on the map is of course a complex question, having as much to do with institutional history as with the value placed on writing or the intellectual labor required to teach it.

What is the value, then, in mapping this space? Creating this map has resulted in several important consequences. First, when I initially drew this map of our institution, we (the WPA and Expository Writing Committee) were feeling beleaguered. In an effort to develop a cohesive program, we developed goals, outcomes, and objectives for our first-semester composition course. Over the course of two years' work, the committee negotiated, discussed, and worked toward retooling the First Year Composition (FYC) sequence to enhance student learning and attain program unity while still maintaining faculty's academic freedom within their classrooms. Throughout the process, the committee was very aware that whatever changes we made to the program would be viewed critically by some of the faculty who teach FYC. During the process, we became overwhelmed with the work and with our own impending sense of confrontation. The map allowed us to see an obvious point that we had known but overlooked—FYC, while taught by English Department faculty and administered by the WPA situated within the English Department, affects the entire university—students, faculty in other disciplines, and accreditation. Faculty across the university expect that students leave the FYC sequence prepared to write in other courses and that by having a cohesive program with clearly articulated student expectations, faculty in other departments gain a better sense of what happens in FYC. Because we teach almost every first-year student in the university, we have an obligation to students, parents, the provost, the Board of Trustees, and accreditation agencies that we have a clear vision

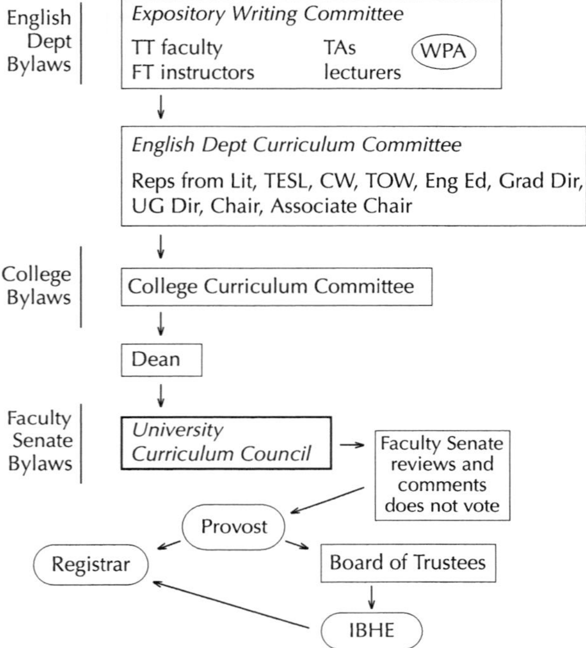

Figure 2

of FYC with an articulated set of student learning outcomes and that we are working to ensure a quality experience for each student. When we began to see the representation before us and the multiple stakeholders in FYC, the committee became—to use the overwrought term—empowered to create a program that would do all of these things, even if it meant that not everyone would agree with the changes.

Mapping the Flow of Work

Using another map, I will demonstrate the flow of work at my institution to highlight sources of potential problems and alliances for the WPA.

Work within our institution follows the cycle outlined in Figure 2. At each level of work, a particular set of bylaws codifies the procedures for channeling the work to get done. Notice that the WPA is missing beyond the first level of the map, which is perhaps more common than not on other campuses. For various political reasons, to have the WPA be a decision maker beyond the local level is precarious. When trying to institute change within a writing program, however, building alliances within the framework is essential, especially at key levels in the cycle (in our case University Curriculum Council, as indicated by italics).

For example, major changes to the writing program curricula (including course descriptions, credit hours awarded, and the like) typically begin with the Expository Writing Committee, which generates a plan, writes the proposal (following approved university procedures), and approves it. The proposal is then sent through various overseeing channels: the Department Curriculum Committee, the College Curriculum Committee, the dean, and the University Curriculum Council (which is part of the Faculty Senate structure). At any point, committees can approve, deny, or request changes to a proposal. Once the proposal is approved by the Curriculum Council, the Faculty Senate at large reviews the proposal and then forwards it to the provost for final approval. (Any new program, such as a new graduate degree, would go beyond the provost to the Board of Trustees and the IBHE.)

Because FYC affects every department and college within the university, certainly few courses would receive as much scrutiny as the FYC sequence. Does this mean that WPAs should be on Faculty Senate and key committees in the faculty governance process? Not necessarily. But it does suggest that having strategic alliances and advocates on those committees is important.

Furthermore, as Porter et al. argue, "[T]here is not one holy map that captures the relationships inherent to the understanding of an institution, all of these relationships exist simultaneously in the lived—actual and material—space of an institution" (2000, 623). By examining figure 2 in relationship to figure 1, we can see that power resides in multiple locations—within the geographic space of the institution (campus) but beyond that physical space as well (the state capital, the Board of Trustees, and the IBHE). To understand where power is located allows us to see how to use alliances to get work done. For an example, I turn to my service experience as a faculty senator, which has allowed me to examine the role of the state board, the Board of Trustees, and accrediting agencies in a much different way than I had ever really thought about as a faculty member. Serving on the Faculty Senate Executive Committee at one university, I witnessed firsthand the importance of these groups to the faculty. During our Executive Committee meetings, the officers discussed strategies to work with, reach out toward, and build connections with these groups to work toward several much-needed fiscal and labor changes. Knowing that the faculty needed a voice beyond the local

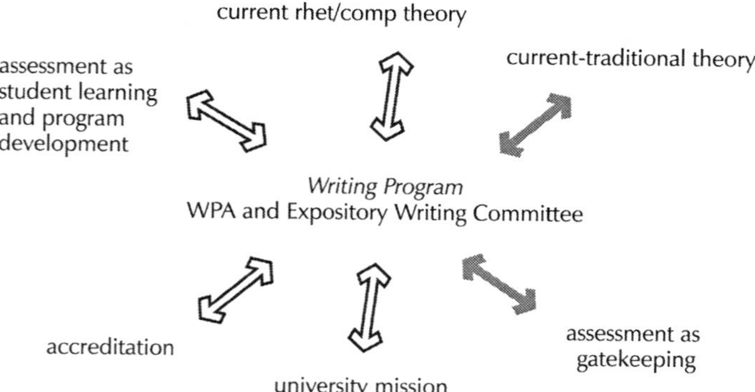

Figure 3

institution, the officers knew that while powerful in some ways, the Faculty Senate body could not get the kind of change needed without the help of these other groups.

I offer one final map that locates the places at which institutional critiques can and are taking place at my institution. As Porter et al. challenge, "[I]nstitutional change requires attention to the material and spatial conditions of disciplinary practices inside a particular institution," (2000, 620) and "[i]nstitutional critique is, fundamentally, a pragmatic effort to use rhetorical means to improve institutional situations" (625).[5] Postmodern mapping illuminates the conditions where institutional critique can occur, and such critique can happen at micro or macro levels and its results may or may not immediately resonate.[6]

This map depicts the tensions at play when we were making changes to our FYC sequence. Prior to hiring an outside WPA, current-traditional pedagogy and theory primarily informed the writing program, and in most years a "common final"—in which students wrote an in-class essay over a common reading which was then scored by a faculty committee—served as a gatekeeping mechanism. These two concerns served as points of tension for the committee as it struggled to change the writing program. As is typical, old habits, pedagogies, or theories die hard, and as the committee and WPA were working to make these changes, we found ourselves occasionally banging our collective head against a wall. Recall that we operated under an umbrella of worry—How would faculty react? How could we make this change happen? Would resistance make all of our changes futile?

At the same time, our institution had become part of the AQIP accreditation process. AQIP requires that universities make student learning visible and have assessment plans in place. Coincidentally, our WPA had gone to the associate provost to ask for money to support the Expository Writing Committee's work to develop goals, objectives, and outcomes. The associate provost realized that our activities would feed directly into his desire to have examples of e-portfolios that made student learning and assessment visible for accreditation. The Provost's Office provided funding for a Web designer (another English faculty member) and small stipends for the initial group's work. We saw this opportunity as a chance to use this power to make needed changes in our program and assessment, although it took the committee nearly a semester to see how the various goals (our goal for program consistency and the provost's goal for visible documentation of student learning and assessment) meshed. Since we would be hard-pressed to show student learning without being able to define what students were supposed to be learning, we were able to develop goals, objectives, and outcome statements that reflected current theories in composition and were aligned with national benchmarks such as the Council of Writing Program Administrators'. To skip to the end of our story, we accomplished what the Provost's Office had hoped, thus making a useful ally. Understanding the points of productive tension on the map, we were able to connect these multiple influences to make a change at the micro-level of our writing program.

INSIGHT LEADS TO MORE SIGHT

What insight does postmodern mapping offer us of WPA work and overcoming the negative emotions of serving as a WPA? First, WPAs may experience negative emotions when they feel they are powerless or are not represented within the university structure. Therefore having a visible representation of the WPA on these kinds of maps gives the WPA a sense of place, a way to view the cycle of work and the WPA's place in it. Just as having a map is comforting and useful when trying to find one's way within a city, having an institutional map—or maps—is useful to the WPA. Being able to navigate within the map is very powerful. Second, mired in the daily grind of administering a writing program, WPAs may sometimes sense that power is located somewhere else, beyond the WPA. As these maps have indicated, though, power does not have only one or two loci, as we may often think; rather, it is webbed within multiple sites throughout the cycle of work within an institution. Postmodern mapping, as Peeples suggests, leads to engaged, active planning. By using these maps to visualize webbed sites of power, WPAs can forge an identity that alleviates the feeling of disappointment, the sense of not getting things done that often permeates the WPA's identity.

5

THE ROAD TO MAINSTREAMING

One Program's Successful but Cautionary Tale

Anthony Edgington
Karen Ware
Marcy Tucker
Brian Huot

At the University of Louisville (U of L), we have thought about mainstreaming our composition courses since at least the mid-1990s. A combination of factors raised the possibility that mainstreaming might be the best way to structure our mandatory writing courses, including the success of mainstreaming in other English departments and composition programs nationwide, the educational reform throughout the state of Kentucky and its attendant focus on writing, and the continually rising admission standards of the university. Our story takes place within this climate. In the fall of 1995, two composition professors—one of whom was Brian Huot—taught special sections of English 101 (the first of two courses required by the university for graduation as part of its general education program) whose enrollments had been reduced to eighteen and consisted of at least five students who might normally be enrolled in a remedial pre-English type of class often called "basic writing," remedial English, or the like. Both instructors who taught these special sections found them to be successful in providing learning experiences for all students, and both professors—to this day—are not sure who the so-called mainstreamed students were. Although this "pilot" certainly proved successful, the resulting cost in reducing first-year writing classes from twenty-six to eighteen was prohibitive, and the idea of mainstreaming was shelved (at least for the time being). However, when mainstreaming became a real possibility, these issues of enrollments and costs were once again important issues that were addressed and understood in different ways. More specifically, even though the WPA, the dean, and the provost wanted to mainstream first-year writing courses, they had different priorities and concerns.

In telling this cautionary but successful tale of how we eventually mainstreamed our first-year writing courses, we hope to continue the efforts that have been accomplished in previous work on mainstreaming (Adams 1993; Gleason 2000; Greg and Thompson 1996; Soliday 1996), contributing information on how incoming students are currently being mainstreamed into first-year composition classes at U of L, and how we as a program arrived at mainstreaming. Our goal is to outline the potential pitfalls involved in any major program change, focusing on how the administrators involved in the decision-making process had different agendas for and understandings of what it meant to mainstream first-year writing. We also hope to delve into areas that past studies have not focused on, namely, to offer our situation as another possible route towards mainstreaming while also highlighting what problems may be encountered and what advice we can offer to programs that are currently considering or questioning a move to mainstreaming. While we doubt that our particular route toward mainstreaming will be followed by any specific institution, we hope that our experiences help others as they move toward or away from mainstreaming, depending upon their institutions and students.

One problem our experience highlights is that a major programmatic change like mainstreaming is defined and valued in different ways by those who occupy different administrative roles. Thus, one focus of this narrative presents a more postmodern view of power, not depicting the actions as a static, one-way exchange (i.e., the administration exerting its power onto the program), but rather as a more fluid process where each participant held various levels of power and control throughout the process. While we would still argue that the power differential in this narrative greatly favored the upper administration, we have begun to realize that the WPA possessed certain levels of power and control that allowed him to influence the final decisions. However, we have also realized that before one can utilize this power, the WPA must recognize it is there. Unfortunately, in this case, our WPA did not always immediately recognize these power issues nor the power he possessed, resulting in problems in the negotiations with upper administration concerning mainstreaming.

Looking more closely at the different agendas allows for a more elaborate view of how power works in discussions about mainstreaming. For the WPA, the major issues cluster around the integrity of the instructional experience for the teachers and students. Questions concerning whether or not the range of writing ability and potential are close enough to foster a productive learning experience for all students are the WPA's paramount considerations. A WPA might assume that a mainstreamed learning and instructional environment requires more attention from the teacher, and this focus is consistent with practices endorsed by national organizations like the Conference on College Composition and Communication (CCCC), which require that remedial or mainstreamed classes should be capped at levels below that for regular sections of first-year writing courses. This concern for enrollment caps might be of special consideration to a WPA (like the one at Louisville) whose enrollment cap was twenty-six prior to mainstreaming, six more than that recommended by the CCCC.

For a dean or provost, mainstreaming can be seen as a cheaper alternative because basic writing courses are usually even smaller than mainstreamed courses. Mainstreaming was politically desirable for an institution that had already outsourced its remedial education to the local community college system. The interest lies in the bottom line for these administrators, since they control the budget for first-year writing courses. As we recount the story of how we mainstreamed, we encountered different conceptions of what mainstreaming can mean to an institution, highlighting the politically perilous position of most writing programs. Since mainstreaming means something different to a dean or provost than it does to most WPAs, and because the WPA in this situation did not understand that the administrators above him were working with different priorities and values, he was unprepared in certain ways for the events that propelled his program toward mainstreaming and was unable to enact the power he had to help make the writing program stronger.

Most substantial programmatic changes in writing administration are supported by local contexts and situations. For this reason, we provide basic information about the program leading up to the decision to mainstream first-year writing courses at a particular institution. While the WPA focused on issues like verifying placement decisions and regular faculty development opportunities for teachers who would be working in a new instructional environment, the dean and provost were interested in and intrigued by the low number of students who were being placed in remedial writing courses. So as the possibility of mainstreaming became more likely, the WPA suggested that class size could be reduced and permanent full-time instructors could be hired to lessen the program's dependence on contingent labor. However, as the dean and provost realized that mainstreaming was a possibility, they thought instead of how cheaply it could be done. With the double whammy of being able to reduce the costs associated with remedial writing courses and bringing recognition to the university's increasing academic standards and stature, mainstreaming seemed like a good idea to various administrators for significantly different reasons.

PLACEMENT PROCEDURES PRIOR TO MAINSTREAMING

In 1997, then president of the U of L, John Shumaker, announced plans for the university to gradually begin "getting out of" the remedial education business. This move solidified the university's ambitions to be a research institution and to improve its reputation as a serious place for higher learning and research. Initially, the move away from remediation entailed the development of a partnership that led to the relocation of remedial classes in subjects such as English and mathematics to Jefferson Community College (JCC), the local campus of the state's community college system. Under the Pathways Program, several of these classes were still staffed by U of L faculty and several of the courses were still held on U of L's main (Belknap) campus. In the fall of 2000, these basic classes fell under the jurisdiction and supervision of JCC, effectively "removing" the U of L from the "remedial business."[1]

This move away from remedial education brought about changes to the ways students were placed into freshman composition classes. Traditionally, students who scored nineteen or above[2] on the verbal component of the ACT test were automatically admitted to English 101 with those scoring thirty or above having the option of enrolling in an honors section of composition that satisfied the two-semester composition sequence in one semester. For those scoring below nineteen, two placement options were instituted. The first was a timed placement essay, usually administered in a large lecture hall for 75–125 students during summer orientation sessions. Up until the 1999–2000 school year, placement essays were read by members of the Transitional Studies Division who were responsible for remedial education before the institution of the Pathways Program. Placement was done in 2000–2001 by Resources for Academic Achievement (REACH). During the 2001–02 year, the assessment of placement essays was shifted to the Composition Program, where composition instructors were responsible for reading and scoring the essays. The figures below show the number of sections of basic writing offered during the last four years it was an option at the U of L.

- Fall Semester 1998 35 Sections
- Fall Semester 1999 32 Sections
- Fall Semester 2000 8 Sections
- Fall Semester 2001 5 Sections

Clearly, a dramatic drop occurred between the 1999 and 2001 academic school years. Of possible significance is that three different groups (Transitional Studies, REACH, and composition instructors) were responsible for placement in three subsequent years (1998–2000), although most of the readers remained the same between 1999 and 2000, the years of the largest decline in basic writing sections. The decline may also be attributed to an increased focus on writing studies within the Kentucky elementary and secondary education system, along with rising admission standards at the university. Regardless of the reason, the point is that fewer students were being placed into remedial classes.

In 1994, the Composition Program at the U of L instituted a pilot project allowing students to submit the portfolios required by the Kentucky Educational Reform Act (KERA)[3] for placement in composition courses. Under this option, students could be placed in all three freshman composition courses (English 099, English 101, and English 102). The first year of this project, we worked with only five schools in the Louisville area but within two years the option was open to all high school seniors from Kentucky.[4] Each portfolio contained three to four pieces of writing; a reflective cover letter that discussed the process of creating the portfolio; and a sheet signed by a school counselor, principal, or teacher verifying the authenticity of the work.

Initially, the readers from Transitional Studies and REACH used a modified holistic scoring approach when assessing placement essays, which utilized a rubric but allowed teachers to assign course designations rather than numerical rankings. When the portfolio project was initiated (and subsequently, the reading and assessment of placement essays was moved to the composition program), we used a scoring system adapted from procedures William L. Smith developed in opposition to holistic scoring at the University of Pittsburgh in the late eighties and early nineties. In Smith's system, instructors with recent experience in English 101 read and assessed student writing based upon their knowledge of the courses and students they taught. Smith found that teachers with recent experience instructing the classes that students were being placed into produced more accurate and reliable decisions than the same readers employing traditional holistic scoring procedures. In addition, several measures were enacted to ensure that the placement procedures were both reliable and valid (Cronbach 1988; Messick 1989; Moss 1992, 1994; Shephard 1993), with rater reliability consistently scoring about 70 percent and feedback from instructors (through the use of a survey) signaling that approximately 90 percent of students were being placed appropriately into the English 101 course.

THE MOVE TO MAINSTREAMING

While our placement procedures were seen as successful based upon departmental surveys and studies and comments from instructors, some questions began to arise. As noted above, the instructors teaching the first-year composition courses continually stated that the students in both their 101 and 102 classes were being placed accurately; thus, we knew that the number of students testing into basic writing did not need to increase. Only seventy-eight students had been put into a basic writing course through the program's placement procedures for the 2001–02 academic year. These numbers made us (and, as we would soon discover, others in administration) question the need for basic writing courses.

In hindsight, this question now seems very important and was basically neglected by the Composition Program leadership (Huot). Since the Pathways Program costs the university a considerable amount of money, this low number of remedial students would be of real interest to the upper administration: by mainstreaming basic writing, the university would really be "getting out of the remedial business" and cutting significant costs. It would also bring some attention and acclaim for the university to say it no longer needed remedial English courses—which was probably true. Although Huot thought that perhaps the remedial option and Pathways Programs were no longer necessary, he failed to realize the political import of the situation and took no action in either making a proposal for mainstreaming or devising the conditions under which the Composition Program would consider mainstreaming. In other words, what we want to stress here is that the move toward mainstreaming did not come from the individuals who should have been most involved (namely Huot and the composition program); instead, it was the administration who put the idea of mainstreaming in motion and it was the administration who tended to control the way it was implemented. As we mentioned earlier, Huot did not recognize the political importance of the situation because he failed to realize that he and the administrators viewed mainstreaming differently. Huot focused on how mainstreaming could positively affect the teaching and learning environment for teachers and students, and this focus did lead to the program receiving smaller class sizes for the first course in the first-year composition sequence—along with gaining more full-time faculty and part-time lectureships to help ease the pressure that would be felt from the increased number of courses that would be included with the move to mainstreaming.

However, the provost and dean had other ideas, focusing more on the political and economic issues related to mainstreaming, a focus that conflicted with future goals that Huot envisioned (such as decreased class sizes for the second course in the first-year composition sequence and better working conditions for all composition instructors—better work spaces, benefits, professional development, and so on).

During a meeting in which various issues about both math and English were being discussed, the Arts and Sciences dean—the chief academic officer overseeing the Composition Program—asked Huot if he thought mainstreaming for composition was a possibility. Huot replied that he favored mainstreaming but the current enrollment cap of twenty-six in composition courses was too much to allow successful mainstreaming. Huot presented the dean with evidence: the CCCC recommendation of twenty students in regular courses and fifteen in remedial. When Huot admitted that he thought eighteen was about right for mainstreamed courses, the dean asked Huot if he would accept an enrollment cap of twenty-two. Huot said twenty-two might be acceptable if it were just an increment and if eventually the number could be twenty or even eighteen. Not being completely politically unaware, Huot also emphasized that the increase in the number of sections precipitated by the smaller enrollment caps could not be absorbed by the current pool of part-time instructors and that these additional sections would need to be staffed by full-time lecturers, since reducing the Composition Program's dependence on part-time labor and its inequitable labor practices had been a long-term goal for the Composition Program. On the other hand, Huot had done the math and knew that even at twenty-two students in composition courses the Composition Program would need to offer thirty-two additional sections, requiring the hiring of four full-time lecturers (who would teach a 4/4 load). In addition, the program would need two additional full-time positions when the enrollment cap was limited to twenty and two more positions for the eventual cap of eighteen. That would be more money than the School of Arts and Sciences or the university could absorb at this time of tight finances and state budgetary shortfalls; thus, Huot left the meeting with a promise that he would forward the figures for the cost of mainstreaming (which he did), but without any real hope of being able to mainstream.

A few weeks later, after receiving a surprising request from admissions for a statement about the new mainstreaming policy for composition courses, the Composition Program informed the English Department chair of the rumor afoot about mainstreaming, and the chair (present at the meeting with Huot when mainstreaming was discussed) agreed with Huot's account of what happened—we were just talking about the possibility of mainstreaming. Shortly thereafter, the department and the program were informed that the administration had committed to mainstreaming the Composition Program as long as the enrollment cap for English 101 was reduced to twenty-two (without mentioning at all an incremental reduction to twenty and eventually eighteen). Furthermore, English 102 would remain at twenty-six, since once students were mainstreamed into English 101, the regular enrollment cap would suffice. Important to note here is that when Huot talked about lowering enrollment caps, he assumed the administration would understand that he meant both courses in the two-semester first-year writing sequence (English 101 and English 102). In contrast, the dean and provost thought Huot meant just the first course in the composition sequence (that is when the mainstreaming would actually take place). In their minds mainstreaming was something that could be accomplished in one semester. It was a simple administrative decision, but for the WPA it was a crucial decision, impacting the teaching and learning environment for over two thousand students and over seventy instructors. The WPA believed in the potential of mainstreaming and the ripeness of the Louisville program for such a change, but he also knew that mainstreaming should be done in certain ways. Clearly, the upper administrators' assumptions were not informed by the literature on mainstreaming first-year writing classes (Greg and Thompson 1996; Gleason 2000; Soliday 1996) or writing development in which certain students can take several years before being able to write acceptably in college (Herrington and Curtis 2000; Sternglass 1997). In retrospect, it seems particularly short-sighted to have assumed that the dean and provost would share a similar understanding with the WPA about the ways students learn to write in college. In addition to lowering the enrollment of English 101 from twenty-six to twenty-two, it was also agreed that the Composition Program would receive its first two full-time lecturer positions.

We thus moved to mainstreaming without the conditions we thought necessary: specifically, lower enrollments and a reduction of the program's dependence on contingent labor. On the one hand, this chain of events highlights that, while the WPA does possess some power when involved in negotiations with administrators, how the WPA recognizes and uses this power plays an important role in how much influence he or she will have. Huot did manage to obtain a reduction in class size for the first semester course (moving from twenty-six to twenty-two students) and the program received new full-time lecturer lines in the process, something that will greatly benefit the program as a whole. Yet, while Huot realized that lower enrollments in the basic writing courses would be appealing to administrators, he did not utilize his full power here by taking the initiative to propose mainstreaming on the program's terms, and was subsequently caught in a bind when the administration made the first move. In this case, Huot missed the opportunity to inform his various supervisors about the complicated nature of mainstreaming and the often-protracted nature of some students' acquisition of literacy in the academy; if he had made the administration more aware of these issues, it is possible that the program would have received more assistance in the move to mainstreaming.

On the other hand, had Huot been more politically aware, he would have also realized that placing only seventy-eight students in remedial courses the previous year had cemented the inevitability of the move to mainstreaming. With the above information in mind, he would have steered any conversations with higher administration in different directions, and Huot could have been more upfront about what was needed. In other words, realizing that mainstreaming was inevitable would have guided Huot to understand the importance of his conversation with the dean and would have prepared him to build a stronger case for the program's needs. We think it is also important to note that although the program was very careful in designing placement procedures and in researching the accuracy and appropriateness of placement decisions, the program's leadership misunderstood the importance of certain political realities, their influence on eventual policy, and their consequences for the Composition Program. Because of our lack of awareness of the political ramifications of a move away from remedial education and toward mainstreaming, we were not prepared when the administration approached us with the idea. While we did our homework in terms of researching the best ways to place students accurately and the resources needed for mainstreaming, we did not adequately understand the political and financial realities that eventually made the move to mainstreaming inevitable. In other words, the WPA and the program possessed power and authority in this discussion, but failed to fully realize and use this power for our best intentions.

CONCLUSIONS AND ADVICE

So what can be learned from our winding road toward mainstreaming? First, it is vital for composition programs ripe for or interested in a move to mainstreaming (or any other major program change) to be prepared: as our experience and our monitoring of the WPA listserv can confirm, substantive programmatic change can be introduced or mandated at any time. Compiling and analyzing enrollment data, discussing current enrollment practices with instructors, and keeping up to date on current research into mainstreaming and other possible substantive changes are all important ways of staying knowledgeable and prepared for any change.

Second, composition directors and staff should understand the political issues surrounding a move like mainstreaming. If the impetus for the move comes from administrators, a director should begin to question why the move is coming at a particular point in time and be able to use this information to address important issues in the current program. This is not to say that we feel the composition program at the U of L was weakened through this move to mainstreaming. We did see a decrease in English 101 enrollments from twenty-six to twenty-two, our current staff received its first two full-time positions, and (most importantly) students are no longer required to take a semester-long noncredit basic writing course. However, we would be lying if we said that the move was perfect and that we could not have done more. Currently, no further discussion concerning a further decrease in enrollments has occurred (for either English 101 or 102) and, as individuals who have recently finished scheduling classes for the upcoming semester, we find the increase in 101 courses greater than the addition that only two instructor positions can satisfy; thus, we have (at least for now) been forced to do the one thing we originally thought a move to mainstreaming would decrease—namely, hiring more part-time and adjunct instructors to compensate for the increased number of courses.

Along with understanding the political ramifications, WPAs should also be knowledgeable about the economic conditions surrounding a move to mainstreaming. It is important for program administrators to be more aware of exactly how much various costs affect, even tangentially, the operation of a writing program. For example, we discovered after the fact that the Pathways Program, in which remedial classes were taught by community college instructors, was an expensive program for the university. Had Huot been more aware of the potential importance of such information, he could have obtained information on the cost of the Pathways Program, preparing himself and the program for the ways in which the university might defer the considerable cost of the program. Being more aware of the costs associated with the Pathways

Program would have made our WPA more sensitive to the need to reduce or cut those costs.

Third, even though this article has focused on what we experienced in our move to mainstreaming, we feel it is vital that a program keep up to date on how successful (and unsuccessful) mainstreaming is (after it has been implemented). At the U of L, we continue to survey instructors about the students in their classes while workshops and informal discussions are continually held with instructors about mainstreaming. In addition, we have discussed the possibility of talking with students about mainstreaming in the future (especially those students who may have been placed into basic writing courses originally). Thus far, we have discovered that mainstreaming is working at the U of L; our instructors have stated that students are writing at similar levels as they were before mainstreaming and the decrease in class size has been continually cited as a positive aspect of the English 101 classrooms.

Why is it important to mention this need to evaluate one's program in a text focusing on writing program administration? For two reasons—first, if programs hope to make more changes in the future, they will need data showing that mainstreaming is working. At the U of L, if we have any hope of achieving our desired goal of an enrollment cap of eighteen in first-year courses, we will need data supporting the fact that mainstreaming is working and that a lower enrollment can produce an even better learning environment.[5] This knowledge can increase a WPA's power when negotiating with upper administration. Second, as other programs across the country prepare to investigate whether a move to mainstreaming is possible, they will need information to support them. This information needs to come from programs that have already successfully mainstreamed. By offering not only information on the pitfalls and successes we experience moving into mainstreaming but also discussing the success (or lack of success) of our mainstreamed programs, we offer other programs some useful information to consider when contemplating and studying whether or not a move to mainstreaming is possible.

In a book chapter on program assessment, Richard Haswell and Susan McLeod (1997) script a dialogue between an assessment researcher (Haswell) and an administrator (McLeod). This dialogue illustrates the different kinds of information researchers, faculty, and administrators want from each other about programs, students, and faculty. While the scenarios Haswell and McLeod describe and work through are based upon changing local conditions, one overriding factor seems to be a critical awareness of the different purposes and rhetorical situations that administrative audiences pose for those of us who work more closely with teachers and students. In other words, had Huot been more critically aware of the needs and concerns of the administrators who hold power over the Composition Program, he would have been better prepared for the push toward mainstreaming. The so-called surprises the Composition Program faced in its move toward mainstreaming were only surprising because of the lack of understanding of the financial and political realities of the university administrators who ultimately hold power over our educational programs.

Casting administrators and program directors in some sort of adversarial role would be easy, but doing so would be both simplistic and counterproductive. Instead, we urge WPAs to become more aware of the financial aspects of their jobs, to know what the university has budgeted and how such costs might eventually impact their programs, and to be aware of what power the WPA may have during discussions. Who should have thought that the price of the Pathways Program would come to be so important to the Composition Program's move to mainstreaming? We hope that our tale about the kinds of factors that can influence the administration and structuring of a writing program are helpful to those who are faced with similar problems and challenges in their own programs. We hope that others can learn from our careful implementation of writing assessment theory and practice as well as from our mistakes and oversights.

6

DEVELOPMENTAL ADMINISTRATION

A Pragmatic Theory of Evolution in Basic Writing

Keith Rhodes

Q: Dr. Phud, how many college professors does it take to change a light bulb?
A: What? Change?!?

CONTEXTS FOR CHANGE IN BASIC WRITING

The college is an unusual organization, a hybrid of business and charity, partly responsive to economic forces and partly insulated from them. Businesses that look only at profits change in response to what people are buying, striving to evolve swiftly in response to changing economic realities. Colleges, by contrast, answer in part to a noneconomic call to enhance human knowledge and wisdom—a difficult call that often goes against the economic grain. Thus, academe comes honestly by the notoriously balky nature of academic change. What other organizations seek to do without even thinking, we must deliberate. We maintain cumbersome processes for making curricular decisions, in part for suspect reasons like simply protecting turf, but mainly to make complex, conscious decisions about balancing economic and noneconomic interests.

Nevertheless, academe has seen a steady erosion of its ability to translate the call to wisdom into operating capital. As a result, it needs quicker, leaner methods of change that can respond more quickly to economic forces. Yet efforts to become more "market-driven" raise new problems. First, we have to question the normal demand for more of everything. We cannot insist on the special privileges of moral capital on the one hand and act like a typical business, questing unreflectively for eternal growth, when that moral capital falters. We can certainly continue to argue for the funding of the call to wisdom; but so long as that argument is losing ground, we have some obligation to consider whether colleges should simply shrink and do less. Second, shifts in the market economy typically affect the whole of academic institutions, with any specific courses largely insulated from direct economic impact. We are unlikely to determine whether English 100 produces any net economic gains for anyone, and even less likely to determine whether changes in its curriculum might also change its economic impact. Instead, the market mostly "buys" whole degree programs based on assumed educational philosophies, then trusts the academic bureaucracy to maintain a curriculum consistent with the assumptions. The purchasing decision, further, is a loose and largely uncoordinated collaboration among students, parents, alumni, foundations, and governments. Thus, generally colleges must "sell" philosophies more than courses, and these philosophies need a broad and varied appeal. Much as college faculty seem to rue the increasing control of admissions personnel over curriculum, such personnel probably are the right rhetorical agents to translate the minutia of our curricular decisions into broad appeals to our constituencies. In turn, faculty must market our philosophies to the ever-expanding numbers of administrative officers on campus.

I have discussed elsewhere how composition programs as a whole might adopt similar lines of thinking in order to "market" whole composition programs (Rhodes, 2000). In brief, I urged that we should emphasize the rhetorical aspect of our curriculum, persuading others that we are the right people to teach much of what first-year experience courses aim to do—if with a "writing-intensive" spin. This plan entails very openly denying our ability to deliver perfectly correct usage. We would focus instead on aspects of writing that we can improve in ways that we can prove more readily (such as invention, fluency, revision, organizational purpose, and rhetorical awareness). We could simultaneously generate the "invention of the university" that both Bartholomae (1985) and any admissions staff want for first-year college students. In this chapter, I want to focus more narrowly on a more particular philosophy that basic writing programs can "sell" to their constituencies. American pragmatist philosophy, as founded by C. S. Peirce but urged upon composition most astutely by Ann Berthoff and her followers, offers an internally consistent way to think about our developmental writing curricula and their marketing. I will discuss how this philosophy has influenced decisions and changes in a basic writing program at a four-year college with an open admissions policy.

Bound up in curricular processes normally designed to retard changes, basic writing usually suffers further from being one of the few subjects in which nearly everyone has a stake, so that several layers of administrators often feel empowered to make decisions about it. As a site of complicated struggle, basic writing can be unusually difficult to change in small increments, and unusually subject to large-scale makeovers. It is highly likely that the current basic writing program at your school was put in place as part of a revolution of some kind, retaining in part the detritus of earlier revolutions. It can seem at times that no method can align all the stars and planets in such a way that any gradual improvement is possible. Further, writing professionals can't always instigate the revolutions they want, nor guide the results once things get going. Yet exactly because so many large, external forces have stakes in basic writing, administrators of these programs can find ways to play off the overlapping power fields to generate changes in their programs. Administrators of developmental writing programs can set in motion processes of gradual evolution by being alert to the different goals of the different constituencies, and by giving up any false ideal of seeing the program as an independent and internally consistent whole of its own. This quieter evolutionary growth is more amenable to being shaped by writing professionals as well. What is needed is the right rhetorical philosophy.

PRAGMATISM AS A PHILOSOPHY OF ACADEMIC EVOLUTION

To manage administrative work's potential for cognitive dissonance, WPAs need to theorize such work as philosophical pragmatism in action, seeing the array of internal and external forces as, in Donald Davidson's potent term, "passing theories" (Kent 1993)—models of coherence that resist final synthesis and resolution, but remain temporarily useful nonetheless. Unlike visions of sheer postmodern play, pragmatism promotes a loose centering by focusing administrators on provisionally welcome results, managing the flux around the program by asking and answering key questions about the health of the program.

While this focus on "results" might smell of positivist empiricism to many a postmodern nose, there is a genuine difference between pragmatism and positivism—a difference that, with unfortunate results in our disciplinary discussions, is more difficult to see without looking through a pragmatist lens. As Ann Berthoff explains best for composition scholars, pragmatism insists that a mediating third position is always invoked by any attempted duality (1981, 41–47; 1989, 1–5). There are never only two choices, despite the natural temptation to see less orderly fields of choice in terms of poles. Simply remembering that any duality is always viewed from some perspective always gives us a third way to see a problem—as when, for instance, we note that subjectivity and objectivity are simply available methods by which to decide what we will assume to be true for purposes of taking action. C. S. Peirce took perhaps obsessive pains to demonstrate that this interpretive triangulation (at least!) of positions as to any idea is virtually a metaphysical necessity, but for our purposes it is enough to note that one need not be either a positivist or a postmodernist, or even just the occupant of some position along a line graphing all possible positions between the poles of positivism and postmodernism. Instead we may choose places in an entire field of attitudes toward reality. A pragmatist pays heed to the durability of social conventions that a deconstructionist might be inclined to dismiss as "not real, but merely conventional"—as if that distinction made a large difference. Social conventions for interpreting reality nevertheless *persist*, regardless of our wishes about them, and so are often better treated as if "real," regardless of our philosophies about them. The ability to demonstrate "results," and with "numbers" when possible, cannot merely be dismissed by any effective rhetoric of administrative change—and Peirce doggedly called pragmatism itself fundamentally a rhetoric (1868).

Of course, a pragmatist administrator will not forget that the fundamental goal is to design a meaningful program, and that none of the "numbers" (or even the more general results) have truly fundamental significance. We should not fool ourselves into believing that one isolated measure has improved and therefore things are better. Yet any effective administrator must work with awareness that single measures will be interpreted for better or worse by others, and some single measures may occupy highly privileged places in the "passing theories" of others who have the power to influence our programs.

Still, I do not mean to imply that what I am calling "pragmatism" as a philosophy simply lapses into "pragmatism" in its most cynical sense. Grounding success in visible results rather than in "theoretical correctness" runs counter to trends that are popular in WPA scholarship. Yet it is not only more responsible to our students but also more likely to get us where we need to go, even theoretically speaking. If our theories are worth having, then they should eventually produce better results when they are applied. If we regard our theories as good simply because they are ours, produced by our discourse community, we design a circular logic that is easily sniffed out as merely self-serving. If our belief alone is the measure of reality, we can believe anything we like. No role would therefore be left for investigation or thinking at all, since mere random whims would serve as well. Such circular logic is incapable of generating externally persuasive arguments for doing anything at all. As Peirce constantly stressed, having a provisional faith in a reality that proceeds in its own ways despite our ideas about it makes sense, since otherwise there is really no point in having ideas at all (1877). If there is no Truth, there is also no point worrying about whether there is Truth—no role at all for critique, falsification, and the entire apparatus of intellectual inquiry. To avoid the opposite trap of positivism, we need only realize that truth-seeking gets somewhere, but never all the way there—better, never perfect. Using pragmatic moderation instead, we can thoughtfully consider the results that would mean the most for our programs, then envision ways in which we can at once produce those results and generate information and communications that lead others to see such results as good things.

When I turn from other philosophies to pragmatism, I turn immediately—and not accidentally—to communication. Pragmatism shares with postmodernism a healthy pluralism when it comes to using results in social interactions. That is because language, always a central concern of pragmatists, always proceeds by way of social mediation. As Davidson perhaps explained best for us under the informed questioning of Thomas Kent, pragmatism holds that language is neither a system of signs without referents nor a direct indication of reality. Instead, language relates to deeper "passing theories" of reference—always somewhat unique, always evolving, but nevertheless recognizable by those who hold "nearby" theories.

To see reality in a pragmatist way, we should imagine a graph with ranges of disparate points grouping into rough coherence around central concerns—passing theories collecting into what Peirce called "interpretants," or broadly shared structures of meaning. While Peirce's term "interpretant" seems rather more idealized than Davidson's passing theories, Peirce probably meant something not much different than Davidson does, in that he often knowingly conflated the conceptual "interpretant" with an individual interpreter to get the right effect (Anderson 1995, 143). As Peirce put it, in his dauntingly formulaic way, a word or other sign "is an object which is in relation to its object on the one hand and to an interpretant on the other, in such a way as to bring the interpretant into a relation to the object, corresponding to its own relationship to that object" (Colapietro 1989, 6; quoted in). Interpretants, then, are like "social constructions," but grounded in both experiential testing and at least the possibility of underlying, universal constructs of meaning-making. As Davidson's more poignant term "passing theory" reminds us, language users may never operate from exactly the same theories of reference, but "nearby" and frequent passings give us a base of experience by which to interpret what is meant. Shared experiences, and here Peirce would include virtually the experience of the cosmos as part of the context, construct "interpretants," or widely shared ways of interpretation. We do not merely pass each other; we signal and respond, developing ways to understand each other. What Peirce and Davidson offer, then, is a means to understand how it is that discourse communities construct shared meaning that works, avoiding both the positivist trap of an ultimately perfect, asocial meaning and the relativist trap of an ultimately meaningless tyranny of the socially empowered.

Unfortunately, such insights into the pliability of language and meaning are not commonly held, even among colleagues on campus. Thus, while composition administrators must not lose sight of such understanding, neither can we forget that many with whom we must communicate will assume that their interpretations are *the* interpretations of meaning and language. I have gone on this long about pragmatism and language because I believe even a simplistic pragmatism is superior to a dangerously relativistic postmodernism when it comes to understanding and influencing our more positivistic peers—and superiors. For those who desire a more thorough version of this argument cast in relatively familiar terms, Ann Berthoff's *The Mysterious Barricades* (2000) is the single best source. In my own nutshell, composition administrators need to be aware that we are engaged in shared processes of making meanings that *by their nature* are partly lost in the translation; and yet we cannot be so smug in the superiority of our philosophy that we forget to apply it to ourselves. There are consequences to pragmatic philosophy when it comes to making changes more effectively, perhaps most importantly changes in attitudes toward ourselves. To guide evolutionary change, one must lose the "I'm OK, You're Not" attitude that so often leads us to vilify administrators. Postmodernism superficially offers a sort of refuge of victimized subjectivity that can encourage composition administrators merely to decry the harm they see being done by more powerful administrators, maintaining an illusory purity of mind and "clean-ness" of hands by protesting without effect. To become instead an active, evolutionary pragmatic administrator is necessarily to be troubled forever by unresolved matters of conscience and complicity. That often is the cost of getting things done.

Still, a focus on action evokes Peirce's point (1878) that clarity of meaning comes largely from clearly understanding the consequences of the actions described. To be consistent, I should start grounding this theory in a context for action: basic writing.

PRAGMATIC ADMINISTRATION IN THE CONTEXT OF BASIC WRITING

First, I hope I can make quick work of the idea that "basic" writing is always local and situational. Mainly, I will focus on problems that have more to do with the situation of basic writing than with the abilities of the students. The words "basic writing" might indeed seem like words without referents if we look basically at student abilities, such that writing pragmatically about the *pedagogy* of basic writing may be logically impossible. Nevertheless, the *situation* of basic writing programs offers several general problems that cross institutions and form the basis for coherent "passing theories" of basic writing. First, composition administrators have to be ready to say whether there should be basic writing programs in the first place; and experience teaches us that no matter how durable or strong a local commitment to basic writing might seem, that commitment can evaporate overnight. This permanent instability at the foundation of basic writing programs adds stress to other matters of commitment, such as whether basic writers should have highly qualified teachers, small class sizes, or writing centers. Further, since there is always a question whether we should permit basic writing, there is also always a question how to define those who will be either excluded from college entirely or admitted only on condition of passing basic writing. Then there is the question by what means we will decide that students have passed this requirement. By no means do I insist that a model of placement and exit testing must happen, or even that it is the best result. It is certainly possible to imagine, and even justify, permitting voluntary placement in an elective basic writing class and a voluntary decision when to leave it; still, the "basic" instability caused by the question whether there should be basic writing makes such a loose structure politically unlikely. Thus, we find instead a general model for basic writing programs that is remarkably consistent across a wide range of institutions.

This general model includes the following points:

- cheap resources—mass placement testing, lower-cost teachers and writing center directors, student tutors;
- barriers to other classes—not always barrier testing, but often restrictions like higher grade requirements for passing into "regular" composition, completion before upper standing, or simply expectations in general education classes of certain levels of competence at aspects of writing that might otherwise be irrelevant to the actual work of such classes;

- relatively little concern that the system maximizes student potential, as opposed to relatively strong concern that the system bars the gates effectively.

If all of these factors are not present at your school, you have an unusual—and possibly temporary—situation. Their prevalence indicates a deep ambivalence to basic writing. On the one hand, it would be even cheaper just to exclude such students—and to the extent the system simply milks most of them of tuition for a while before turning them away, exclusion might be genuinely kinder as well. On the other hand, both the persistence of basic writing and the passionate commitment of its adherents point to an enduring, democratic *hope* that students we would otherwise exclude can make it somehow, given half a chance.

That enduring, widely shared democratic hope is clearly a powerful force for positive change, strong enough to work against serious counterforces. Indeed, for a basic writing administrator, perhaps it is *the* Force, the one our metaphorical Jedi masters would have us trust and use—the central theory to which the broadest range of passing theories can relate. Thus, it makes sense to start a program of evolutionary, pragmatic change by seeking results that would be consistent with this hope. While different administrators might seek different ends, clearly some of the larger ones simply reverse the tendencies noted above:

- ensure that basic writing has resources equivalent to those used for similar purposes;
- replace barriers with informed choices;
- focus less on whether underprepared students might "slip through" and more on whether basic writing programs enhance their success.

The provisional goal, then, of basic writing administration might be idealized as helping students learn how to use relatively potent resources to their advantage as students, workers, and citizens. Of course such a goal warms the hearts of dedicated composition teachers, but more importantly it clearly has important corresponding goals in the "passing theories" of others on campus. Yet just as clearly there will need to be, at best, transitional stages—and most likely, compromises—along the way to this embrace of optimism. We can thus look more simply at whether our choices result in an increase or decrease in the general values of resources, choice, and development.

A CASE STUDY: RESULTS AT MISSOURI WESTERN

I had nearly an ideal test case. In my own work as an administrator of a basic writing program, I had the chance to test these ideas in fairly steady application, if for a brief time. Missouri Western State College is an open-admissions four-year school whose entering classes often have close to a majority of students who would be placed in developmental writing classes at virtually any other school, and perhaps only a literal handful of students who would escape basic writing classes at elite colleges. Its English faculty entirely embraces its role as a writing faculty. With no graduate programs, it has no temptation to justify using TAs to cover classes. Its tutoring center has a professionally qualified and active basic writing teacher assigned to a thorough paraprofessional training system for preparing undergraduate writing tutors. These tutors, as well as the student assistants who lead small-group lab sessions for basic writing, mostly come from an English Education program that strongly features informed writing pedagogy. The dean to whom I reported valued our work and understood our constraints. As a consequence, the basic writing program as I came to it was relatively robust already, and had been managed well by capable predecessors. The campus as a whole focuses on student development as its primary concern, and several well-supported offices on campus were able to assist me in studying the results of our programs. I came to Western only after having spent a few years learning the ropes and honing my philosophy of administration at another campus where managing basic writing had been a good deal easier, and where a highly effective professional colleague had managed writing placement and collaborated with me in studying the results. In sum, I was ideally positioned to aim toward ideal goals for basic writing.

Here is what I found. First, I believe pragmatist thinking can support some moves if we realize, paraphrasing Pogo, that we have met the enemy, and it is us. For example, with mostly cheap resources available, our very hopes tempt us to use as much of them as we can; but as with other cheap resources (like Big Macs), more is not always better. By cutting the associated small-group lab hours from two to one per week, I was able to raise wages for the lab assistants and seek to hire only the most committed and skillful prospects, even while reducing the average size of the groups from seven to five. If there have been any reductions in student preparation as a result, we haven't been able to find them. The administration went along with this change with little comment, and no wonder: it saved money, opened schedules, helped students feel a bit more in charge, and softened the extent and degree of student complaints about the course.

Second, pragmatic thinking permits knowing that compromises perhaps are not as bad as they seem. I have committed the heresy of participating in a change from placement by universal timed writing (with no right to challenge the placement) to placement by English ACT scores (with a right to challenge the placement by means of a timed writing). This change could be the subject of an entire article in itself, but the most interesting result is that students overwhelmingly think it is a good thing. Our students nearly all have ACT scores already, so it is not a matter of taking an extra test. They are strongly advised that they can take an extra test if they wish; but consistently with information I had gathered and studied before the change, most of them think their ACT score is reliable enough. As a result, we have simply purged the strongly negative residual influence of having a mandatory placement put students in a basic writing class. With the time and goodwill we have saved, we have been able to improve our efforts at informing students when to challenge a lower placement—and when to self-place in a lower course. It is more than just an aside to note that the successful movement toward Directed Self-Placement (DSP) has specifically pragmatist roots (Royer and Gilles 1998).

Third, since I was able to choose losses that I could suffer, I had a stronger impact when I insisted on gains, particularly in resources. Even in times of fierce budget cuts, our basic writing courses were less likely than courses in the regular sequence to be taught by part-time adjunct instructors; and the part-time adjuncts who taught the course have stronger connections with the program and the other teachers than is true in the other composition courses. In times when the department steadily lost positions (or more often their equivalent in lost released time), upper administrators agreed to hire a full-time instructor for basic writing. When highly qualified student tutors were not available, upper administrators agreed to hire qualified adjunct teachers to run the lab sessions, despite the additional cost. While this result came mostly because of good leadership before and above me, the department consistently hired candidates with genuine professional expertise in teaching basic writing. Against the tide of budget cuts, we sustained lower percentages of class-size increases than in equivalent classes even while holding on to an ideal that all basic writing students deserved a fully qualified teacher. Basic writing classes had equal priority with other nontechnical courses for being held in computer labs.

As in most of the writing world, of course, getting to an actual study of results has been the most difficult. Still, conditions were such that I could afford to find bad news. Having done things that others found sensible, I was expected to act sensibly again, whatever the results. Collaborating openly with others, I could afford to find whatever we would find because I was largely trusted to keep seeking improvements.

Yet in the middle of that process, I decided to leave my position at Western for another opportunity. I have meant the example more as an illustration than as a measure of pragmatist theory, thinking all along that many of you will be saying "but I do that"—and rightly so. Far from seeing my own pragmatism as unique, instead I see pragmatism as more coherent with what most composition administrators find they should do—simply to put a normal set of compromises and maneuvers in a more defensible, principled, and optimistic context.

CONCLUSION: A DIFFERENCE THAT MATTERS

Part of why academia is so slow to change is that it is so strongly idealistic. If changes don't conform with ideals, they are discounted and ignored; and sometimes opportunities slip away. Then the weight of lost opportunities comes crashing down, a crisis occurs, and change is compelled by unreasoning forces. This pattern seems much the same whether the ideals are posited as "hard" reality or negotiated as the consensus of a strong community; either way, the ideals don't permit a great deal of innovation, of counterintuitive thinking, or of getting along well with those of other ideals. Despite the common sense that postmodernism entails freedom or play, unfettered discourse communities would determine reality, if anything, more thoroughly and pervasively than any objective could. Skeptical of both positivism and nominalism, a pragmatist administrator can accept a wider range of changes and find value in a wider range of possibilities, doing so in ways that are not only highly responsible intellectually but also more genuinely "in play" than postmodernism otherwise permits. To a pragmatist, nothing is determined (yet), either by objective reality or by social construction. While by nature academics may need to remain balky, pragmatism can at least take out Professor Phud's exclamation points and ask a simple question: Change? Then it will only take three professors to change a light bulb: one to call for proposals, one to do it, and one to peer review it.

7

INFORMATION TECHNOLOGY AS OTHER

Reflections on a Useful Problem

Mike Palmquist

For a number of years, I have been troubled by what Richard Young, following Dewey, taught me to think of as a *felt difficulty*—a sense of dissonance, inconsistency, and inappropriateness. My difficulty dates to my initial efforts, shortly after I had become WPA for the first time (a curious reward for earning tenure), to expand the role of information technology in our composition courses. My work in computers and writing had convinced me of the benefits of using computers to make writing the focus of activity—as opposed to discussion—within our writing classrooms. It had also convinced me of the role network communication could play in expanding the classroom and improving communication among students and teachers.

As might be expected in an English Department with two computer classrooms and two open labs—one established in 1980—my colleagues strongly supported my efforts to increase our use of technology. Our curriculum was reconfigured to make better use of network communication tools and word processing software. We conducted workshops to acquaint our adjunct faculty with recent developments in the instructional uses of information technology. We expanded our emphasis on technology in the training program for our graduate TAs. And we developed instructional materials for distribution on our online writing center to support instructors and students.

Our efforts were largely successful. Over the past several years, the number of writers making use of our Web-based resources has risen dramatically (in the 2003–04 academic year, more than 1.6 million visits were made to our writing center Web site). Our instructors, as a group, now think of our course management software not as a novelty but as a necessity—to the point where problems with our server produce a predictable flood of concerned e-mail messages. And the competition for courses taught in our computer-supported classrooms continues to grow.

Despite this progress, however, I'm troubled. I'm troubled not by the extent to which our instructors have embraced information technology in their teaching—although some have certainly embraced it more than others—but rather by the manner in which they have embraced it. I am troubled by a sense that most instructors view technology as an add-on to their courses—something that is considered after the important work of planning a course and developing daily lesson plans is complete. I am troubled, most of all, by a sense that writing instructors as a group have not considered how information technology has changed not only the tools we use to produce writing but the context in which we write, read, learn, and teach.

In the graduate seminars I took with Richard Young, he taught me to value and nurture felt difficulties. He suggested that we should think of them as the first step toward defining a useful problem. Like many other good thinkers, Young saw problems as generative constructs. In fact, he envisioned rhetoric and composition—a field he helped found in the 1960s and 1970s—as a discipline based not on an arbitrarily defined set of foundational knowledge, but rather on the formulation, consideration, and solution of problems. That is, he articulated a vision of rhetorical studies—and, by extension, of writing pedagogy—that rejected a modernist, foundational approach in favor of a postmodern ideal of reflection, adaptation, and extension.

Perhaps it is my graduate training that allows me to feel an odd sense of satisfaction about the disconnect I'm seeing between the instructional promise of information technology and its impact on our courses and curricula. From my perspective, the more thinking we can do about its role in our teaching and writing, the better. I welcome this essay as an opportunity to focus my thinking about the issue.

FROM FELT DIFFICULTY TO PROBLEM DEFINITION

Although I've been uneasy for some time about how we—as teachers—approach technology, my felt difficulty came into sharper focus after I returned from sabbatical following my first three-year tour of duty as WPA. During a meeting in August, when our faculty met to plan our orientation for our new graduate TAs, we talked about the changes that had been made to the syllabus. With some concern, I pointed out that many of the technology-supported activities we had put into the syllabus while I had been WPA—such as the posting of drafts to class discussion forums and out-of-class peer reviews—had dropped out of the syllabus.

I was concerned that our new program director had made these changes in an attempt to diminish our reliance on technology. But that wasn't the case. She had simply forgotten to include them. I did not need to worry, she told me (or words to that effect). We could add the technology in later.

That exchange helped me begin to transform my felt difficulty about teaching and technology into a defined problem. Eventually, I came to the conclusion that resistance to technology was not the issue—at least among my colleagues. Far from it—over the past two decades our program had earned a reputation for its innovative work with technology. The issue, in contrast, was the perception among some of my colleagues—and, for that matter, among writing teachers in general—that technology is something that is added on to our curricula after we have completed the real work of designing curricula and developing syllabi.

In making this observation, I am not discounting the widespread use of word processing software (and its associated tools) or classroom management systems (e.g., WebCT, BlackBoard, SyllaBase). Nor do I want to suggest that the contributions that can be made to writing instruction by the World Wide Web and e-mail have been overlooked by our field. I am concerned, however, that as designers of writing curricula we seem to regard the integration of important technological tools in our syllabi and lesson plans as an extracurricular activity.

This conception of information technology is rooted deeply in our conceptions of what it means to be a teacher—and, for that matter, of what it means to be a learner. It serves to exclude consideration of technology-supported instruction as anything but *other*—that is, as an add-on, an embellishment, an extra. For many WPAs and curriculum designers, technological support is something that is added to a nearly finished curriculum, something that might extend the reach of a syllabus or lesson plan, or something that can help students and teachers extend a classroom. It is not, however, considered one of the foundational elements—and here I am thinking once again of a modernist conception of "foundational"—of a writing curriculum.

I could point out, of course (and I will), that a number of technologies *are* considered foundational by writing teachers: textbooks, pens and paper, classroom equipment, desks, chairs, and so on, to touch only the surface. These technologies, however, are not seen as technology per se. They are invisible parts of a teaching context that shapes the type and quality of instruction provided to our students. I could also point out that most curriculum designers use word processing software, e-mail, and the Web as they create syllabi and lesson plans. In the end, however, I am forced to concede that even as they use them, most writing curriculum designers do not recognize how established and emerging information technologies—including interactive, Web-based instructional programs and network communication tools—might contribute to the teaching and learning of writing.

This lack of understanding is a problem, I think, because our conceptions of what it means to write, to be a writer, and to learn to write should take information technology into account. In particular, we should recognize that information technology makes possible more than additional—or even better—strategies for meeting our teaching goals. It also makes possible new teaching goals. Recognizing this possibility is important for all teachers of writing, but it is particularly important for WPAs, who often construct program-wide curricula and coordinate faculty development programs. Treating technology only as a new set of tools for achieving our existing goals allows us to think of it as something other than what it actually is—a critical element of our writing and teaching context, an element that we must consider as we develop not only our pedagogy, but our theories of pedagogy.

IF IT'S NOT RESISTANCE, WHAT IS IT?

My argument is tempered by my awareness of the important strides we have made in understanding how information technologies can support the teaching and learning of writing. Since the early 1980s, computers and writing scholars have learned a great deal about the design and pedagogical applications of word processing software, style and grammar analysis software, computer-aided instruction, network-communication tools, and hypertext technologies.[1] Equally important, computers and writing scholars have learned much about the effective design of technology-supported writing courses, including those taught in computer-based classrooms, traditional classrooms, online contexts, and hybrid settings in which classes sometimes meet face-to-face and at other times online.[2]

This work has contributed in important ways to our teaching and scholarship. It has not, however, led to fundamental inquiries into our goals as teachers and writers. Instead, it has tended to address the development of specific tools and, with the notable exception of some Multi-user domain Object Oriented (MOO)-based instructional innovations (Haynes and Holmevik 1998; Jordan-Henley and Maid 1995a, 1995b) and explorations of the use of hypertext (Bolter 1991, 1993; Kaplan and Moulthrop 1990;

Moulthrop and Kaplan 1991), the use of those tools to support instructional goals consistent with long-standing instructional practices.

Instead of using technology to transform writing and the teaching of writing, we remain in a transitional stage where new technologies have been used largely to improve upon earlier—and, one might argue, largely modernist—teaching and learning practices. Rather than reconceptualizing writing textbooks so that they take advantage of the latest interactive technologies, we have—using the Web—built bigger, better, and more accessible textbooks. Rather than considering how writing instruction might take place most effectively online, we have developed course management systems—such as WebCT and BlackBoard—that present analogues of those classrooms on the Web. Our teaching and composing practices, consequently, remain firmly shaped by the legacy of the printed page and the institutional models of classroom instruction that dominate traditional education.

My analysis is likely to seem at odds with the perceptions of computers and writing scholars who rightly consider themselves an adventurous group. Our field, as the scholarship I've referred to above indicates, has been nothing if not innovative. I am not arguing, however, that we have stood still as technology has marched on. Instead, I am suggesting that we have failed to capitalize on a number of opportunities to rethink the way we teach and our students learn.

More specifically, I am not concerned that our field has suffered from a general resistance to education reform (Evans 1993) or a reluctance to consider how technology might contribute to instructional innovation (Albaugh 1997; Clegg, Konrad, and Tan 2000; Cox, Cox, and Preston 1999; Crawford and Gannon-Cook 2002; Groves and Zemel, 2000; Herling 1994; Lee 2001; Mumtaz 2000; Noblitt 1997; Persichitte, Tharp, and Caffarella 1999; Stocker 1999; Surry and Land 2000). Nor am I concerned strictly about problems with the diffusion of innovation through our field (Reigeluth and Garfinkle 1994; Rogers 1995). Instead, I am worried that our commitment to a particular conception of what it means to teach—a way of seeing, a terministic screen, to use Burke's terms—has made it difficult to discover how technology might change what we try to accomplish and how we accomplish it. As Szabo and Sobon (2003), citing Cuban (2001), note, teachers use instructional communication technology "to support their existing teaching strategies, rather than explore its transformative potential."

In a similar vein, Dooley (1999) observes, "The greatest single educational system barrier for an innovation is the system itself. Teachers teach in the manner in which they themselves were taught." The power of the "system" is difficult to overstate. Durrington, Repman, and Valente (2000), for example, found that the extent to which individual instructors are embedded in a social network is negatively correlated with their willingness to adopt technological innovations. That is, the more instructors are involved in their profession, the less likely they are to innovate.

RESISTING THE MOVING AVERAGE

Perhaps it is the system—or, more accurately, the systems—that deserves blame. The educational structure in which most of us work makes it difficult to find time to reflect and reconsider. In the name of making educators more "productive," "responsive," and "efficient," we are pressed to do more with less, to pack far more into our days (and we might as well add mornings, evenings, and nights) than is reasonable or appropriate. In the midst of this pressure to produce, we are bombarded with claims about the values of various technologies. Reasonably, many of the most thoughtful members of our profession resist. Leslee Becker, one of my colleagues at Colorado State University, recently confessed that she has been a longtime resister. For a time, she said, she had viewed our department's plan to distribute its newsletter via e-mail as a small part of a grand scheme to dehumanize us all. Once our electronic newsletter had been forced into her inbox, however, she found that she didn't mind reading it on the screen (and that it wasn't all that bad that a few more trees were left standing). Reflecting on the experience, she observed that her resistance might have had more to do with lack of time to learn the possibilities of a new technology than with anything inherently problematic about that technology.

The time demands associated with learning new technologies certainly contribute to the problem with which I've been wrestling. A rich understanding of the capabilities and characteristics of a given technology is an essential prerequisite to careful thinking about how it might change our teaching and learning. When we lack the time to do all that we're asked to do, however, we can't learn the new technologies as fully as we might like, let alone carefully consider their pedagogical implications. Instead, we put in the time needed to return graded drafts to our students, plan our next classes, carry out the myriad activities associated with life in the academy, and (when we can) piece together a working knowledge of these new tools for writing and teaching.

Clearly, directing my criticisms concerning a lack of reflection about technology toward writing teachers who work far more than is reasonable would be both inappropriate and ineffective. Instead, allow me to express my concerns about a higher education system that, despite its goal of reflective engagement with ideas and issues, seems far too susceptible to the pressures of economy, efficiency, and productivity. Although there are significant differences among institutions of higher education, individually and categorically, some of the shared values that cross institutional boundaries work against the kind of reflection and innovation that might allow these institutions to become more economical, efficient, and productive. These values include a commitment to scholarly excellence and funded research that all too often distracts faculty and administrators from a commitment to excellence in teaching.

Consider the rewards structure at our leading comprehensive research universities, as well as at a growing number of private and public four-year institutions, where faculty teaching responsibilities are set at a level that—at least in theory—should allow them the time to reflect on their teaching methods. The rewards structures at these institutions lean heavily toward publication and funded projects. Savvy faculty, and in particular savvy junior faculty, see all too quickly that innovation and reflection about teaching is valued far less than other forms of academic work such as publication, service, and outreach. Teaching, even in programs where it is highly valued and carefully evaluated, is often rated in such a narrow range (80 to 90 percent of the faculty in a given department, for example, might be evaluated as "above average") that faculty quickly learn that putting additional effort into developing curricula and rethinking their teaching activities will do little to differentiate them from other members of the department. To ensure tenure and promotion and to increase their salary, they learn, it is best to publish, obtain funding for projects, or engage in distinctive forms of service.

In more concrete terms, a faculty member might be faced with deciding how best to spend a set amount of time—say forty hours over the course of an academic term. The choices might include writing an article, developing a funding proposal, serving on a committee for a professional organization, and revising the curriculum for a course. At many universities and colleges, publication or a successful grant project will do far more to enhance an annual evaluation rating than will service on a committee, and service on a committee will do far more than redevelopment of a curriculum. In advancing this argument, I am not suggesting that teaching is not taken seriously at these institutions. In fact, many of these institutions use a wide range of strategies for evaluating teaching including peer observation of classroom teaching, review of teaching narratives and portfolios, evaluation of course curricula, and review of student evaluations. When indications of problems are found, programs put significant effort into addressing those problems; when those problems are not resolved, the impact on retention, promotion, and salary can be significant. However, beyond these extreme cases, the *differential* contribution of teaching evaluations, at many institutions, can be quite minimal. If twenty out of twenty-five faculty members receive the same teaching evaluation, those evaluations will play little or no role in determining differences in merit among those twenty faculty.

In far too many cases, we work within a rewards structure that supports and rewards the perpetuation of proven teaching methods at the expense of reflection, reconceptualization, and innovation. If we are to make progress in considering the impact of information technologies on the teaching and learning of writing, we must begin with efforts to alter that rewards structure so that efforts to transform our teaching methods are viewed in the most favorable light during merit, promotion, and tenure decisions. Those efforts might include direct support for teaching innovation (already in place at many institutions) and funding for experimentation with information technologies in instructional settings. They should also include the recognition that innovation will not necessarily lead to improvements in teaching and learning. Taking reasonable risks—that is, risks that are calculated on the basis of careful thinking about teaching and learning—should be rewarded even when the outcome is something other than what is desired.

The bottom line—to borrow a phrase from those who so highly value economy, efficiency, and productivity—is simple: if we begin to reward reflection and innovation concretely—that is, with increased salaries and favorable decisions concerning tenure and promotion—we will see more reflection and innovation.

IS THERE A CONCLUSION IN HERE?

Changing the rewards structure in higher education is a daunting task. It may well be that none of us can make a difference—but that all of us can. We may need to rethink our understanding of how information technology can transform teaching and learning not one by one, but as a field.

WPAs can—and should—play a critical role in this process. At many institutions, WPAs are charged with setting the direction of writing programs through curriculum development and faculty development activities. They are often seen as leaders within their local institutional context and, in such cases, are typically well placed to make arguments about the importance of taking seriously the role of information technologies in teaching and learning. WPAs might, for example, consider the growing number of tools offered in conjunction with new writing textbooks, such as interactive Web sites and exercises, commenting and review tools, and information management and analysis tools. They might explore the implications of technologies such as hypertext and network collaboration tools for writers and writing instruction. They might consider the role productivity software—such as word processing, desktop publishing, and Web editing packages—can play in enhancing students' understanding of visual rhetoric and the design of written documents.

Although much of the thinking I'm calling for is something that would of necessity be done by individual WPAs, it need not be viewed as a solitary activity. WPAs have the backing of a strong national organization, the Council of Writing Program Administrators, and can contact other WPAs relatively easily through the WPA listserv e-mail list; the WPA Web site (www.wpacouncil.org/); regional and national conferences; and *Writing Program Administration*, the council's refereed journal. Moreover, WPAs can take advantage of the work of colleagues who have already been considering these efforts, such as those who converse regularly on e-mail lists such as TechRhet. By working in collaboration with other WPAs and with writing scholars who share an interest in exploring the role of information technology in teaching and learning, we can affect not only our own instructional efforts but also—through our work as program leaders, curriculum developers, and faculty development coordinators—those of the faculty and administrators with whom we work. Essentially, we can work as agents of change not only at our local institutions, but also within the larger field of writing studies.

We might begin this process by reexamining a maxim many of us have lived by since computers first made an impact on writing instruction: technologies should not drive instruction; instead, each technology should be considered in terms of how it might be used to accomplish our teaching goals. In calling for a reconsideration of this maxim, I am not advocating the widespread adoption of curricula that valorize digital communication over print communication, as is suggested by some interpretations of the remediation argument advanced by Bolter (1991; Bolter and Grusin 1998). As important as these arguments are, I am confident that, just as writing did not replace speaking and television did not replace radio, digital texts will not fully replace print texts (or, perhaps more to the point, hypertexts will not replace linear texts). I want to argue, instead, that we should carefully consider how new information technologies—such as the Web, virtual reality, and online collaboration systems—can expand our understanding of what is possible in writing instruction.

This argument is not based on a rejection of what has been learned by past generations of writing instructors. As Johndan Johnson-Eilola (2002) observes, "At the risk of sounding middle of the road, I want to suggest that postmodernism is not about replacing the old with the new" (438). Instead, I am arguing for a postmodern sensibility that allows for openness to new possibilities. I am arguing that we should continuously challenge our (pre)conceptions of teaching and learning in an effort to strengthen the work that we do.

Paul F. Velleman, 1998 winner of the Educom Medal for outstanding contributions to improving undergraduate education through information technology, suggests a framework within which we might consider the role of information technology in our teaching and learning. "I think that IT [Information Technology] has great potential to improve teaching and learning," he observed, "but only if and when the necessary investments are made to ensure that the technology actually enhances education rather than its simply being used to deliver the same old course or to substitute for face-to-face teaching" (Rickard 1999).

Making those investments will enable us to consider how the contexts within which we teach and learn are altered by innovations in information technology. It will also help us recognize how our instructional goals might account for those innovations. Most important, it will help us continue to help our students participate in and contribute to the discourse made possible by those technologies.

8

COMPUTERS, INNOVATION, AND RESISTANCE IN FIRST-YEAR COMPOSITION PROGRAMS

Fred Kemp

Writing instruction has traditionally drawn its legitimacy from an essentially Platonic and largely intuitive presumption that perfect form in writing exists and that successful writing students should model their writing on it. Our long-term dedication to prescriptive grammar and the modes of discourse have both drawn from this presumption and fed it, supporting hundreds if not thousands of years of teacherly admonition first to discover this ideal and then to emulate it. The usual handbook rules of writing, of course, are incrementalized aspects of this form: step-by-step directions leading to the idealized end product.

Postmodernist notions of local knowledge and the authority of discourse communities completely undermine such sclerotic concepts of effective writing, and writing instruction specialists have largely adopted these notions and rejected fixed models of effective writing in favor of adaptive principles usually generalized as the "rhetorical" concerns of audience awareness and responding to context. The problem is that an effective and universally accepted pedagogy has not arisen from a rhetorical rather than prescriptive emphasis in writing instruction. There are reasons for this, but the problem of a lack of accepted pedagogy based upon postmodernist emphases is most acute in large composition programs in which classes are taught by graduate students or paraprofessionals. In effect, the professionally trained scholars—in many cases the WPAs—are saying one thing and many of those who actually do the teaching in the classrooms are defaulting to something similar to what James Berlin and others have called "current-traditional" instruction, or the age-old effort to peel away error until only the ideal expression remains. No matter what we at the top of the theory food chain are learning and espousing, what composition students actually encounter is largely a nineteenth-century approach.

A hugely significant proportion of first-year composition students are thus affected not by a failure of rhetorical or instructional theory but by a failure of administrative implementation. Large university composition programs face a daunting revolving door of graduate-student faculty that, for a variety of reasons, don't buy into the authority of *kairos* or peer interaction or the drafting process. Instead, intuitive ideas of how people should learn to write better are perceived of as "natural" or "what has always worked" and quickly defeat more sophisticated concepts arising from the scholarship in the field. Many graduate students, like students everywhere, are good at recognizing on which side the bread is buttered and responding appropriately during orientations and workshops, but once inside the classroom, when the door is closed, often default to "tried and true" methods that have certainly been tried but hardly ever been proven true. This action is not the result of malevolence or intellectual sabotage, but of human nature, which often rebels when first engaging counterintuitive theoretical propositions. Some of these graduate students will recognize later in their career the value of what they couldn't recognize in the first several years.

But the problem remains that most of the country's first-year college students are undergoing writing instruction that is not effectively informed by the best thinking in the field. And the problem lies not with theory but with administration, not with ideas but process. Those of us trained in English studies are pretty good with ideas but maybe not so good managing organizations or—dreaded term—human systems. We constitutively don't like human systems, seeing in them an inevitable diminution of individuality, transforming people into the railroad ties described in Thoreau. But we are confronted by the need, if we wish to have any effect at all on what people actually do, to translate ideas into action—into widely distributed action—and if we want our instructional ideas to actually affect what students do to learn to write more effectively, we need to better understand how people must work together to achieve more than any single one of them could. Our effort to transform first-year composition at Texas Tech University is not, as some have said, a response to pressing fiscal demands or a response to pressures from our higher administration, and certainly not a manifestation of our will to control. What we've done at Texas Tech is attempt to merge postmodernist principles of peer interaction and contextualist writing in the usually inhibitive environment of first-year composition. We think we are learning a great deal about our students, our teachers, and—given the response of WPAs—about our colleagues across the country.

A CHANGE IN COMPOSITION AT TEXAS TECH

In the fall of 2002 the first-year composition program at Texas Tech University implemented a series of instructional and administrative changes that could well prove to be the closest thing to a genuine paradigm shift in composition at the university level in over a hundred years. At Texas Tech the role of "teacher" has been divided into two separate instructional roles, that of "classroom instructor" and "document instructor." In its rawest form, the system separates classroom instruction and draft commentary. The grading and commenting on student writing is spread throughout the writing program, done anonymously, and most student writing receives two readings, with the grades averaged for a final grade. In its first semester of implementation (the fall of 2002), over 91,000 pieces of student writing were entered and successfully evaluated and commented on, but not by the classroom instructor. In the last two years, we have evaluated an average of 110,000 pieces of student writing a semester. We are calling the integration of our local Web application with this separating of classroom and document roles "ICON," for "Interactive Composition Online."

ICON is enabled by database-driven Web software written at Texas Tech (TOPIC) for the explicit purpose of supporting a large state university first-year composition program. Students turn in their documents through Web browsers, do their peer critiquing online, and receive their comments and grades online. The database manages the huge distribution of student writing, critiquing, grading, and professional commenting. The Web application handles the considerable logistics of distributing documents for grading and commenting; managing quotas for the document instructors; sharing syllabi, assignments, and writing criteria across the system; managing how many critiques are conducted by whom for whom; assigning late and no-turn-in penalties; maintaining the grade books and absence accounting; and performing a dozen other information management tasks that such a large and necessarily coordinated enterprise entails. At any minute from noon to midnight we can see up to 150 students working on the system from dorm rooms, the library, university labs, and apartments—turning in work, critiquing, accessing their progress, and sending e-mail from the Web application. In my seventeen years working in computers and writing, I have not seen of, heard of, or read of a "paperless" composition instruction engaged so coherently in affecting so many students and instructors.

We have, of course, encountered serious problems—probably the most interesting of which does not concern the computer application or database, the pedagogy, the students' ability to handle computers and the Web, administrative resistance, or a lack of committed, energetic, collaborative effort from our faculty and staff. The most interesting problem has been the resistance of the teachers themselves, a mix of a little over fifty graduate students (equally divided between MA and Ph.D. students) and seven lecturers (or paraprofessionals). What I have called the "psychology of loss" dominated the thinking of most of these intelligent and genuinely dedicated people in ICON's first semester—in spite of numerous orientation and training sessions, extensive attempts to explain the benefits of such a program, and almost universal acceptance of the advantages of what we are trying to do by nearly everyone but the teachers themselves. The rest of this paper will describe those benefits and advantages in relation to a maddeningly difficult-to-articulate sense of sheer "wrongness" on the part of those who have been teaching in the traditional "self-contained classroom" mode.

I believe that what we are doing at Texas Tech is a clear model for composition instruction that will be replicated in many locally specific incarnations in the next ten years, although certainly not accepted universally or perhaps even by a majority of large composition programs in that time. The reason for a lack of acceptance will rest not in instructional value or technological difficulties, but in the "psychology of loss" that we are encountering—a mostly unstated and unexamined attitude that permeates the principal motivation of those who become English teachers. When challenged, in what I consider to be our genuine desire to understand the downside to what we are—at great personal and professional effort—trying to accomplish, those who are troubled by our attempts at a gut level can really say nothing concrete. They agree logically with the advantages and benefits of our changes, but it all continues to seem wrong to them and, personally, a deprivation of sorts. Future changes of this magnitude in English composition programs will undoubtedly encounter such an attitude, perhaps to the extent that English departments further distance themselves from a public perception of relevance and currency.

HOW DOES ICON WORK?

Most controversially, class time in ICON is reduced to half of the usual two class meetings a week, and class size is increased from the previous cap of twenty-five to thirty-five students. To compensate for lost seat time and larger classes, the online assignment schedule is nearly doubled, to over thirty writing assignments a semester. We are making the clear assumption that writing instruction is improved when the principal effort for the student is shifted significantly from listening and discussing in a classroom to writing itself and receiving peer and professional commentary. We are moving the center of gravity of teaching from what happens between teacher and students in a classroom to what happens between teacher and students in a piece of writing. Ideally, of course, we would like both, but the exigencies of time and effort make emphasizing both nearly impossible to carry off in a large composition program.

One of the usual arguments against large class size is that it increases the grading for the teacher. Program directors have assumed, and I think correctly so, that more students probably means fewer writing assignments and less robust written commentary, simply because of the load on the teacher. But ICON provides a means of increasing and professionalizing the commentary without placing the burden of such grading on the classroom instructor. The necessary trade-offs end up benefiting the learner.

The basic assignment unit in the curriculum is the "essay cycle." The essay cycle includes drafts, peer critiques, writing reviews, and—in the research course—annotated bibliographies. The pattern of assignments in the essay cycle is repeated weekly and usually includes three turned-in written assignments: a draft, two prompt-driven peer critiques of other students' drafts, and a writing review, which reflects on previous efforts and feedback and projects changes for a new draft. The student develops the writing review from the comments received from peer reviews and the program's "document instructors." The next week proceeds to a second revised draft, new peer critiques, and another writing review.

The typical essay cycle repeats this pattern over three weeks. Therefore, a semester in 1301 (the initial composition course in first-year composition) requires four of these essay cycles, with each subsequent essay's criteria growing more rigorous in a movement that begins with the typically conceived "personal essay" to a concluding "classical argument," modeled on coherently defended academic writing. All these documents are submitted to TOPIC, a Web application that stores the documents in an extensive database (Microsoft's SQL) and then makes them available for a myriad of purposes. Document instructors will read them, comment on them, and grade them. Drafts for peer critiquing and for instructor commenting are stripped of identifying information and directed to staff and peers automatically. Drafts are read by at least two document instructors and any differences in grades reconciled or, if the difference is too great, made available to a third reader who is not informed that he or she is a third, rather than a second, reader.

Following commentary and grading, the student writer can read the commentary and see how the grade affects the compilation of the student's overall grade for the course. As soon as peer critiques are completed and the student writer has completed his or her two critiques of others' drafts, the critiques are available and are used (together with document instructor commentary) for writing the writing review—a critical assessment of what needs to be changed for the subsequent draft. Additionally at this point, the document instructor's commentary and grading can be reviewed by administrators and rated and commented on.

This and much more information related to the students' turned-in writing assignments (a little over thirty a semester) is held in fifty-eight database table fields (integer, text, dates, and Boolean types) associated with each piece of student writing. The prodigious and complex movement of various kinds of writing and assessment could logistically be managed only through a digital document management system like TOPIC and accessed by students, instructors, and administrators only through a dispersed global medium like the Web and Web browsers. Using paper, ICON's current scale of interactivity and automatic distribution would be impossible and, undoubtedly, never attempted. ICON is a true instructional and administrative application of the Internet and digital capabilities.

But do students learn to write better, engaged as they are in all this writing and critical reflection of their own and other students' efforts? The technology infrastructure is clearly driven by a peer-interactive process pedagogy extending back to the early work of Peter Elbow, Kenneth Bruffee, Ann Ruggles Gere, and other advocates of drafting and peer review. More about the pedagogy later, but now I will consider some rather obvious benefits of the system to assigning and handling student work.

BENEFITS TO ICON

I don't have enough space to present the program in its full richness and complexity, but the principal gains, instructionally and administratively, are as follows. I have listed them in descending order of importance.

By objectifying the grading, we remove the long-standing student complaint that some teachers are biased. What my daughter has called, when she heard about what we are doing, the "suck-up value" is mostly eliminated. So is the charge that a particular teacher simply doesn't like a student for such and such a reason and has therefore given him or her a bad grade. The classroom instructor avoids Elbow's "contraries" of coach and cop and becomes simply and significantly the coach, the mediator, and the students' advocate. If a student finds the grade received from the document instructor to be problematic, then he or she appeals to the classroom instructor and defends an increase, which the classroom instructor can provide depending on the effectiveness of the defense in terms of the shared criteria.

By distributing grading and commenting across the entire system of fifty-seven professionals, we have *required* all those engaged to share the same criteria and terminology of effective writing. Nobody likes the idea of coercion in English departments, but the simple fact is that eighty sections of the same course should, in all rationality, be teaching and evaluating in terms of the same general criteria of what is effective and ineffective writing. Such has not been the case in the courses that I have supervised and, it seems clear to me, not in the courses of the great majority of composition programs in the country, no matter how we WPAs may have finessed the whole requirement for consistency. In Texas Tech's composition program, ICON, a grader who is not evaluating in terms of what the classroom instructor is teaching quickly comes to light, as does the classroom instructor who is not presenting the criteria that the pool of document instructors is basing their judgments on. In some ways, we have turned our students into *quality control agents*, for they are the first to recognize discrepancy between what we say we teach and what we look for in our evaluations. There is a kind of "truth in teaching" dynamic in our program that gives me hope that even writing instruction can be handled fairly across a large group of students.

We can, *as a system*, turn our pedagogy from one that values seat-time in class to one that values writing, critiquing, rewriting, and reflection. For years I have promoted peer interaction and a process model of multiple drafting in teaching orientations and workshops, mostly to no avail. The graduate-student classroom teachers, principally interested in their own literary, creative writing, or technical communication studies, constantly devolve to what Seymour Papert has called "teaching by advice." It is, frankly, much easier to talk in front of a room than it is to assign many pieces of student writing and respond to them competently. ICON requires from thirty to thirty-five pieces of student writing a semester, all of it graded and commented on by document instructors. The focus on numerous pieces of student writing and on commentary as a separately engaged act allows us to train effective and specific commentary in ways not possible previously.

Training of new graduate-student faculty is hugely facilitated. We experience about a 30 percent turnover of graduate-student composition instructors every year, for the usual reasons of graduation from the MA and Ph.D. programs and of moving on to sophomore level literature, creative writing, and technical communication classes. At least 50 percent of our incoming graduate instructors have never taught in a classroom or experienced any kind of teacher instruction or, for that matter, taken the class (freshman composition) that they are teaching. A considerable portion of our teachers, perhaps as high as 75 percent, state openly that they are not interested in teaching composition as a professional goal or a personal interest. ICON allows for a graduated integration of these folks into the classroom instruction and document instruction tasks, as opposed to the old process of putting them through a class in teaching composition and then giving them one or two self-contained sections, often a traumatic experience both for new teachers and their students.

Those graduate students, and this may include as many as 20 percent, who do not want to teach composition but want to be employed as graduate part-time instructors, can, *if they want,* not ever handle a classroom but simply fulfill the terms of their employment by responding to student documents online. For those Ph.D. students in the semester of their dissertation defense, or for technical communication MA students who want to go into industry and not teach at all, this option is a godsend.

The separation of document commentary from classroom instruction admits possibilities for complex management of discipline-specific writing and writing across the curriculum that can allow engineering students, for example, to write about engineering subjects in a composition class, or engineering students in an engineering class to write documents that are "document instructed" by English Department graduate students. Plans for both are underway.

The stunning amount of discretionary data that is captured by the online interaction of so many pieces of writing, critiquing, and commentary gives us a sort of running assessment of correlations between assignments and student writing, student writing and instructor commentary, and peer critiquing and reflective judgments on effectiveness—all of it tied to grades, retention, attendance, turn-in rates, and student evaluations.

There are many other advantages to ICON, certainly not the least of them being oversight and accountability. Since all student writing, commentary, and grading is online, administrative staff can monitor the quality and timeliness of such work. Many teachers look askance at this, of course, but we should not privilege the prerogatives of the graduate-student instructors over the instructional gains that we hope for the freshmen. People who are conscientious and proud of the work they do should not balk at having that work reviewed. The collection of large amounts of data relating to the efforts of students, instructors, and administrators allows for what is being increasingly called "course-embedded assessment." The data necessary for collection and distribution of so much student and instructor writing is to a considerable extent the data that reveals the effectiveness of the various writing and evaluation tasks in which the participants engage. The objective nature of student writing evaluation provides a consistent ongoing measure of writing effectiveness that does not require outside testing and evaluation.

Even more important than oversight and accountability is the "learning organization" character of ICON. The extensive amount of data collected in the system during its normal instructional process can be "fed back" into the system in a feedback loop that informs the participants in the system of what and how the system is producing and how best each individual member can improve the process. Web interfaces are constructed that configure and display the data the system collects to students, teachers, and administrators in a way that informs them, on-the-fly, of how their efforts (collective and individual) are influencing whatever "product" of the system is defined. An example is that all second readers of a draft must read the comments posted by the first reader. What is "good" or "bad" about such comments (reviewed anonymously, of course) makes an impression upon that second reader, and undoubtedly influences further commentary by those second readers (who become first readers on other documents). In this way, good commentary tends to drive out bad and the entire commentary system experiences what we consider an automatic norming of draft commentary.

That, of course, was not the original perception of many of the graduate-student instructors and the lecturers. And herein lies the most intriguing issue in the implementation of ICON at Texas Tech University, what I am calling the "psychology of loss." When confronted with the advantages to undergraduate students in terms of consistent and coherent across-the-board writing criteria, active learning (writing-based, not listening-based), objective assessment, distributed work load, and so forth, the usual response is agreement, but with the additional comment: "But this is not why I became an English teacher."

The tension, therefore, is between the instructional advantage for students and the personal predilections of the teachers. And a number of those teachers make the argument that, in essence, what is good for them is also good for the students. The general proposition is that "something" happens personally between teacher and student in the self-contained classroom that will be diluted or eliminated when the assignments and evaluation are spread across the system of 2,600 students. Something will be lost.

I am not entirely unsympathetic to this point of view, often sincerely and emotionally conveyed to me in the numerous discussions I had with the instructors over the spring and summer of 2002 who were destined to be most engaged in these changes. I think I understand the desire to influence young people personally and the reasons why teachers resent any forces that seem to interfere with that presumed relationship. But my constituency is the 2,600 undergraduate students who take composition courses each semester. As WPA for Texas Tech, I have invested a sense of personal mission in giving all those students the best and most consistent instruction I can. My own personal "psychology of loss" has been played out year after year when a minority of first-year students, perhaps no more than 5 or 10 percent, has encountered erratic, possibly random, and even harmful instruction. Ten percent of the first-year students in our program may seem inconsequential, but that percentage can number 260 individual young people. Maybe I can discount them as a percentage, as a batting average, but I cannot discount them as 260 individuals who can be seriously affected by their experience in their first few classes at the university. Of course, the number could be higher. Lacking the kind of data capture that ICON provides, we are only guessing at the previous system dynamics.

It is a systems problem, and English departments are notoriously resistant to (even repelled by) systems problems. But if we are to escape essentially nineteenth-century models of instruction and take full advantage of the new information management and distribution capabilities of the Internet, as most other professions have, then we must look at the deep-seated attitudes of our teachers and compare their hopes and fears to the advantages new processes can provide our students. If we are indeed losing something by rearranging the student-teacher relationship the way we are at Texas Tech, then that loss must be better articulated by those who most feel it. On the other hand, those of us promoting what we consider to be changes for the better must understand these difficult-to-pin-down attitudes and address them specifically or risk experiencing unexpected and sometimes shockingly passionate resistance.

THE REASON FOR ICON

ICON is the result of a nearly twenty-year exploration at Texas Tech of what was called at first "computer-assisted," and then later "computer-based," writing instruction. The English Department at Texas Tech was among the very first departments on campus to have a "microcomputer lab" for instructional purposes (1985); the first department to schedule classes full time in the "lab"—soon to be called the "computer-based writing classroom" (1988); the first department to install Ethernet connections throughout all offices and computer-based classrooms (1989); the first department to deliver instruction from its own computer servers (1989); and the first department to establish its own Web servers (1993). Belying the usual perception of English departments as technologically backward and loving it, the English Department at Texas Tech has actively sought out new pedagogical uses for computer technology and especially computer networks.

At the heart of this long effort (and its affection for computer networks) has been the conviction that students learn just about anything better through structured peer interaction—in the case of writing instruction, by reading each other's writing and responding to it in accordance with well thought-out prompts. The prompts guide critical investigation of the elements of effective writing, and by so doing establish an explicit understanding of those elements in the peer reviewers. The act of explicitly articulating the effectiveness or lack of effectiveness of a piece of writing back to the writer firms such understandings in the mind of the peer reviewers and strengthens their ability to assess their own writing critically during revision. The peer reviewer is the one who gains most from the critical act, although the writer gains too as the skill of the reviewer increases.

The problem with such peer interaction has always been logistical. It is difficult if not impossible to distribute or "publish" the students' writing across a wide group of readers. Using copy machines for such purposes has always been awkward and expensive, and the amount of paper such machines produce inhibits the sharing of comments among students; students end up with stacks of papers that get read only by the most diligent. Although writing theory almost exclusively centers upon cognitive issues (how students learn), I've found that the most inhibiting issue in peer interactive or collaborative learning to be simply how to get the right words distributed to the right people.

And here is where digital electronic media present a specific value for those who want to distribute student writing among peers. When one clicks "send" on an e-mail, that message can be sent to a thousand people (or ten thousand) as easily as to one, and for the same cost and practically instantaneously. The same is true for a piece of student writing.

In fact, computer networks are miraculous publishing devices. Scholars in the humanities have for too long focused on dogmatic assumptions about computers based upon classic works such as *1984* and ignored the rather obvious fact that publishing and publication capabilities are immensely increased by digitalization and computer networks. Words, through computers and computer networks, can be duplicated and distributed with practically infinite iteration, at practically zero time, and at practically zero cost. The core of the humanist capability—the written word—experiences greatly enhanced replication and distribution through the computer.

This increase in publishing capability should provide a benefit for those who want to see students reading more of each other's work, and it does. Student writing which is put online can be viewed by any number of students and responded to—with no copying or paper costs, no transmission costs, and no costs whatsoever outside of maintaining the infrastructure (which is usually in place for other purposes anyway). There is a long-standing argument, of course, that some students don't have the computer access that other students have; but in fact, as the computer becomes more and more a standard instrument in the homes and apartments of people (and even more so an assumed tool of higher education), the "computer-access" argument declines in relevancy.

THE PROBLEM WITH THE PEDAGOGY

There is a problem with what might be called a "peer-interactive pedagogy" that directly addresses the difficulties encountered at Texas Tech with the three-year implementation of ICON. The peer-interactive pedagogy assumes that students learn most effectively by working with each other about and through their own written documents, not by listening to teachers in a classroom or memorizing writing concepts from textbooks.

Defending such an idea with teachers who may not be inclined to consider the matter so intently becomes a problem in a large composition program. The focus must be drawn to what it is specifically that enables one writer to write effectively and causes another to write less so. Can one person teach another how to write effectively by providing what might be called "general writing advice"? The model for depending on "general writing advice" draws from an intuitively powerful sense of mentorship, the presumably unassailable notion that the novice learns at the feet of the expert. It seems reasonable that those who wish to write better should study the texts and listen to the words of those who are more effective writers. Experienced writers try to distill their own "writing knowledge" into various forms of "general writing advice" in order to inculcate in the novice the rules, habits, and experiences gained through study and experience. These "rules, habits, and experiences" are encapsulated in more or less generic form in textbooks, instructional material, classroom lecture, and (among more enlightened instructors) in classroom activities of one kind or another.

The assumption is that *how* to write well can indeed be so encapsulated, transmitted, and reconstituted in another human being. Most writing instruction is based upon a not closely examined assumption that the *stuff* that enables effective writing can and should be managed as a sort of freight moved from one place to another. From this assumption arises the usual dependence on textbooks, teacher prescriptions, and drill and practice. A teacher moves the freight however best he or she personally thinks will "get through" to the student, and the presumption is that some textbooks and some instructional presentation gets the freight through more competently and with less loss in transit than others.

The presumption at Texas Tech under ICON, however, is that learning to write well does not actually engage the "freight" that the field is so eager to move from expert to novice, that such freight (which I am calling "general writing advice") is the result of a kind of self-conscious analysis that certainly hones one's ability to analyze writing but does not directly assist one's writing ability. Writing is largely an unconscious act that engages a huge set of relatively hidden decisions determined mostly through habit and based upon one's "verbal ear." Most people who write well have achieved the requisite skill by doing a lot of reading, usually beginning at an early age—developing a sense of how the written word is effectively manifested through sheer reading experience in much the way that spoken languages and dialects are acquired. A facility with "the King's English" is most capably gained by being around people who speak it a lot, and the same is true of writing ability.

This presumption of how one learns to write well would seem to encourage a return to reading-intensive writing courses (the "reunification" of reading and writing in composition courses that many of my graduate students yearn for), but it doesn't. The reading habits and "verbal ear" acquired over ten or fifteen years cannot be gained in fifteen weeks of force-feeding essays by E. B. White or even Erma Bombeck to nineteen-year-old freshmen. Those who read a lot like to read, and those who read very little don't like to read, and that rather self-evident dynamic cannot be reversed in a first-year composition course without coercive measures too draconian to contemplate. For most of the nineteenth century, the written word was the principal means of distance communication, nightly family entertainment, and access to the revealed word of God, and as such was intimate to the daily activities of the educated and about-to-be-educated. The current competition that the printed word encounters among information and entertainment sources is too evident to be detailed here, but one need not look to failures in modern schooling and writing pedagogy to see why Johnny and Susie don't write well: Johnny and Susie are now engaging hour by hour a confusing welter of verbal and visual activities that strip the printed page of its once transcendent allure.

So far it would seem that a presumption that one cannot learn to write better by assimilating "general writing advice" and trying to translate it into specific writing habits, or by catching up on fifteen years of lost reading in a fifteen-week course, would seem to make any writing instruction a hopeless business. But there is another way to "jump start" writing ability even in nineteen-year-olds that does not require a lot of memorization or reading (or at least the memorization of writing precepts and the reading of great essays, neither activity being suited to the temperament and patience of most of our composition students): this pedagogy can be called "peer-interactive process pedagogy."

Most good writers have what I call in my introduction to teaching composition course an "unarticulated capability" in writing. They write well and make few errors, but until they become teachers themselves, they are often at a loss to describe what syntactically or even stylistically they are doing well. When one has assimilated effective writing habits (usually through all that out-of-school reading), one does not need a self-conscious analytic knowledge of what one is doing. It is only when a writer tries to critique another person's writing that such analytic terminology comes into play, a problem that often constitutes a year or two of angst for new English teachers. Establishing this "articulated capability" in writing, building, and applying an analytic nomenclature in order to report back to a writer the characteristics of effective or ineffective writing does two important things: (1) it allows for a self-conscious negotiation of those characteristics, and (2) it brings them into conscious play when the critiquers write and revise their own words.

What a "peer-interactive process pedagogy" employs is an extensive set of student activities that requires students to explain writing elements or the characteristics of effective writing *to other students.* It is only through the act of articulating specific characteristics of writing that the students learn those characteristics and develop a personally useful nomenclature of effective writing that then can be brought into play when writing decisions are needed. It is certainly important what the student knows, but that knowing is achieved principally through the act of telling. It is also through the student's telling that the evaluators can determine whether the student does indeed know or not know what we presume we are teaching. The huge amounts of distributed feedback such a pedagogy requires can only happen, as I said above, in a database-driven Web application.

This peer-interactive pedagogy makes sense to the composition theorists at Texas Tech, but it doesn't necessarily make sense to teachers who have responded well, even affectionately, to a mentorship model. The mentorship model is deeply invested in the assumption that learning is tied to the personal, perhaps even inspirational, relationship between a teacher and a student. And almost all of us in teaching have arrived here because we wanted to be like one of our own teachers. We have found something powerful in one or more teachers we have had in the past and want to be like those who have so influenced us. Nothing could be more natural.

What complicates this desire in the case of graduate students teaching first-year composition is that the teachers and the students are thrown together in a coercive situation. Few general education first-year composition students want to be taking composition, and few English department graduate students want to be teaching composition. The former don't see a need for it, and the latter desperately want to teach literature or creative writing to students who want to learn about literature or creative writing. The academy has managed to thrust large numbers of people together who don't particularly want to be together. Most of the courses that one takes in college are, we presume, taken by people who want to take them and are, we also presume, taught by people who want to teach them. First-year composition is, in this regard, quite aberrant.

Some English graduate students who are teaching composition want to invoke the mentorship model, sometimes quite emotionally so, and are very often disappointed when their students do not respond as they themselves responded to their own teachers in the past. Being new teachers, they are often influenced by romantic notions of teaching that don't fit the first-year composition classroom well. Complicating all of this is the fact that composition courses engage a skill, writing, that bears large psychological implications about one's intelligence and education. One may not be able to "do" math or biology and not feel too bad about that lack, but to not be able to "do" writing well suggests deeper personal deficiencies. Criticism of one's writing strikes hard, even with those we tend to think of (perhaps fallaciously) as intellectually unsophisticated. The disconnect between the presumed relationship between first-year undergraduate students and graduate-student teachers in composition that both sides are sometimes harshly aware of makes a mentorship model of instruction impossible except in the rare cases of graduate-student teachers who have an overwhelming charisma and transcend the attitudes described here. If you are a very likable person, then the problems related in the last two paragraphs disappear. Unfortunately, likeability is not teachable.

So the central problem we experienced in the fall of 2002 is that we had a pedagogy that depended on student peer interactivity opposed to a teacher base that wanted, expected really, a more personal relationship between students and teachers, what I am calling the "mentorship model." Peer interactivity, especially in the writing-intensive distributive model that ICON employs, dramatically reduces the influence of the personality of the teacher. To detractors, of course, that means an assembly-line mechanistic model of instruction that undercuts the humanity of writing itself. To those who support the peer-interactive online pedagogy, it means better learning about writing. We at Texas Tech, in regards to first-year composition and that alone, have decided that a raw dependence on teacher experience, enthusiasm, and talent reveals distinct liabilities in too many cases to ignore. If we care about our freshmen, we cannot assume that the graduate students who enter our program are all capable, dedicated, and—most importantly—pedagogically informed teachers.

Frankly, past assumptions about this group of people—most English graduate students who teach first-year composition—have rested upon two beliefs: (1) writing is something that graduate students in English understand in an "articulated capability" sense, and (2) that knowledge of how to teach is either innate in everyone who can read good literature or is essentially unimportant. Both beliefs, based upon my long experience, are completely false. Writing well and *knowing* about writing well are two different things. Second, knowing how to read and interpret literature has nothing to do with knowing how to teach, especially knowing how to teach writing. It has only been a disregard of both the college freshmen student *and* the nature of writing skill itself that has allowed so many universities to staff first-year composition courses with English graduate students without the kind of caveats that we have applied at Texas Tech.

That said, as so many of my administrative colleagues remind me, writing skill among college students remains dismal. If how first-year composition is taught continues to be as problematic as I describe, what can we do?

A SYSTEMS APPROACH

My suggestion, which will remain highly controversial, is that we shift the principal instructional responsibility from the individual teacher to the *system* of instruction we employ. That is what we have done at Texas Tech. We have attempted to create in ICON a means by which students manage their own learning. They learn by *doing* things that *teach* them things. They don't learn by attaching themselves or their ideas to a teacher. The system gives them writing problems, and they solve those writing problems, and then they go on to other writing problems. They are a part of a complex set of writing interactions that informs them about writing itself. The teacher is there as a help, not a guru. The teacher assists them and doesn't indoctrinate them.

I have long understood why teachers become teachers, principally because I myself became so engaged for the same reasons. We as program administrators have an obligation to encourage our graduate students in their enthusiasm to teach. We also have an obligation to provide our first-year composition students as fine an instruction in writing as we can. Indications moving into ICON's second full year are that once over the hump of a new and strange experience, supported by a well-coordinated team of faculty and graduate-student assistants, our graduate-student instructors eventually grow aware of the instructional benefits of our program—both to our students and to them. For the academic year 2002–03, we served 4,394 students and graded and commented on 139,704 pieces of student writing, including 43,682 essay drafts and 58,189 peer critiques, an average of about 31 documents per student per semester. Our student evaluations regarding teacher effectiveness in the spring of 2003 were the highest ever recorded for the composition program, and the perceived increase in our consistency and instructional rigor has led the provost to eliminate College Level Examination Program (CLEP) exemptions for composition courses. I believe that other colleges and disciplines on campus are beginning to believe what was once highly suspect—that composition instruction at Texas Tech is coherent, accountable, rigorous, and (above all) useful for their students.

Is ICON a solution to the multiplicity of problems affecting composition programs across the country? Unlikely, at least as a package. All such solutions are local. It is not the computer networks or the software that succeed but the local mix of personalities and resources. However, ICON provides an administrative model that for Texas Tech, at least, is pulling us out of holes we have become far too familiar with. More importantly, we have encountered the dark side of such seismic changes in a composition program—the unarticulated fears of teachers that too often make change unthinkable—and have survived the backlash. Our unabashedly systems approach, so automatically unpalatable to many, should provide at least a conceptual alternative to what has become on many campuses—after the glory days of the "New Rhetoric"—a discouraging business indeed.

9

MINIMUM QUALIFICATIONS

Who Should Teach First-Year Writing?

Richard E. Miller and Michael J. Cripps

Who is qualified to teach the first-year writing course? Only scholars who have earned doctoral degrees in rhetoric and composition studies? English professors? Part-time lecturers with an interest in literacy? Graduate students working in the language arts? Anyone who wants to? Anyone who can be made to? Anyone who will?

One could argue that the discipline of composition studies was brought into being at the moment institutions for higher education began to explore all available solutions to the perennial problem that is student writing. Or put another way, one could say that composition studies as a field is simply the concatenation of local institutional responses to the challenge of providing fundamental writing instruction to first-year students. Seen in this light, the teaching of writing is always ultimately a local matter, and so too is the question of who is best suited to do this work, since the answers to this question can only be sought within the inevitably narrow field of possible solutions that are marked out by local institutional constraints. Thus, we contend that treating the question of who should teach composition as a philosophical, pedagogical, or (most commonly) moral matter distorts the reality that prevails in every writing program in the country; the question of who teaches first-year writing is determined not only by the local WPA's philosophical, pedagogical, and political commitments, but also by a host of variables entirely beyond the local WPA's control; the pool of possible applicants in the region; the home institution's history with writing instruction; the financial well-being of the home institution; and who happens to be department chair, area dean, and provost at any given moment. By drawing attention to these local constraints and the role they play in shaping the available solutions to the problem of staffing the first-year course, we maintain that all WPAs are always working in a compromised space—one that is never fully under any one person's control, never fully a reflection of one's own sense of what is best or ideal, never anything more than a temporary realization of what is best (under the circumstances) for the time being.

While we don't see our position as distinctly postmodern, the fact that we have chosen to eschew a single, overarching narrative in this essay in order to provide a multi-perspectival account reflects our own unease with grand narratives. Our four overlapping versions of the Rutgers Writing Program's approach to staffing freshman composition are meant to foreground both the multiple forces at play in the narrative and the locally relevant measures of success. Our contention is that this condition of local responsiveness is common to all WPAs.

WHO IS THE FIRST-YEAR WRITING COURSE FOR?

How Graduate Students Outside the English Department at Rutgers University Found Themselves Working for the Writing Program

Version One: It's All About the Numbers

In 1991, the Writing Program at Rutgers University first opened the doors of its many classrooms to doctoral candidates from across the academic disciplines. Since that time more than 250 future teachers and scholars with training in fields including history, political science, sociology, linguistics, philosophy, classics, economics, art history, physics and astronomy, French, and Spanish and Portuguese have spent two years teaching freshman composition. Thus, in little more than a decade, the Writing Program has made it possible for more than twenty thousand entering students to receive training in how to generate successful academic prose from advanced graduate students whose primary specialization is neither in English nor in composition. While we recognize that many professionals in the field will see this fact as a betrayal of the noble effort to professionalize the work of writing instruction, we feel that such responses are unwarranted. Likewise, we see little value in touting the approach the Rutgers Writing Program has taken to solving its staffing problems as either an unqualified success or a model that can and should be transported to other locations. For us, praise or condemnation of what might be termed the "Rutgers Solution" is beside the point: the only response to the "Rutgers Solution" that we see as having any intellectual merit rests with understanding how this particular response to the challenge of staffing the first-year course emerged as both a reasonable and a possible alternative within the local context.

To this end, it is best to begin with some facts about how the Writing Program has grown since 1991. In the fall of 1991, the Writing Program ran 177 sections; in the fall of 2003, the Writing Program ran 308 sections. In 1991, the Writing Program had one tenure-track faculty member on staff: Kurt Spellmeyer, the program's director. In 2003, the Writing Program had a total of three faculty members: Kurt Spellmeyer, in his nineteenth year as the program's director; Richard Miller, who served as the program's associate director for seven years before becoming chair of the department; and Mary Sheridan-Rabideau. Between them, these three faculty members staff four sections of writing a year—two in the fall, two in the spring. That is, while the Writing Program now offers 130 more sections each fall than it did a decade ago, the number of courses staffed by its tenured and tenure-track faculty has grown by two sections. This is one way to describe the contours of our local staffing problem: putting aside the question of how those 177 sections were staffed in 1991, how do you staff the extra 130 sections each fall?

The answer that comes immediately to mind, of course, is to hire more faculty. With the 2/2 teaching load at Rutgers, the math here is quite straightforward: sixty-five tenure-track faculty would do it. That's it: just hire a faculty larger than the entire English Department, larger even than any other department in the entire Faculty of Arts and Sciences. Setting aside the cost represented by such a proposal, the fact that hiring on this scale is unprecedented both at this university and in the discipline of composition nationwide, and the entirely justified moral imperatives that the working conditions of writing teachers be improved in just this way, one is still left with the harsh reality that over the past decade the *total* number of faculty lines allocated to all the disciplines in the Faculty of Arts and Sciences (FAS)at Rutgers University has only increased by ten. Ten lines total to accommodate the growth and development of areas of research as diverse as biomedicine and women's and gender studies. Ten lines to accommodate a FAS-wide increase of thirty-five thousand student enrollments annually. What this means, in short, is that both within the Writing Program and outside it in the other departments, the phenomenal growth in the student population has not been—and cannot be—absorbed by faculty on the tenure-track.

So if faculty lines are not a possible solution in this context, what's the next best approach? From a purely managerial perspective, one might think about getting those already teaching in the system to take on a heavier teaching load, but here local conventions make such a thought quite literally unthinkable: while class sizes have grown dramatically across the disciplines (a development that amounts, obviously, to a de facto increase in teaching load), union rules and the conventions at research universities nationwide guarantee the maintenance of the tenure-track faculty's 2/2 teaching load. And indeed, locally, the problem of staffing all those additional writing sections was made all the more challenging by the university's decision—a decision, needless to say, that everyone in the Writing Program strongly and actively supported—to *reduce* the teaching load of TAs from three sections a year to two sections a year. This, then, is the local situation: at the very moment that enrollments in Writing Program courses are skyrocketing, one of the program's primary resources for meeting student demand—TAs in the English Department's graduate program—had its teaching capacity reduced by one-third. In concrete terms what this meant was that, at the very moment the Writing Program found itself scrambling to cover those extra 130 sections, it lost coverage in 72 sections formerly taught by TAs on a 2/1 load. That's a swing of more than 200 sections in need of staffing; that's a swing larger, in itself, than nearly every writing program in the country.

More students seeking a college education and TAs receiving a lightened teaching load: these entirely laudable developments combined to produce a local staffing crisis of truly extraordinary proportions. As union negotiations for the reduction in TA workload proceeded throughout the early 1990s, the Writing Program sought relief from the university's central administration. What might have been the most obvious response, that is simply increasing the number of TAs allocated to the English Department to make up for the shortfall, was impossible in the event: with seventy-two TAs assigned to the department, English has a resource pool that towers over all the other disciplines in the Faculty of Arts and Sciences. Under the circumstances—where the History Department, for example, has only sixteen TAs to work with—there was no credible way to argue for adding thirty-six more TAs to the English Department to assist with covering the staffing shortage exacerbated by the reduction in the TAs' teaching load. And so it was decided that the best solution was to allocate to the Writing Program thirty-six additional TA lines that would then be distributed to qualified advanced ABD graduate students in the other FAS disciplines. That's one version, then, of how TAs from outside the English Department came to be teaching in the Writing Program. In this version, it's primarily a matter of the numbers, of fooling with the ledger to move the available labor around to get the job done.

Viewed from the perspective of sheer scale, successful writing program administration is the ability to put qualified instructors in front of students. In this respect, the program has done pretty well. At a time when the annual number of sections offered grew by 86 percent, the Writing Program tripled (from one to three) the number of composition faculty. What of adjunct labor, a perennial solution to the problem of staffing the first-year course? In 1991, adjunct faculty taught 34 percent of the courses offered by the Writing Program; in 2002, a year in which 329 courses were offered during the fall term, adjunct faculty taught 29 percent of the sections. Remarkably, the Writing Program also came to rely less on TAs over the same period, from 50 percent of all sections in 1991 to 45 percent by 2002, as a result of the program's success in securing more than fifteen full-time, non-tenure-track WPA and instructor positions to assist in covering the increase in the total number of courses offered annually. In fact, by 2002 nearly one-third of all composition courses were staffed by instructors with a full-time commitment to composition research and/or instruction.

Version Two: A Matter of Scale or Increasing Capacity to Do More of What We've Always Done

This partial solution to the Writing Program's staffing problems didn't arise unbidden from Zeus's skull, though: since the late eighties, the Writing Program had staffed a handful of courses with doctoral candidates from history, political science, and art history. And indeed, one graduate student in anthropology, Darcy Gioia, so distinguished herself during this time that she was assigned control over one of the Writing Program's three writing centers, then over the Writing Program's first computer classroom. She steadily rose through the ranks to become one of the program's first permanent administrators, coordinating the basic writing course, designing and overseeing the university-wide placement test, and handling all matters having to do with scheduling. Gioia's success, and the program's success at placing a handful of advanced graduate students from disciplines other than English in the first-year course, suggested to all involved in thinking through these staffing problems that the Writing Program could pull off placing roughly a fifth of its curriculum (70 sections out of 500 total) in the hands of teachers who had no previous experience either with English as a discipline or composition as a field of research.

To some it might seem that this set of decisions represents a betrayal of the first-year student, since it places the needs of the Writing Program beneath the needs of the graduate school—where the goal is just getting more students from across the disciplines to complete their degrees, whatever the cost. Such a judgment might be warranted, were it not the case that the Writing Program's highly evolved administrative structure depends on having all of its teachers submit their work in the classroom to regular review. This administrative structure was already in place when the TAs from disciplines other than English arrived en masse precisely because the staffing of writing courses at Rutgers has *always* required the employment of a teaching faculty whose primary commitments rest somewhere other than with the teaching of writing. That is, even before the explosion in course offerings over the nineties, the Writing Program's courses (like those in many writing programs nationally) were almost entirely staffed by a teaching faculty composed on the one hand of graduate students working in an English department whose course offerings are exclusively focused on literary studies and, on the other, of an ever churning and changing pool of part-time lecturers whose qualifications were almost exclusively drawn from the literary and creative arts. Given this local history, Kurt Spellmeyer, the program's longtime director, designed and put in place an administrative structure that applies the same grading standards across all the sections and ensures the program's teaching faculty provide consistent instruction. Spellmeyer has achieved these goals by adopting a single required textbook for the required writing course; by mandating attendance for all new teachers in the program at a weeklong, extensive training session in the program's pedagogical approach; and by instituting regular one-on-one meetings with *every* teacher in the program *every* semester to assess the work being produced in *every* classroom.

This well-established administrative structure, unique among writing programs of this scale, was ready and waiting when the TAs from the other disciplines arrived. And so, in a certain way, there was little about how the program went about its business that needed to be changed by this new arrangement: the new TAs just needed to queue up for fall orientation, regularly attend the mentoring sessions, and sign up for midterm and final folder review and everything would proceed as it always had. To be sure, scheduling became considerably more difficult, since the program had to work with 108 TAs to staff the same number of sections that had been previously been staffed, under the heavier load, by 72 TAs; and there was the additional problem of expanding the number of mentoring sessions offered for new teachers outside the English

Department, since this sector of the teaching faculty had increased dramatically. But these are primarily problems of scale. That is, nothing *new* had to be built to accommodate this change.

In this version, success is measured not in the number, educational level, or scholarly commitments of writing instructors but, rather, in terms of curricular integrity. Can a Writing Program expand by well over one hundred sections, draw in thirty-six ABD student-teachers with no background in writing instruction, and still remain basically the same? The Writing Program had a highly articulated professional development apparatus that provided instructors with the tools necessary for writing instruction and students with a consistent educational experience. But the apparatus of intensive weeklong orientation workshops for one hundred new instructors each August, hour-long midterm and final folder reviews for instructors in each course, and mentoring sessions for new instructors is administratively labor intensive. The challenge was to expand the number of administrators capable of handling this responsibility. Over the period from 1991 to 2002, a time when the number of courses offered grew by 86 percent, the Writing Program expanded its staff to fourteen, a 100 percent increase in WPA positions.

So at the local level, over the last decade the size of the Writing Program grew dramatically because of demographic shifts and shifts in admission standards, two developments over which the program had no control. Fiscal constraints and the broader commitments of the central administration resulted in the provision of some relief from this growth in the number of sections offered in the form of TA lines designated for advanced (ABD) graduate students from disciplines other than English. Because of the Writing Program's administrative structure, we were confident that we could provide the TAs from the other disciplines with the training they needed to succeed in the classroom; we were confident because we had years of experience training creative writers, journalists, and screenwriters to work within our system; we were quite prepared to handle resistant teachers, given our many years working with graduate students in English who saw the composition classroom as a distraction from their scholarship. In sum, we fashioned a viable solution out of the available options, and we did so thinking that the TAs from the other disciplines were the only players in this game who were going to have to change; at the time, none of us could see how dramatically bringing a cohort of teachers with different perspectives, commitments, and disciplinary biases would change the program itself.

Version Three: On Unintended Consequences

Although no one involved in administering the Writing Program saw it coming, introducing nearly forty interdisciplinary TAs to the revolving pool of teaching faculty in 1996 set in motion a host of internal adjustments that have done nothing less than transform how the Writing Program defines its mission to itself, to the English Department, and to the university at large. This didn't happen all in a flash; it wasn't the end result of a summit meeting, a faculty retreat, or even a flurry of engaged memos. No, the change came about slowly, occasioned by the commodity that has, historically, been prized above all else in the field of composition: experience.

There is no way to provide a full or an accurate account of how the subtle and substantial changes in the program's mission came about. With the arrival of a new force of teachers, new training challenges arose and new conversations were started. One place these challenges and opportunities surfaced was in the one-on-one folder reviews, where the new TAs brought their papers and their assignments in for review with one of the program's many administrators. For new instructors, folder review is primarily a mechanism for professional development that supplements the large summer orientation and the ongoing meetings of the smaller mentoring groups. Under the best of circumstances, during midterm folder review problems with assignments, comments, evaluation, and classroom practices can be detected early enough for the instructor to make the necessary pedagogical adjustments to bring the affected section back in line before final grades are submitted. Final folder review is less concerned with faculty development than with ensuring that instructors have normed their evaluations of their students' work to the program's standards.

Because folder review serves both a pedagogical and an evaluative function, it is inevitably a site where learning occurs and conflict arises. When the TAs from outside the English Department joined the program, the required text for the first-year course was David Bartholamae and Anthony Petrosky's *Ways of Reading*, long the industry standard for programs committed to providing an intellectually demanding writing course driven by challenging readings. The Writing Program's adoption of this text in the mid-1980s and its steadfast defense of a writing pedagogy that asked students and teachers to read some of the university's most respected theorists secured the program's reputation as a site where serious work was being carried out. The view of the program's strengths was altered, incrementally, by the accumulation of reports of folder reviews with TAs from disciplines other than English. Prior to the inclusion of scholars from across the disciplines, we saw *Ways of Reading*'s focus on the close textual analysis of cultural studies texts as a universally valued literacy skill; TAs from outside English showed us that this approach was really a discipline-specific methodology that did not readily transfer to writing for history, philosophy, or political science. Because the program is founded on a commitment to taking student writing seriously, it followed as a matter of course that the reports of these student-teachers warranted attention.

Partly in response to the concerns raised by TAs from other disciplines and partly in response to Spellmeyer's and Miller's weariness with having worked out of the same text for more than two decades between them, the Writing Program began to pilot a new set of readings for its first-year course. This eventually resulted in Miller and Spellmeyer's coedited volume, *The New Humanities Reader*, which brings together essays and book excerpts by prominent scholars across the disciplines writing for a broad, educated audience about some of the most pressing concerns of our time. Although it didn't start out to do so, *The New Humanities Reader* represents the coeditors' dawning recognition that the discipline of composition has largely been shaped by the question of who should teach the first-year course, when a better question to ask is: who is the course for?

If the first-year course is for all students, regardless of intended major, then one could argue that the course shouldn't serve as an implicit proxy for the English Department or its values. If the course belongs to all the students and is staffed by a teaching faculty with an expertise drawn from across the disciplines, then, it seemed to follow that, since the first-year course could never prepare students to write in every discipline, the best pedagogical response might well lie with challenging students to build connections *across* disciplinary boundaries to generate responses to pressing contemporary problems. So reconceived, the first-year course moved from being a course centrally concerned with close reading and close textual analysis to a course that asked students to use their writing to engage with a set of problems that belong to no one discipline: the place of religion in secular society; the fate of democracy in the jobless future; the biogenetic engineering of food and the prospect of environmental devastation. So whereas early in the 1990s, a first-year student at Rutgers might well have started her year reading and writing a response to Stanley Fish's "How to Recognize a Poem When You

See One"—working with a text, an author, and a methodology readily familiar to graduate students in English—first-year students at Rutgers this year might well have started the semester reading and writing about the roots of human compassion, drawing on essays by the cultural anthropologist Jonathan Boyarin, the zoologist Stephen J. Gould, and the primatologist Franz de Waal. Recognizing that the first-year course belongs not to the English Department or to its graduate students, but rather to the first-year students—in all their heterogeneity—thus reflects a parallel acknowledgment that the ability to teach the first-year course does not reside exclusively with the English faculty, its graduate students, or even (more broadly) with those who have studied the literate arts.

This was not the only unintended consequence that followed from trying to find other sources for staffing the first-year course, though it is certainly the most intellectually stimulating result, since it has meant that the program's deliberations about how best to serve the first-year students have been relieved of the need to maintain fidelity to something as abstract and as distant as "the profession." Although Spellmeyer did foresee that bringing graduate students outside the discipline of English into the Writing Program would assemble a whole cast of stakeholders from outside the department who would develop a commitment to the program's success, no one involved in managing the program over the past decade foresaw just what would happen when the TAs from the other disciplines completed their two years in the Writing Program and returned to their home departments. While we are only now collecting data on the lasting effects of this experience, we have considerable anecdotal and circumstantial evidence that shows this initiative has influenced the teaching of writing across the disciplines at Rutgers, enhanced the employment opportunities of the advanced graduate students who have participated in the initiative, improved the completion rate of these same students, and materially changed the composition of the Writing Program's administrative team.

While coauthor Michael Cripps is in the process of a fuller analysis of this initiative, we can report with confidence that informal conversations with TAs from disciplines other than English confirm that there is, almost inevitably, some transfer of the program's process pedagogy as well as its commenting techniques; many participants report in addition that they have returned to their home departments with a greater willingness to assign papers in discipline-specific courses. In effect, the practical experience of teaching writing puts these TAs in a position to break down the conventional wisdom in many disciplines that either their undergraduates already know how to write a sentence, paraphrase, summarize, organize ideas, and develop an argument or they'll never be able to learn. At Rutgers University, this interdisciplinary TA experience may be the only, and therefore the best, way to spread writing across the curriculum.

We also have evidence that suggests the Rutgers Writing Program's initiative has materially improved the job prospects for advanced graduate students and newly minted Ph.D.s from disciplines other than English with experience in the composition classroom. Given the conventional wisdom in all disciplines other than composition regarding the writing abilities of undergraduates these days, a young scholar who comes to a job interview with both expertise in a discipline *and* experience teaching writing clearly has an edge over a candidate who has no such experience and can only join others in lamenting the current decline in literacy. In political science, a discipline with which the Writing Program has a particularly close relationship, graduate students are routinely told that a two-year position as a TA in the Writing Program will certainly improve their chances of landing a tenure-track position in political science. This narrative is not a fiction. No one would claim that the experience working as a Writing Program TA is the primary reason political science Ph.D.s secure good jobs: the program in political science and the research records of its graduates are obviously the most important factors in determining which candidates secure access to permanent employment. However, in a highly competitive academic job market, aspiring scholars need any edge they can get and two (or more) years as a composition instructor seems to provide that edge.

If the evidence of this initiative's influence on writing across the curriculum at the university and on job placement is mostly anecdotal at this point, the evidence within the Writing Program that this initiative has had a profound impact on the career trajectories of a number of graduate students is quite easy to document. As the Writing Program grew during the nineties and the number of teachers involved in this grand project increased, the only way to maintain the supervisory structure that lies at the heart of the program was to increase the number of assistant directors of the program as well. Soon, advanced graduate students from disciplines other than English began to compete with advanced graduate students in English for these prized administrative positions and for the growing number of full-time instructor positions in the program. And sure enough, because the ability to teach writing successfully within this local system is not tied to a disciplinary affiliation, advanced graduate students from art history, comparative literature, history, and political science have, over the past decade, joined advanced graduates from the English Department as being the most qualified candidates to carry out these central administrative jobs and these full-time teaching duties.

The value of gaining experience helping to administer the Writing Program is clear. Over the past decade, every single one of the more than twenty assistant directors of the Writing Program who have gone on the market with a completed dissertation has landed a job: nearly all of them have accepted tenure-track positions with a WPA component, positions in English departments teaching literature, or positions in composition; some have gone on to be university administrators (assistant program director, assistant dean, program director); and one is a managing editor in the textbook industry. Out of this group, five WPAs have come from disciplines other than English: one now holds a tenure-track position in the University of North Iowa's History Department; two are associate deans, one at Rutgers, the other at Pace; one, a graduate from the political science department's doctoral program, teaches writing full-time at the Penn State-Erie, the Behrend College; and another graduate of the political science program (a coauthor of this essay) is an assistant professor of English in the CUNY system. To our way of seeing, it is unmistakable that this experience adds value, improving the employment opportunities of those who acquire the skills required to teach first-year students effectively and the skills required to handle all of the administrative challenges that rise in the wake of such a large, complex pedagogical effort.

One final unintended and welcome consequence of this initiative is worth noting: the political value that comes with extending support to graduate students from other departments. When the Writing Program offers eight TA lines to history or political science, year after year, those departments become potential allies of the program. In political science, those eight lines nearly double the number of graduate students the department is able to fund through TAs in a given year! Indeed, when one adjusts for the ABD requirement, the Writing Program TA funds more graduate students each year for some FAS departments than any other source. Graduate program directors recognize that this arrangement enables more doctoral candidates to make significant progress on their dissertations and that everyone benefits from it. The obvious material benefits the interdisciplinary TA program brings to graduate programs across the Faculty of Arts and Sciences translates into both broad-based, generalized support for the Writing Program and a deeper understanding of its policies and procedures. While the Writing Program has not actively sought to mobilize this support from other disciplines, this arrangement yields a potentially important source of political capital that helps insulate the Writing Program from having its TA lines cut. More importantly, this initiative has established the Writing Program as a central player in all university-wide initiatives that involve undergraduate education: indeed, in 2003 the vice president of undergraduate education worked in concert with the directors of the Writing Program to craft a grant proposal that called for integrating the program's pedagogical approach to intercultural issues into introductory courses across the disciplines. This effort, in turn, attracted a $365,000 grant from the Bildner Foundation to establish a program for advising university faculty interested in constructing a more coherent undergraduate curriculum. Who would have thought such developments would have followed from being driven to reconsider the question of who should be allowed to teach first-year students how to write?

In this version of events, success is defined as the ability to establish effective administrative and pedagogical connections within the local context. Has the Writing Program established a web of institutional affiliations that enable its administrators to influence decisions made outside the program's own structure? Is the Writing Program engaging the university community in conversations about writing in which the WPAs listen, learn, and adjust? These questions are central concerns of WPAs charged with Writing Across the Curriculum (WAC) (and of WAC programs generally), and the ability to provide and modify structured responses to these questions is essential to the health of any writing program. The impact of the TA experience on the job prospects for new Ph.D.s in a variety of disciplines, the inclusion of doctoral candidates and recent Ph.D.s in the ranks of full-time instructor and WPA positions, and collaborative grants to improve linkages between courses in the undergraduate curriculum are all indicators of a healthy program. Success in "A Matter of Scale" is measured by absorption and institutional continuity; in "Unintended Consequences" success requires a willingness to listen and to change. The inclusion of TAs from disciplines other than English led Kurt Spellmeyer and Richard Miller to reframe a fundamental question in composition, from "Who should teach the first-year course?" to "Who is freshman composition for?" This alternative perspective led, in turn, to the eventual publication of a reader that encourages students to read and synthesize ideas in multiple disciplines.

Version Four: It Ain't All Roses

Obviously, not everyone involved in this initiative has rated it an unqualified success. Indeed, course evaluations consistently show that some students do not value TAs from outside English; in this way, they reflect the broader assumption that such work is the proper preserve of those who teach English, rather than of any intelligent person in the process of entering a profession where writing plays a central role. What these students don't—and can't be expected to—know is that, in terms both of formal training in and actual experience with writing instruction, there is no clear or discernable difference between first-time English TAs and the first-time TAs from other academic disciplines. That is, a first-time English TA, drawn to Rutgers by its outstanding graduate program in literatures in English, is not, a priori, better prepared than an advanced graduate student in art history or political science or physics and astronomy to begin the hard work of teaching first-year students how to read with care, how to draft a thoughtful response, or how to use revision to produce a supple argument. That there is no clear and consistent difference between the performance of beginning graduate students in English and advanced graduate students from the other disciplines is evident from the folder review process. Administrators in the program consistently find that the alchemical mixture of an aptitude with language, an interest in its problems, and a desire to assist others in acquiring greater fluency on the page is much better at predicting success in the composition classroom than is one's disciplinary background. What the students don't know, the discipline of composition also doesn't know: no discipline can claim exclusive ownership of or access to this alchemy.

Of course, not all the graduate students who have participated in this initiative have relished the experience of teaching in the ways the program requires, of reading and responding to student writing, and of working closely with first-year students. For the vast majority of TAs in the Writing Program, composition instruction is a job they perform so they can make progress on their research. Since the program is realistic about the place of the TA in graduate students' conceptions of their professional aims, it does not ask, require, or even expect instructors to agree with its pedagogy in any philosophical sense. Everyone knows that most TAs from disciplines other than English will work for only two years in the Writing Program, teach their requisite four sections of freshman composition during this time, and then return to their disciplines to pursue their careers.

The interdisciplinary TA program is not designed to recruit future compositionists; it is designed to help meet the staffing demands of the first-year course. The weeklong orientation at the end of the summer, the ongoing meetings of the mentoring groups, and the folder review process work together to ensure that everyone involved in this enterprise has the support necessary to meet the Writing Program's standards. The Writing Program's concern is not to convert any of its teachers to its method; it does demand, though, a practical adherence to its pedagogy during the term of employment. Consistency in the number and type of writing assignments across all sections of the program's writing courses, consistency in pedagogical approach, and consistency in the application of the shared evaluative criteria are all that is required; these three consistencies make it possible to provide over ten thousand students each year with a common learning experience in their writing classes.

Given these constraints, as one would expect, some of the program's new instructors simply do not work out because they are unwilling or unable to adhere to the pedagogy. Some TAs (in English, as well as in other disciplines) chafe against the organizational apparatus that secures a consistent pedagogy. Some interpret folder review to be an unwarranted intrusion into their classroom, a violation of intellectual freedom, which some understand as the right to teach or do whatever they want in the course. For others, the issue is less philosophical than practical: to teach writing well is hard work and nothing can be done to change that fact. And still others, although overtly willing to give the program's approach a try, struggle to learn the pedagogy and implement it effectively in the composition classroom. These familiar challenges, which accompany any serious pedagogical venture, don't go away just because one has redefined the available labor pool. But in this case, we can also say with confidence that the challenges don't get any steeper than they ever are. In this version of our narrative, success is best measured by the program's institutional response to the question: who should teach the first-year course? Does opening the course up to instructors from fields as diverse as art history and physics mean that anyone can teach freshman composition? Yes, and no. There is no disciplinary prerequisite, and the program does not demand loyalty oaths. But all instructors must demonstrate in summer orientation the ability to work within the Writing Program's pedagogy. Instructors are taught to read and comment effectively on student writing; they learn to draft focused writing prompts that enable students to explore their own positions in relation to a set of readings; they discuss and draft lesson plans that can engage students in conversations on both issues in the readings and specific writing skills; and they practice norming to the rubric that all Writing Program instructors follow. Instructors who either come to the orientation with these skills or develop them over the course of the week are deemed qualified to teach in the Writing Program, with the understanding that twice each term they will meet with an administrator to share teaching strategies, to discuss student writing, and to ensure that grades are normed to the program standard. In our experience, we have found that over 90 percent of TAs from outside English are capable of meeting these criteria for teaching writing, so long as we provide them with a week of orientation and support them with a semester of mentoring and several hours of folder review.

CONCLUSION

In their introduction to this volume, Sharon James McGee and Carolyn Handa identify *chance* and *process* as two features of postmodernism that apply to WPA work. While our approach to administration may not be distinctly postmodern, our narratives of the Rutgers Writing Program's inclusion of TAs from disciplines other than English demonstrate just how much writing program work is open to chance and how much a writing program is always a work in process. The university's decision to reduce the annual teaching load for Writing Program TAs from three to two courses created a potential staffing crisis over which the Writing Program had almost no control. And the solution, a decision to enlist TAs from outside English in the teaching of the first-year course, was hardly foreordained. We made up our solutions as we were going along, arguing for additional resources and responding to new problems as they arose. The dream of administration is that it is always possible to plan in advance; the reality of lived administration is that improvisation—of making do with what is at hand—is always at the heart of this work.

Does it matter who teaches the first-year writing course? This is one of the questions that has propelled the abolition movement in composition, because to suggest that the answer to this question might be no is to imply that there may be no deep or lasting scholarly merit to the field. We think that this question can only be answered locally. At Rutgers, the structure of the program that Kurt Spellmeyer has designed and overseen for nearly two decades makes it possible for graduate students with no more training than one can receive in a weeklong orientation to begin teaching the first-year course; ongoing mentoring sessions provide carefully timed pedagogical support to assist with faculty development; and the midterm and end-of-term folder review sessions provide oversight and quality control. This highly elaborated program, which itself was constructed in response to how Rutgers has historically handled the challenge of staffing the first-year course, provides the structure first-time teachers require to succeed in our classrooms. That may sound like a solecism, but it is the solecism that resides at the heart of any writing program: the program, designed in response to and in concert with local constraints, defines what success means locally and then cultivates the conditions whereby others can succeed according to local standards. Or perhaps put in more familiar terms, all we've really been arguing is this: the field within which any writing program works is a rhetorical one populated by real people, real histories, and real institutions—and that field both constrains and helps define the range of possible options at any given moment. Our sense of what was possible changed dramatically when we stopped asking who should teach the first-year course and began to ask who the course was for. While our answer to this question is a local one, the question is one that can travel.

10

THE PLACE OF ASSESSMENT AND REFLECTION IN WRITING PROGRAM ADMINISTRATION

Susanmarie Harrington

In truth, assessment has always been just another kind of research designed to provide us with information about student performance or the performance of the programs we design to help students learn.

—Brian Huot

Assessment is, as any reader of this collection doubtless knows, one of the hottest words in higher education today as well as one of the most irritating. Many a dean, provost, accrediting agency, or faculty colleague heralds assessment as a cornerstone of academic work, embracing its potential to inspire reflective practice and to generate new ideas. Peter Ewell, senior associate at the National Center for Higher Education Management Systems and renowned researcher on institutional effectiveness, argues that "assessment constitutes a powerful tool for collective improvement that is highly consistent with core academic values and . . . infusion of the logic of assessment directly into classroom and curricular settings is perhaps the most powerful means we have at our disposal to transform the logic of pedagogy itself" (1999, 147). Such a statement is consonant with composition's disciplinary values—much of our research and core disciplinary values are associated with a desire to transform pedagogy. But from a faculty view, program assessment often seems externally driven (by accrediting bodies, for example), inconveniently timed, focused on trivialities, and an activity that takes up time better spent generating classroom materials or conducting disciplinary research.

WPAs can't afford to take up these attitudes, if for no other reason than they find themselves in the midst of campus assessment efforts; any campus serious about general education is likely to be asking questions about the effectiveness of first-year composition programs (not to mention the fact that on many campuses, any cranky colleague who wonders why the student who "can't write" passed first-year composition may be capable of setting an assessment inquiry in motion). In this chapter, I look at ways a reconceptualized view of program assessment can change the way we do our jobs for the better. Using my campus's recent experience with the Consultant-Evaluator Service of the Council of Writing Program Administrators as a touchstone, I will develop principles to guide administrative efforts with program assessment integrated into the daily work of a program.

Such work is essential to our efforts to make sense of the multiple levels of discourse that a WPA addresses on a regular basis. I argue here that it is our responsibility to make assessment activities the cornerstone of our administrative work, for to do so is to interact with the most important questions facing our local professional lives. Assessment done well can be perhaps the most important route to crafting an understanding of our programs. As the introduction to this volume notes, we interact with multiple hierarchies and are dependent on bureaucracies we are often trying to change. A postmodern analysis of writing programs as open structures—always in process and dispersed through the university in complex ways—opens new possibilities for the ways we see ourselves and for the ways we help others see and interpret our work. New approaches to assessment offer the chance to shape our own stories—not in a grand narrative that will dismiss postmodern complexities, but in a multifaceted and multi-voiced story that creates a fluid and proactive program identity.

REHABILITATING ASSESSMENT

Any argument that aims to make assessment the central work of a writing program should probably begin by establishing some common ground with people who are rolling their eyes and thinking "oh no, not another call for more assessment." So let me preface my ultimate argument with a preamble: assessment is, to some extent, what teachers do all the time. If we think of assessment not as the thing we need to do for the accreditors, but rather as a way to find out what's worked and not worked in the past so that we can move into the future, it seems like common sense. What teacher doesn't regularly stop to consider what students have learned in a given day, week, or unit? Assessment done well simply encourages us to ask—often in conversation with our colleagues—questions that are at the heart of any teaching enterprise. Assessment can be a form of values clarification. Bob Broad argues eloquently for a particular way of reconceiving assessment notions (to move beyond the use of rubrics), asserting that communal assessment addresses four questions:

> How do we discover what we really value?
> How do we negotiate differences and shifts in what we value?
> How do we represent what we have agreed to value? And
> What difference do our answers to these questions make? (2003, 4)

These questions can apply, rightly, to any kind of assessment activity. They are rooted in rhetorical values. If we consider assessment as a way to find out something we want to know, it becomes a valuable part of our work. If we further consider assessment as a way to shape inquiry and the representation of our values and accomplishments, it becomes the foundation of all the work we do.

It is not always easy to view assessment that way, particularly in an environment where demands for information about, say, a department's goals for student learning and an assessment plan in relation to those goals seem to come down from on high at the busiest point in the semester. Traditional notions of faculty work haven't included attention to communal assessment. Teaching has traditionally been a private affair: we teach with our doors closed, we rarely team-teach in American colleges and universities, and the patterns of specialization in many four-year schools mean that people don't always teach the same courses. At institutions where teaching loads are more generalized they are typically higher, and there may or may not be time in the work week for common conversation about teaching. Different sections of the same courses don't always use the same texts. Assessment mechanisms that require people to articulate common goals, common outcomes, or common evaluations can seem to violate that privacy. To the extent that assessment makes teaching public, it is at odds with the traditional position teaching occupies in our professional lives. This tension is probably a good thing, although that's an argument outside the scope of this chapter.

Another factor leading some faculty to resist assessment is our training. Most English faculty are not trained in writing assessment, and few faculty in any discipline are trained in assessment more generally. Assessment thus seems unfamiliar and threatening (and to the extent that assessment and grading are related terms, burdensome and argument-producing). Brian Huot's extensive scholarship on assessment has offered the field multiple strategies for broadening the role of assessment in composition. In *(Re)Articulating Writing Assessment* (2002), Huot attempts to rehabilitate the term *assessment* by couching it in terms that faculty already endorse relating to research, shifting the discussion from assessment as *strategy* to assessment as *inquiry*. His overview of writing assessment's history correctly notes that writing assessment has been viewed as technology, defined in terms of the methods used rather than the underlying questions (see his chapter 7 for the full argument). In other words, people confronted with an assessment challenge frequently ask "Should we use portfolios? What scoring guide should we create?" rather than asking "What do we want to know about our students or our program?" Given that much writing assessment research has been conducted by people outside of English and the humanities, it is not surprising that many English faculty find such research hard going.

Despite the efforts of scholars like Huot, Yancey (1998), and White (1998) to bridge gaps between fields, most WPAs aren't comfortable with assessment. We still view assessment as a burden rather than an opportunity. But what would our jobs be like if we took assessment seriously? After all, as administrators we nurture curricula that help students suss out their values as they conduct reasoned inquiry; we encourage our colleagues to participate in faculty development opportunities that support faculty values; we conduct research to develop knowledge in the field. If assessment addresses fundamental questions of value and helps to construct knowledge, it deserves to be front and center in our administrative work. If we conceptualize *administrative activities as a dynamic triangle of relationships among research, reflection, and administration,* we will establish a rich and generative foundation for our writing programs. In making this argument, I build on Huot's contention that assessment is an outgrowth of writing research. Through reflective assessment, writing programs can become agents—agents who learn from the past and plan for the future. Here I want to outline some fundamental assessment principles which WPAs can use to structure a reflective approach to assessment (see figure 1).

REFLECTION AS THE FOUNDATION OF AGENCY

We readily accept reflection as essential for learning in many other settings. In any class that uses portfolios, the reflective piece (transmittal memo, writer's memo, writer's letter, self-analysis—it goes by many names) is a key component, and it may well be the first place readers look when they begin to assess the portfolio. As practitioners, we are urged to be reflective, to look back at our own teaching practices and to research them (Schön 1982). Almost a century ago, John Dewey urged

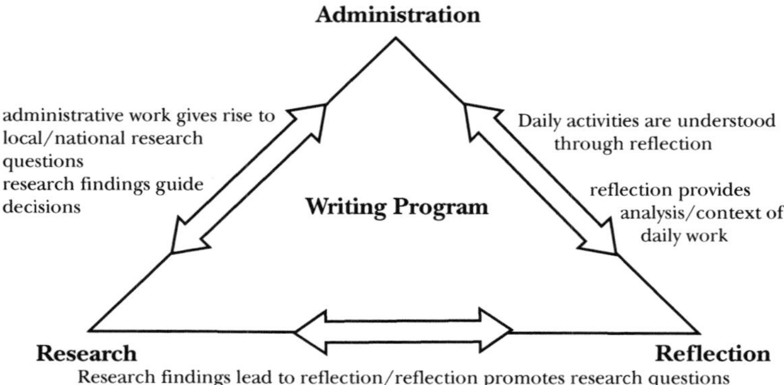

Figure 1

educators to consider the connections between thought, democracy, and education. In *Democracy and Education*, Dewey argued that "education means the enterprise of supplying the conditions which insure growth," an enterprise connected to learning at any age (1916/1944, 51). For Dewey, reflection and thought are synonymous, and it is reflective experience which carries the most meaning, promoting development. Reflection offers the opportunity to understand "the relation between what we try to do and what happens in consequence" (145). Most discussion of reflection is aimed at student learning. It can be most profitably applied, however, to issues connected to programmatic learning and administrative work.

I am not the first to explore the question of what reflective administration looks like. The move within WPA circles to promote a scholarship of administration has encouraged much excellent local research with broader applications (see, for example, the fine essays in Rose and Weiser's edited collections *The Writing Program Administrator as Theorist* (2002) and *The Writing Program Administrator as Researcher* (1999), as well as the essays in Diana George's *Kitchen Cooks, Plate Twirlers, Troubadours* (1999) for only a few examples). Such research, written with an audience of the discipline at large, has obvious benefits for the field. It vividly illustrates how WPA work can fulfill the two criteria for intellectual work noted in the Council of Writing Program Administrators Statement "Evaluating the Intellectual Work of Writing Program Administration": "First, it needs to advance knowledge. . . . Second, it results in products or activities that can be evaluated by others." How this research filters back into the sponsoring institution, and how a writing program as a whole can participate in such research, is an open question. Thinking of administration as research prompts us to define questions, to gather information, to analyze patterns, and to draw conclusions. It prompts us to use empirical evidence from our own programs as the basis for local decisions, and it prompts us to set our local evidence in a national or disciplinary context. Considering issues of research has helped us increase the professional profile of writing program administration. Huot's conceptualization of assessment as research into student—or program—learning focuses attention on assessment as inquiry and reinforces the importance of informed decision making in administration.

Considering assessment as research doesn't necessarily address issues of program evolution, however. Research projects can be discrete entities, even if we consider a research agenda to be something that unfolds over the course of a career. Most researchers develop different lines of questions that may or may not be related to each other. As teachers, we work with our students to foster self-awareness about writing processes and products. As administrators, how do we foster increased self-awareness in our programs? I suggest we look to the same strategy we use with our students: reflection. Using reflection as an administrative and assessment tool moves us toward inquiry and research, but also moves us to ask questions like "What is the program learning?" "How is that learning occurring?" and "Where do we want to go next?"

Let's start by looking at Kathleen Blake Yancey's notion of reflection. As she puts it, reflection is "dialectical, putting multiple perspectives into play with each other in order to produce insight. Procedurally, reflection entails a *looking forward* to goals we might attain, as well as a *casting backward* to see where we have been" (1998, 6, original emphasis). In Deweyan terms, such thinking "is the intentional endeavor to discover specific connections between something which we do and the consequences which result, so that the two become continuous" (Dewey 1944, 145). The simultaneous looking forward and backward with a pragmatic eye involves assessment questions: what have we done, what difference did it make, and is what we have done consonant with our goals, principles, and direction? In Yancey's work, reflection is as much process as product. It is "the dialectal process by which we develop and achieve, first, specific goals for learning; second, strategies for reaching those goals; and third, means of determining whether or not we have met those goals or other goals" (6). While the literature on reflection in composition universally addresses issues of student learning, Yancey's definition of assessment can easily be applied to administrative work. What processes can we establish, as administrators, which lead to meaningful goal-setting? What specific strategies do we use to reach articulated goals? And how do we know what has been accomplished?

Yancey's comprehensive treatment of reflection offers several categories of analysis. First, she examines reflection-in-action, "[T]he process of reviewing and projecting and revising, which takes place within a composing event, and the associated texts" (13). Reflection-in-action is what most of us commonly associate with reflection: writer's memos or reflective essays. This type of reflection is largely a public affair, written for an audience and tangible. Constructive reflection, on the other hand, is "the process of developing a cumulative, multi-selved, multi-voiced identity, which takes place between and among composing events, and the associated texts" (14). This is largely private work for students, although there are ways to use public assignments to nurture constructive reflection. It is developed over time, and involves invention of a self. It is an abstract affair. Yancey says it is valuable "for what it captures *between and among and outside and inside the drafts: the writer inventing him or herself*" (68; original emphasis). We can easily see the ways in which the work of a writing program is analogous to the work of a teacher: programs develop curricula, grading standards, and make policies, and those actions all have clear analogs in a classroom with its own syllabus, grading constructs, and policies. Considering the ways the work of a writing program is analogous to the work of a student is less common but important to do. Yancey celebrates the ways teachers can access the "*between and among and outside and inside*" of student work, and as administrators we too can access those dimensions of the everyday program work we do. This access can throw light on the kinds of texts we produce and identities we develop for the program itself. In my program's history, our work with the C-E service was a key moment in our reflective history. The act of reflection and research helped capture the inner dimensions of the program, holding them up for evaluation and contestation.

ASSESSMENT AS REFLECTION: INVENTING IDENTITY

One of the basic challenges facing WPAs is that of identity. Many directors work without job descriptions, or have job descriptions that go unnoticed by other colleagues. A common theme in WPA scholarship, and an implicit rationale behind the Portland Statement, is that WPAs need to define their work as intellectual work. The C-E service exists to help evaluate and develop writing programs, and one rationale for bringing in outside consultants is that outside voices may carry weight with department and campus administrators who oversee a writing program. In effect, one job of the C-E service is to help educate the campus about the identity of the writing program. Thus the C-E service models one kind of reflection and assessment.

A short overview of the C-E process is probably helpful here. Campuses requesting the C-E service work with the C-E coordinators (currently Deborah Holdstein and Edward White) to articulate their needs so that appropriate C-Es can be assigned to the campus. The formal part of the process involves four stages:

- The program completes a self-study that identifies key issues it faces.
- The program hosts two C-Es, who remain on campus for a day and a half. They interview faculty, students, and key administrators, including the chief academic officer.
- The C-Es send a detailed report to the campus following the visit, offering suggestions for future action.
- The program writes a formal response to the report, planning ways to implement or otherwise act on the suggestions.

The self-study guidelines ask for a comprehensive set of materials addressing issues of program history, staffing, curriculum, resources, and material support. The self-study is the key to the entire visit, as it lays out the program's agenda for the visit, and introduces the campus to the C-E team. It constructs a primary frame for the visit. It also puts a public face on the program, committing one version of the program to paper. It serves as an authoritative history.

My program's self-study was an interesting enterprise, as we discovered that seemingly factual matters were, in fact, open to dispute. (I should note that our program has a wealth of administrative riches: there are six people with administrative responsibilities for different aspects of the program and we work together in a collaborative structure that eliminates some of the loneliness single WPAs may feel; see Harrington, Fox, and Molinder-Hogue 1998 for a more complete description of our history and working relationships.) Without any kind of previous program history to guide us, the dates and priorities associated with major shifts in the program were hard to capture. In addition, the motivations for past hiring decisions and administrative moves were remembered differently by different people, and these competing histories led to conflicting understandings of the present. We had divergent views of whether particular events had served to marginalize the Writing Center or whether efforts had been made to bring the Writing Center into a focal position in the Writing Program; indeed there was dispute about whether or not the Writing Center was even properly part of the Writing Program, and dispute about why the program's administrative committee was set up as it was. Were all members equal or were some serving as, in effect, outside consultants to others who were doing the day-to-day work of the program? There were also different understandings about whom, if anyone, the director of writing supervised. All these views had been left unarticulated (precisely because of the conflicts they uncovered) until the job of constructing a program history became necessary for the self-study.

When I began the job of compiling the self-study from texts and charts written by my colleagues, my first impulse was to reconcile the histories. But to do that would have meant selecting one version of history and program structure, and I decided to simply let the histories stand parallel in the self-study. This process ensured that every voice was heard, and it illustrated both for us and for the C-Es how our issues had emerged. I thought back to this process as I read Yancey's words about constructive reflection: she says that student writers "see themselves emerge as writers with practices and habits that transcend specific texts. Working in the particular, they mark and map the general" (59). This reflection is exactly what happened as we wrote our self-study: working with the particulars of the past, we recognized general patterns that characterized our working relationships. We realized that we had consistently been unable to discuss the relationship between course teaching assignments in classrooms and in the Writing Center, we had consistently been unable to discuss administrative goal-setting, and we had consistently been unable to discuss issues about hiring faculty into new courses. We became aware of habits of (mis)communication and practices associated with faculty and curriculum development. These communication failures were the products of various accidents (whose office was near whose), departmental policies (vagueness in the relationship between how annual reviews were conducted and the responsibilities of course directors), and a department culture that valued individual goal-setting, not collective goal-setting (so the relationship of my goals as director and the goals of a course coordinator or Writing Center coordinator were never examined). For the most part, we found much to celebrate in a long history of collaborative work. But we also noted patterns of disconnection and isolation that allowed frustrations to build over time.

Turning back to the triangle in figure 1, we can see the relationships among my program's experiences as a multidimensional continuum, with reflection being the point on the triangular continuum that fuels the relationships between administration and research. Through reflection, my colleagues and I came to understand the daily activities that comprised the history of our program. Individually, we could have listed the major shifts in program history (e.g., major hirings and faculty departures, the introduction of writing process, the introduction of portfolios, key changes in placement practices). But those events or experiences did not mean the same things—or even mean anything—to us. Dewey would characterize our experiences as having elements of "hit or miss or succeed" to them, in that we understood *what* had happened, but we did not see the connections among our discrete experiences (144–45). Through reflection we began to move toward understanding how our experiences were related to each other, although imperfectly at first. As we reflected on the text that emerged in the self-study, we interpreted our experiences, generating additional questions. Thus the reflection generated administrative activities—building the paper trail necessary for the C-E visit—as well as research questions. In the short term, research questions sent us to our college archives to answer some specific questions: What year did full-time non-tenure-track faculty first get hired? When was the Writing Center established? In the longer term, the questions also generated a larger research project on academic ranks. Some of the questions raised in the self-study (as well as a university-wide initiative to convert part-time to full-time positions) propelled us to examine Indiana University Purdue University Indianapolis (IUPUI) faculty experiences in light of national issues. This project is generating a coauthored article (Harrington, Williams, Fox, Weeden, and Worley) as well as various department policies and position statements on promotion criteria for lecturers and a statement on qualifications for teaching courses at different levels.

ARTICULATING PRINCIPLES FOR REFLECTIVE ASSESSMENT AND ADMINISTRATION

As the person coordinating our C-E experience, I spent a good bit of time reflecting on the process, particularly as I organized the follow-up work as we responded to the report. In order to successfully negotiate the fault lines exposed during the process, we had to address issues of values. What values could we agree on that would help us forge a plan for the future? Exploring those questions led us to realize that there are five assumptions built into the way we handled our self-evaluation which we can take as cornerstones for any reflective assessment process.

- Programs need to set their own agenda. Starting with the self-study, it's important to articulate a program's themes, challenges, and goals. As Ed White pithily put it in an online discussion on the WPA listserv, "Assess thyself or assessment shall be done unto thee."
- Outside voices are good. Multiple perspectives help develop insight. Marcia Baxter Magolda makes the same point about student learning, that students are best positioned to become what she calls self-authors if they are led to understand that "*knowledge is complex, ambiguous, and socially constructed in a context*" (Broad 2003, 4; original emphasis; quoted in).
- History is useful. Understanding the past is a helpful guide for the future. Shirley Rose has argued that "archival research allows us to evaluate what we have done well in the past and what needs further development by providing us with the facts and figures necessary for identifying significant changes and trends. Archival research on our programs encourages and allows us to take a long-term perspective on the development of the program by aiding us in constructing the "big picture" (1999, 108).
- Programs need support from the top and the bottom. While this metaphor is perhaps needlessly hierarchical, it is important that programs get support from the campus administrators who are ultimately responsible for budgets and resources as well as support from the faculty who carry out the program every day.
- Programs need a plan for addressing the future connected to local values.

In short, the C-E model urges a reflective approach to assessment, a simultaneous looking backward and looking forward, working with multiple perspectives in order to move ahead. Classroom reflection models this dialectic process for us. Reflection during the semester provides a safe haven for students to slow down, stop, and write about their learning. I made reflection central to the administrative tasks associated with the C-E process. Although the meetings were fast-paced and eventful (one big difference between an administrative committee's reflection and a student's reflection is the larger number of voices in the conversation at once), considering our work as reflection made it easier to do. It allowed us to tolerate ambiguity and to invite interpretation.

The final response report is the documentary heart of the assessment process. In our case, the report's appendices are the most telling. Our report included the following sections:

- Background to the C-E visit
- Recommendations of the consultant-evaluators and actions taken in response

- Challenges that remain
- Appendix A: Budget request from the Writing Steering Committee [a new committee formed in the wake of the C-E process to craft the emerging writing major, create opportunities for faculty to develop new courses, and to support closer coordination between first-year courses and the major]
- Appendix B: The Writing Steering Committee report, 2001–02
- Appendix C: English major: Concentration in writing and literacy [a new track in the English major]
- Appendix D: Writing Coordinating Committee (WCC) report, 2001–02 [the Writing Coordinating Committee handles first-year composition, a two-course sequence, and the Writing Center]
- Appendix E: WCC three-year plan
- Appendix F: WPA job descriptions
- Appendix G: Professional development plans for lecturers, Department of English

Our report documents reflection-in-action. We needed to craft a public document that recorded (and indeed would shape) our thinking. Having a public document to work on helped focus our writing. The simple fact that we needed to write a report galvanized two different committees—the Writing Steering Committee focusing on the major, and the Writing Coordinating Committee on first-year writing—to get something done in order to have something to report (in that respect, we aren't so different from our students working to meet a deadline). Yet the more important aspect of our reflection was constructive reflection. This form of less-tangible reflection is not explicit in the text itself, yet it is perhaps the most important benefit of the C-E process. Composing a three-year plan (see appendix A) enabled us to construct a new public identity as a program, offering better job descriptions that addressed challenges like the place of the Writing Center in the Writing Program. The three-year plan also announced an agenda for the program in advance. It enabled us to *claim our own priorities and become more proactive and public.* We formed an identity rooted in our past accomplishments, looking toward the future. We named the formation of a teaching community as a public priority. This was a profound development in the history of the program.

Assessment is the crux of the three-year plan. Over the three-year period (a length of time chosen as it corresponds to the terms of service for each administrator), each major portion of the program (the Writing Center and our four core courses) receives assessment attention. Through assessment we announced our priorities, for we defined our agenda in part by announcing what it is we need to know in order to do our jobs well. In some cases we already know what we want to know (does our Stretch Program improve retention and student performance, for example); in other cases, the particular questions will be developed later. But by planning a range of assessment schedules, we ensure that each portion of the program receives administrative attention. By naming our priorities, we took control of our own agenda, and set up a working schedule that didn't seem jam-packed. We also reorganized administrative roles so that an administrative position is associated with each priority area. As programs to link writing courses with other first-year courses have proliferated on our campus, we wanted someone to have responsibility for those programs; hence we eliminated one position and created a coordinator of special programs. Our schedule is busy, to be sure, but it is one we can live with. And so we construct a public and shared identity using our multiple voices, allowing for conflicts, and aiming for shared articulation of values.

INVENTING A PROGRAM

I will close with the proposal that regular and reflective assessment is the best way to ensure that the writing program (re)invents itself. Only if we understand what we have already done can we look to the future in an organized fashion. Assessment allows us to see ourselves better if we adopt a reflective stance as we research our practices. Gathering empirical evidence about the work we have done, asking ourselves how this work has crafted an identity for the program and how it defined different administrators in relation to each other, and then forming a plan to move toward new goals cultivates a productive administrative cycle. The process treats the writing program as a unit with the same care with which we approach our students each semester. And it allows us to use assessment to help ourselves do our jobs better, serving students, faculty, and ourselves in a humane and focused manner.

The triangle of relationships between administration, research, and reflection ensures that a writing program becomes a learning unit, drawing on inquiry to sustain momentum and using planning and assessment tools to set directions, limits, and boundaries. WPAs as individuals and writing programs as entities easily become overcommitted (see Holt 1999; Holt and Anderson 1998; for a fascinating discussion of the WPA attitudes about work); we can also easily become enmeshed in the regular work of staffing courses, ordering books, developing curricula, and handling complaints. Indeed, to get all that work done is an accomplishment. But to frame that work so that we can learn from it requires assessment; to understand that work requires reflection; to put the work in context requires research. Each point on the triangle reminds us to balance the work, and to keep the different dimensions of our work in dialogue with each other.

Seeing administration, reflection, and research in a dynamic relationship means that we would take a number of steps.

- Make time to stop and reflect. Whether using the C-E service, a periodic department or internal program review, or an end-of-year retreat or focused meeting, administrators and faculty should find time to think about common goals and values. In particular, reflection-in-action can be implemented after key events. Reports on workshops can summarize and interpret faculty comments on their work.
- Craft texts that reflect values and priorities. Having a program plan serves several uses. It keeps a program's agenda on the minds of those both in and out of the program. Other texts that can reflect and communicate values include curricular documents, newsletters, guidelines for common assessments or portfolio meetings, charges to committees evaluating textbooks, or Web sites. We represent ourselves as we write, and the textual record is a key part of programmatic identity.
- Seek out research opportunities. Research opportunities may be formal and lead to publication (for example, we researched the effect of switching our placement test to an electronic format) or informal, aimed at in-house uses (we are currently examining enrollment patterns to explore differential faculty workloads in the department).
- Find opportunities to share those texts with program constituencies. Whether via Web sites, memos, curriculum documents, motions in meetings, or general announcements, use texts to promote a public identity grounded in the values that assessment reflects and shapes.

Bob Broad has done more than anyone to study the connection between assessment and value. The assessment triangle I propose is another way to represent the activities that are driven by our core values, and which in turn shape those core values. In *What We Really Value*, Broad argues that assessment is useful precisely because it leads to a public articulation of values, as well as a public grappling with important open questions. He advocates a process he calls dynamic criteria mapping (DCM) to get at the heart of a program's values. DCM involves first collecting information about what faculty actually value as they read student texts (in a discussion of sample texts, scribes would record the terms faculty use as they explain why they evaluate the samples as they do), and then analyzing that data to represent the collective values. DCM requires careful attention to detail—as he notes, the process of articulating and mapping a program's actual instructional values takes time. For one, data collection should occur after the semester or quarter, so that faculty are not simultaneously working to teach and reflect on that work (2003, 131). Broad cautions that "the analysts [must] work slowly and methodically from those data through small steps of abstraction and reconceptualization" (132–33). Once it has been determined what faculty *do* value, the program can turn its attention to discussing what they *should* value (133). The final step involves a public document and additional resources that display for students, faculty, and any other interested parties what the program values (134). These maps and sample papers should be periodically revisited to ensure that the program's public articulation of its values remains current. Note that Broad's DCM process occurs mainly on the administration/reflection side of the triangle. But if research were applied to the questions that emerge in the debates about what a program does and should value, then the conversation becomes all the richer. Indeed, research would help move the program along toward the next mapping period. So looking at all sides of the triangle promotes a full and lively program.

There are as many ways to explore the triangular relationships among research, assessment, and reflection as there are writing programs. DCM and the C-E program are only two possible ways in which the research/administration/reflection triangle can be engaged. Ultimately, a multidimensional approach to writing program administration rooted in reflection will nurture a writing program that learns over time. Our field has been enriched by scholarship advocating that individual administrators see their programmatic work as part of an ongoing intellectual project. We will be similarly enriched by a view of reflective assessment that leads to programs, not simply administrators, taking on intellectual work. If we conceive of the program as a living and learning unit, we will build on our teaching and research experiences to shape the futures of students and faculty.

Appendix A

WCC THREE-YEAR PLAN

This three-year plan will be updated and extended each year. Each program administrator has an individual three-year plan for his or her area; those area plans are more detailed. The committee plan enables us to coordinate administrative work and strengthen ties between areas of the program.

In setting up this first three-year plan, our priorities included work that will

- build a more vibrant teaching community;
- increase coherence across and within courses;
- coordinate assessment across the program;
- increase faculty involvement in planning and programming;
- provide common resources and common celebrations of student/faculty achievement.

The plan is by necessity more detailed in the early years than in the more distant years. Each year, the plan will be extended and elaborated as needed. At the first meeting of each academic year, the committee will schedule reports on pressing projects for the year in order to ensure oversight of its plans.

2001–02

Administration/Assessment

Develop peer observation proposal
Finish three-year plan
Redesign Web sites
Hold assessment seminar
Preliminary assessment of English W130

Curriculum

Pilot W231 curriculum
Update all curriculum guides
Create English as a Second Language (ESL) W131 guide

2002–03

Administration/Assessment

Review placement needs
Review honors course needs
Begin University Writing Center assessment
Develop handbook for UWC
Review UWC fellow recruitment strategies
Assess Stretch Program
Begin assessment of W131 online
Assess W131 (particularly grading)
Assess revised W231

Curriculum

Implement revised Stretch, W131, W132, W231, and W396 curricula
Begin addressing issues of text selection in W131
Cultivate connections for two linked versions of W132
Articulation project (W132, W210, and W290)
Complete UWC technology grant work
Offer peer-tutoring graduate course as independent study

Faculty Development

Implement community of inquiry

2003–04

Administration/Assessment

W132 assessment
Program coherence assessment
Review links with university college courses
Review reading in Stretch Program

Curriculum

Implement new readings in W131
Offer linked W132 sections (two maximum)

Faculty Development

Provide orientation for all faculty on Stretch Program

2004–05

Administration/Assessment

Review of writing and literacy concentration and connections to introductory courses

Curriculum

Publish book of student writing from introductory courses

11

NEW DESIGNS FOR COMMUNICATION ACROSS THE CURRICULUM

Andrew Billings
Teddi Fishman
Morgan Gresham
Angie Justice
Michael Neal
Barbara Ramirez
Summer Smith Taylor
Melissa Tidwell Powell
Donna Winchell
Kathleen Blake Yancey
Art Young

Clemson University conducted its first Writing Across the Curriculum (WAC) Workshop in 1989. It was an entirely voluntary grassroots affair: there was no mandate, no administrative support, and no extrinsic reward for participating. Sixty of Clemson's approximately nine hundred faculty signed up for a one-day workshop and journeyed to a retreat center eight miles from campus where they met, talked, and shared strategies for incorporating writing activities into their classes. During the next few years, Clemson faculty as well as visiting scholars conducted several more well-attended workshops on a variety of WAC topics that included responding to student writing, writing to learn, and collaborative learning. The common themes for all of the activities were the use of WAC strategies to encourage students as active learners and to support instructors as interactive teachers. This faculty workshop approach to WAC, which in a modernist sense is the program's primary mode of delivery, is a familiar one for beginning WAC programs.

In 1990, the R. Roy and Marnie Pearce Center for Professional Communication was established at Clemson University with a generous gift from the Pearce family. As a result, the WAC initiative expanded to focus more broadly on Communication Across the Curriculum (CAC), thus strengthening its interdisciplinary emphasis by explicitly embracing oral, visual, and digital—in addition to written—communication. The Pearce Center was founded for three interrelated missions: CAC on the Clemson campus, collaboration with South Carolina schools, and partnerships with industry and the community. This three-part charge serves to connect our Clemson-specific mission of enhancing the developing language and thinking abilities of our students with community activism, school-to-work partnerships, and civic responsibility. These changes in our mission marked the beginning of a postmodern turn in our endeavors. Instead of writing workshops functioning as a stable, recognizable site for CAC, the program became more multidimensional and more about multiple functions than a location (Derrida 1978, 280). We no longer focused on writing as the only medium; we no longer separated written and oral language from visual and digital learning; we no longer viewed the Clemson campus as our only space; and we broadened our audience beyond faculty to include community and corporate partnerships. During the first half of the 1990s, however, faculty workshops continued to be the primary engine that drove the CAC initiative, the topics broadening to include speaking across the curriculum, service learning, visual communication, and teaching with technology. Our endeavors were recognized in 2001 when *Time* magazine and Princeton Review honored Clemson as the "Public College of the Year" on the strength of our CAC program and its impact on campus culture and teaching throughout the disciplines. Despite these successes, however, attendance at our faculty workshops had steadily declined since the mid-1990s. Whereas early workshop enrollments ranged from thirty to forty, they dropped to twenty and thirty, and then dipped into single digits.

So what was our problem? Clearly faculty were still interested in communication as evidenced by their continued participation in CAC alumni events and the use of WAC/CAC techniques in their classrooms. Our successful model of interactive faculty workshops had even sparked significant competition for faculty participation in interdisciplinary workshops. During the past six or seven years, new campus entities were developed to help faculty improve their teaching effectiveness. Examples include the new Office of Teaching Excellence and Innovation; the newly endowed Rutland Center's Ethics Across the Curriculum; the campus-wide Service Learning Cooperative; the Office of Distance and Continuing Education; and the Collaborative Learning Environment, a course management system from our new division of Educational Technology Services with workshops for faculty on how to use this new e-environment in pedagogically sound ways. Other interdisciplinary workshops were sponsored by women's studies, African American studies, and the Office of Assessment. While we welcomed the increased attention to teaching innovation and effectiveness, we recognized that we were now having to compete for participants. Particularly at a school that is placing increased emphasis on research, grant funding, and graduate education, finding faculty members with the desire, the time, and the resources to participate in CAC workshops became increasingly challenging.

This decline in faculty participation in workshops is not unusual in mature, or "second-stage," WAC and CAC programs. In "The Future of WAC," Barbara Walvoord addresses directly the sustainability of WAC programs initiated and nurtured by faculty workshops:

> I think WAC also must fundamentally reexamine its old micro-level concerns, particularly its traditional workshop-plus-follow-up model, its leadership, and its theories of faculty development, and the delivery of services to faculty. . . .
>
> The word "follow-up" reveals an underlying assumption that the centrally located workshop led by a writing specialist is the key transforming event, which needs only "follow up" to maintain conversion. That thought pattern spells demise or stagnation once the recruitable faculty have been through a workshop. WAC must see itself not as a transforming workshop plus "follow-up" but as part of a sustaining set of services, a network, a culture, within the university, that supports ongoing, career-long, self-directed growth for faculty. (1996, 72–73)

Walvoord has described one aspect of the situation we were facing at Clemson, and her postmodern prescription for the future of WAC coincided in many respects with our own planning for the further development of our CAC initiative. In our effort to remain a catalyst for faculty-centered educational and cultural change, we have become more open to chance opportunities to network and partner with a variety of organizations both on and off the Clemson campus.

Even as we realized that traditional faculty workshops could no longer be the singular focus of our CAC program, we continued to value the interdisciplinary faculty workshops that have changed and continue to change Clemson's culture. The problem, as we saw it, was that workshops had become routine. Clemson's Strategic Plan and Roadmap both call for substantially more interdisciplinary faculty collaboration in teaching, research, and service. The good news is that faculty frequently participate in workshops, symposia, and other interdisciplinary teaching and learning exchanges. Even Clemson's president, James Barker, routinely convenes interdisciplinary colloquia on topics such as science and society and academic integrity. The bad news, however, is that faculty no longer attend our CAC workshops in the numbers they once did.

As one solution to the decline in workshop participation, many WAC/CAC programs viewed the establishment of required writing-intensive courses as central to institutionalizing and, thus, sustaining themselves.

However, Clemson's CAC program never pursued this strategy, believing that curricular requirements that are reluctantly embraced would need to be monitored, further reducing writing- and speaking-rich courses to an identified handful. Independent of the Pearce Center, the university in the mid-1990s did institute the curricular option of writing-intensive and oral-communication-intensive courses; however, with a few exceptions, academic departments never embraced this opportunity, preferring instead to have their majors fulfill general education requirements with courses such as technical writing and public speaking taught by faculty in English and communication studies. In the fall of 2003, as part of a proposal to revise general education, the University Curriculum Committee voted to end the writing-intensive and oral-communication-intensive requirements.

The dubious nature of writing-intensive courses as represented on the Clemson campus as well as our own decentered vision for CAC within broad local, national, and international arenas means that we have not pursued aggressively "writing in the disciplines" (WID), which many scholars have suggested as the next step for WAC. For example, Jones and Comprone write, "Finally, and most importantly, WAC pedagogy needs to use research into discipline conventions to create more effective rhetorical approaches to WAC courses" (1993, 65). They continue, noting that David Russell calls for discipline-specific research on writing and discourse communities that may enable disciplines to "eventually . . . design the pedagogical 'scaffoldings' . . . , curricular structures built of meaningful experiences with language, which will lead students through progressively more sophisticated engagement with each discipline through its discourse" (65).[1]

Such scholars argue for a greater emphasis on WID because knowledge is socially constructed and academic language is constituted by the written conversation of particular discourse communities (for example, history or physics). They often see studying each discipline's rhetoric as essential to the growth of WAC theory and practice as well as a force for change locally and nationally. And such research, curricular changes, and pedagogical scaffolding are important theoretical and applied work for WAC as well as rhetoric and composition and technical communication programs. However, for our work at Clemson—which encourages participation and collaboration with schools, industry, and civic groups—we promote pedagogies and scaffolds that are interdisciplinary rather than discipline specific and that promote personal reflection and social action as ways that students can write, speak, design, and digitize to make a difference in their own lives and the lives of others. We want CAC at Clemson to work across as well as within communities, both on and off campus. This commitment to civic values implies that CAC will never be a quick fix for educational or political issues. CAC here is fundamentally about systematically changing our campus and, since our campus does not exist in a vacuum, about changing the larger cultures in which schools, colleges, industries, and communities exist. Thus a solution will not be found in a workshop, a curricular change, a focus on technology, assessment, or any other grand narrative for educational change—but it may be found in all these and more in paratactic combinations.

Consequently, the highly visible problems of lack of attendance at faculty workshops and the continued challenge to institutionalize curricular revisions have become an exigency to rethink our primary goals. We plan to work for educational change on our campus and nationally through the interconnectedness of our commitments to work collegially with every discipline, department, and program on our campus in support of common goals; to develop mutually beneficial partnerships with South Carolina and the nation's secondary schools; and to develop mutually beneficial partnerships with corporate and nonprofit organizations, especially as they relate school to work expectations, performance, and critique. In this process, we developed and continue to plan, implement, and assess a variety of new and always provisional partnerships, projects, workshops, resources, clients, and delivery systems that allow us to join with others on and off campus in continually learning and changing as we together educate students and wider communities in using writing and communication to make a difference in our lives. To quote Barbara Walvoord again, "WAC . . . must dive in or die" (1996, 70).

In what follows, we provide brief descriptions of some of the CAC initiatives with which we are currently involved and suggest how each plays an important role in fulfilling our mission. We combine new approaches with familiar ones, establish a diminished role for faculty workshops without abandoning them, and reimagine a future for CAC at Clemson based on an active partnership with our students as well as with other people and organizations at Clemson and in the community. First, we introduce three new models and modes of delivery for interdisciplinary collaboration: the South Carolina Institute for Ethics and Reflection (SCISE), the Poetry Across the Curriculum initiative (PAC), and the Summer Reading Program and Presidential Colloquium. Next, we describe three reinventions of the traditional workshop model, some involving new workshop structures and new clients: the thematic series, the focused two-hour workshop, and the graduate school partnership. Last, we describe the Class of 1941 Studio for Student Communication, in both its physical and virtual spaces, a facility and a facilitation that suggests Ihab Hassan's "open in time as well as in structure or space" (1987, 93). This new kind of studio, designed by the Pearce Center faculty to enable students and faculty to collaborate on communication projects in a variety of new and old media, will establish a presence for CAC on campus that cultivates new opportunities to ensure that CAC at Clemson will never again be only faculty workshops led by a writing specialist and a few writing-intensive courses.

SCISE

Having determined to dive in, we began looking for ways to better address the changing needs of the university while still meeting the three-part mission of the Pearce Center. One particularly attractive opportunity was a three-way partnership with Clemson's Rutland Center for Ethics and the university's Darla T. Moore School of Education. Together, we developed SCISE, a summer institute that targets teachers and teacher educators throughout the state (although we have had attendees from other states and even other countries). These workshops, which are conducted during the summer to allow practicing teachers to attend, focus on current trends and issues of concern to education professionals. Faculty facilitators act as instructors, discussion leaders, and role-playing participants in order to help bring about experiential as well as reflective learning on a range of related topics including pedagogy (both for K-12 teachers and university teacher educators), ethics, and the uses of communicative and reflective practices in the classroom.

SCISE combines small group discussions, scenario-based problem solving, reflective writing, and collaborative presentation. Participants begin with discussions of the core concepts which, for the past two years, have centered on incorporating ethical awareness into class discussions and activities. Then they are presented with various scenarios and are asked to identify and justify ethical decisions. During the initial discussions, participants are introduced to some major schools of philosophical thought. Because many K-12 (and other) educators have little familiarity with teaching ethics, it is first necessary to define key terms, review central concepts, and "practice" the methods and approaches that workshop participants will later use with their students. Once key terms and vocabulary are in place, facilitators lead increasingly complex scenario-based inquiries in which new topics are introduced and often argued. Facilitators demonstrate how the various philosophical "tools" can be used as strategies for making more reasoned decisions. The next step is to show participants how these strategies can be taught as a mechanism for resolving ethical dilemmas, again with the goal that participants will later follow similar procedures with their own students. Workshop sessions typically end with reflective writing exercises that are collected and responded to by facilitators.

A single day's discussion topics might include a brief introduction to Kantian deontology, virtue ethics, and utilitarianism, all of which might be applied to questions about colonialist paternalism. Rather than addressing the topic in the abstract, however, participants might be asked about when intervention in the cultural customs of another country might be warranted. Is it morally justifiable to intervene, for instance, in situations where women's dress is proscribed? Does it matter if, along with other mandated codes of conduct, women are not given access to higher education? Are we justified in trying to change another culture to prevent the practice referred to as "female circumcision"? When does it become our moral duty to interfere, and when are we ethically obligated not to get involved or not to impose our own standards on members of another culture?

Although discussion topics range from abstract instructional scenarios like the classic, "if four people arrived at the emergency room and you had to choose between saving the one most critically injured or saving the other three," to highly topical real-life political questions such as the ones outlined in the last paragraph, they share a common thread of civic responsibility—particularly with respect to elementary and secondary education. Additionally, the methods of the institute itself—small group discussion, free writing, reflective writing, dialogic problem solving, cross-disciplinary collaborations—all are in keeping with the mission of the Pearce Center even though the look and feel of this institute is very much different from our traditional communications workshops. In the process of building ethical knowledge and pedagogical strategies among participants, there is a blurring of the traditional hierarchical relationship between ethics and rhetoric—relocating them in language and as interdependent. As Faigley, interpreting Lyotard's approach to ethics, writes: "Lyotard relocates ethics in the material practices of reading and writing. In a traditional view of the relationship between rhetoric and ethics, ethical values pre-exist rhetoric. Rhetoric in the traditional view becomes the means to persuade people to be ethical. In a postmodern theory of rhetoric, there is no legitimate preexisting discourse of values for rhetoric to convey" (1992, 237).

There are several features of SCISE that make it unusual not just for us but for WAC/CAC activities in general. The partnerships with ethics and education faculty as well as the emphasis on content area (in this case, ethics) rather than communicative strategies may seem, at first glance, to make this less about communication and more about pedagogy and ethics. In fact, however, SCISE provides a very focused, very communication-intensive series of activities which have WAC/CAC principles at their core. Institute participants, too, are somewhat nontraditional for WAC/CAC activities. Rather than being the interdisciplinary mix that WAC/CAC coordinators hope to attract, the SCISE participants come from a variety of disciplines, all of which are related to education. While there have been no engineering or math faculty present, the range of ranks and responsibilities of the participants provides a variety of perspectives and concerns which serve to enrich the discussions as participants negotiate the topics under consideration. What finally, however, makes the SCISE and the Pearce Center a useful symbiotic relationship is the emphasis on "communication to learn," which functions as the central pedagogy for the workshops and is complemented by exploratory reflective writing. The SCISE workshops afford a unique opportunity for the Pearce Center team to work directly with not only teacher-educators but also the teachers who will be utilizing WAC in their K-12 classrooms in fulfilling the three-part mission of the Pearce Center.

POETRY ACROSS THE CURRICULUM

Poetry Across the Curriculum (PAC) is in its fifth year, and forty faculty from more than twenty disciplines and over two thousand students have participated. Such a project is one way to address the CAC issue of "follow up" in faculty development and at the same time embark on a new area of emphasis with a delivery mode not based on workshops led by a "writing specialist." While many college catalogs announce curricula based on critical thinking and *creativity*, this project (in collaboration with other people and organizations) seeks to integrate creative thinking and expression into courses throughout both the curriculum and the campus culture. To participate in this project, rather than attend an isolated workshop on why and how to incorporate PAC into the classroom, faculty participants meet regularly to contribute their knowledge and experience with this innovative teaching strategy, to generate collaborative scholarship on teaching and learning, and to value and promote opportunities for imaginative representation and expression in disciplinary contexts. As part of this PAC project, teachers ask students to write poems in courses across the curriculum in order to gain new perspectives about the content they are studying and to develop their creativity through imaginative language play. Poems suggest an accessible cross-disciplinary discourse for probing, imagining, and resisting specialized disciplinary knowledge and discourse. Elsewhere, Art Young has described this impetus for resistance as "writing against the curriculum":

> The purpose of Poetry Across the Curriculum, as we conceive it, is to provide opportunities for students to use written language to engage course content in meaningful ways, not to teach them to be better poets. For many students, creating a poem provides a way into disciplinary discussions in which the writers' own poetic language engages, recasts, and critiques disciplinary knowledge without having to conform to the discourse conventions of an alien discourse. (2003b, 475)

Poetic writing activities give students opportunities to make personal connections to the material they study and to reflect on new academic knowledge and experiences. Most teachers describe a poem "as anything you want it to be," thus creating an open space for play with language, media, ideas, and experience and for performing, exploring, identifying, or blurring the tensions within and among them. And when such playful language activities are made social by sharing in groups or at public readings, they enable students and teachers to build classroom communities based on a respect for language and on a connection to texts and to each other in which further learning and growth occur, sometimes in surprising ways.[2]

Our ongoing PAC project (2000–04) involves occasional academic and social get-togethers coordinated by professors of biology, English, and psychology who are codirectors of the project. PAC participants attend regular lunch meetings to discuss issues and experiences that arise in their classes. Each year, we publish an anthology of selected student poems from each participating class; print editions of whole sets of poems from particular classes such as biology, horticulture, music, and psychology; award "certificates of achievement" and bookstore gift certificates to selected authors for merit; and publish selected poems on the Web (people.clemson.edu/~apyoung/focus_on_creativity.html). We print student poems from every participating teacher's class on special

PAC stationery for posting on office and departmental bulletin boards. Each spring, poets and their faculty mentors read students' poetry in the university library as part of Clemson's "Arts in April" festival. And an interdisciplinary group of faculty holds an evening meeting each spring to discuss the future of the project and to analyze and evaluate over a hundred student poems.

Many of us are excited about what the PAC project has yielded for our teaching and learning, and we plan not only to continue the project for another year but we are also expanding its goals. An interdisciplinary team of PAC participants is developing a 2004 pilot project for our classes tentatively called Creative Response for Learning (CRL). Our goal is to open and expand possibilities for students' imaginative responses to academic subject matter beyond poetry to all forms of creativity: graphics, music, stories, performance, parables, video, hypertext, quilts, e-poetry, photography, poster design, sculpture, mixed and fused modes and media, publication, and other fascinating genres and media that we know our students will generate. The opening of the Class of 1941 Studio for Student Communication (discussed later in this chapter) promises to be an enabling space for the collaborating, planning, designing, composing, presenting, and performing that we imagine for ourselves and our students participating in the CRL pilot project. We know there will be new challenges as well as new possibilities, and we know that if and when we decide to open the project to all Clemson faculty, we will be greeted with questions like "How can I make and assess assignments that encourage students to use photography or multimedia, when I don't know anything myself about using and judging art forms in my classroom?" Although we may not arrive at a satisfactory answer during our pilot project, we are familiar from other contexts with such questions about oral presentations, written documents, digital portfolios, and the writing of poetry. In many instances, we trust answers will emerge through our collaboration with our students and colleagues and through our partnering with other organizations and projects, such as the state's schools and Clemson's "Arts in April" festival.

PRESIDENTIAL COLLOQUIUM

Clemson instituted its Presidential Colloquium four years ago when our president selected as the theme for the year "The Idea of a University." Throughout the year students in first-year composition read works that covered every aspect of the topic from Cardinal Newman's early thoughts on the purpose of a university to the will of Thomas Green

Clemson, which created Clemson as a land-grant university, to visions of how computer technology will increasingly shape university life. Richard Lanham came to speak to the students about what discourse has come to look like and where it may take us in the future. A series of additional outside speakers, plus lecturers and panels representing a range of Clemson faculty and administrators, kept the topic before the first-year students as well as other students and faculty throughout the year, and the theme became a topic for PAC and for an essay competition sponsored by our Rutland Center for Ethics. The theme gave the campus a year-long focus for communication across the curriculum.

In each subsequent year, the president has worked with faculty to come up with a topic that will interest faculty and students across the curriculum. One year the focus was "Science and Values: New Frontiers, Perennial Questions"—until the events of September 11 forced us to reconsider what we wanted our students thinking, reading, and writing about, and we shifted in midyear to focus on ethics in time of war. We moved from asking about how the "Brave New World" of cloning and other areas of medical research forces us to rethink our values to the topic "Values Revisited: The Brave New World in Time of War." Again, hundreds of our students were thinking, hearing, reading, and writing about images of the enemy (How do we handle our relations with international students who now look like the enemy?); America's history in time of war (What was the campus like during World War I, World War II, and Vietnam? How does Bush's statement after the World Trade Center and Pentagon attacks compare with Roosevelt's on the day after Pearl Harbor?); and women in the military ("What Did You Do in the War, Grandma?"). We have gone on to focus last year on academic integrity and this year on the human and social costs of admission to the American educational system.

Broader involvement campus-wide, if for a shorter period of time, came this year when we joined numbers of universities across the country in instituting a Summer Reading Program. One of the most gratifying results was that we were able to involve both faculty and staff from all over campus, 165 of them, from administrative assistants to the provost and president. These volunteers met over lunch in the spring to get their copies of Richard Rodriguez's *Hunger of Memory* and some general guidelines for leading a discussion of it. Then on the day before classes began they watched as three thousand or more students streamed into the coliseum from all over campus to hear the author speak about his life and the writing of the book. After the presentation, faculty met with students in small groups to discuss the book and Rodriguez's remarks. Before they arrived the students each wrote a brief response to the book, a piece of writing that in future years will be the first piece in each student's digital portfolio.

Getting faculty from all disciplines involved has been an important step toward breaking down disciplinary boundaries. We plan to continue to draw in faculty from across the campus by selecting works for the Summer Reading Program that are not viewed as fitting only into the domain of literary studies, as has been the model for a number of summer reading programs elsewhere.

VARIATIONS ON AN OLD THEME: THE EVOLUTION OF CAC WORKSHOPS

As we programmatically expand the purview of the Pearce Center to include new initiatives such as SCISE, PAC, and the Summer Reading Program and Presidential Colloquium, we would be shortsighted to abandon features of our program that have been foundational to the long-term success of the CAC initiative at Clemson. Rather than rigidly clinging to past successes in the area of faculty development workshops, we have begun to experiment with variations of the tried-and-true workshop model that has garnered such positive responses throughout the history of the program. As we enter this new phase at Clemson, we want that which has worked well for us in the past to evolve into something that will continue to meet our ever-changing audience, environment, and purposes. Recently, we began to rethink the traditional workshop model that has been a staple of the program since its inception. In response to the current environment at Clemson, we are exploring variations in both delivery and audience.

Workshop Series: Plagiarism and PowerPoint

Desiring a longer time frame for depth and coverage but understanding the reality of busy faculty schedules, we have begun to offer communications workshops in a series over the course of a semester or an academic year. Multidimensional topics like plagiarism and PowerPoint effectiveness—two issues we have covered at Clemson in such a series—would be a challenge to "cover" in a full-day workshop format. For this reason, we began offering workshops in two different types of series. In the first we offer a number of separate workshops centered on a specific theme. These are identified as a series in the promotional materials, and attendees commit to any number of individual sessions. Our first foray into this model of delivery focused on the vexing problems associated with plagiarism, an initiative that arose from several intersecting goals of the university and the Pearce Center. We were looking for ways to continue to provide useful, topical offerings while at the same time coordinating our efforts with those of the university colloquium series, which for that academic year was organized around "Academic Integrity and the Integrity of the Academy." Our goals shifted from attempting to provide a "survey" that addressed the most critical elements of the topic to a series of semi-self-directed inquiries from which workshop participants could build a set of "best practices" or, in some cases, simply a more sophisticated understanding of key issues. In our first meeting on academic integrity, we began by attempting to define plagiarism in the context of our home disciplines. While the participants were initially skeptical of the usefulness of this discussion, it became painfully clear within the first ten minutes that the entire two-hour period could be devoted to this task. Workshop participants not only had differing ideas regarding what constituted plagiarism, they also wanted to contest the ways in which other disciplines defined the problem. Based on discrepancies between the disciplinary understanding of plagiarism, we spent a large portion of the first workshop examining problems students might have negotiating several disciplines within a semester and committing to define plagiarism clearly within our classroom settings. The absence of a universal understanding of plagiarism across disciplinary, cultural, and other contexts then became a foundation for the remaining workshops in the series. By shifting from a coverage model or workshop delivery to one in which depth and focus were the primary goals, we hoped to provide maximum benefit to participants who were unable to attend the entire series.

The second type of workshop series enlists a group of participants to commit to a number of shorter workshops on a designated topic for a period of time, usually a semester or two. At Clemson we have twice offered this type of series on PowerPoint as a pedagogical delivery method. As an area, PowerPoint provides the entire range of CAC content—written, oral, visual, and digital communication—and targets pedagogical issues upon which the Pearce Center has built its reputation. It's also a CAC topic not without controversy: some sign up for the workshop because they are heavily invested in the technology and think it has revolutionized teaching for the better while other participants find that PowerPoint necessarily leads to student passivity and the reduction of subject content to bulleted lists. In fact, many of the PowerPoint tip sheets one finds online suggest no more than six bullets per slide and six words per bullet (the six-by-six rule). Those of us who have battled with students over a predetermined format cringe at the thought of content becoming subservient to the formatting limitations of the medium.

But dismissing PowerPoint as a pedagogical delivery system is not an option for some in the academy. In our first meeting this year, we began the workshop with personal introductions that included an opening statement of interest in PowerPoint in which one participant discussed a difficult predicament. The personnel committee in her science-related field critiqued her first year of teaching because she did not use PowerPoint; however, after she adopted PowerPoint the second year she found her students disengaged from the content of her lectures and more critical of her teaching methods on the student evaluations. Others felt a similar departmental pressure to use PowerPoint in their teaching, especially with the increasing population of students in their respective classes, though some were more confident than others in its effectiveness.

Because the group remains consistent over time, content can build upon itself in this model to achieve greater depth and breadth of coverage. The sustained effort does not significantly infringe on the workload of the participants because meetings are held at reasonable intervals—in our case once a month for the two-semester series—and the framework allows for reading, exploration, and activities to be completed in between meeting times that enhance the discussion and application of the topic. In response to the concerns articulated in the first session, we have since followed up with a number of conversations and mini-presentations centering on uses of PowerPoint that engage students in active listening and learning, thus in effect discussing differences and tensions in the modernist and postmodernist perspectives on teaching and technology. All participants brought in sample slides demonstrating good teaching within their respective disciplines that in turn fostered lively discussion regarding students, teaching, and engaging pedagogy: the type of discussions that interweave communications, technology, and teaching and that reflect the values of the Pearce Center.

Stand-Alone Two-Hour Workshops: CAC Topics

In an evolving program, the stand-alone workshop, however, is not without merit. One alternative we have explored is cutting the length of the workshops from a full day to two hours, offering each workshop at least twice on different days and at different times to allow for scheduling conflicts. While the two-hour workshops contain significantly less content than the full-day ones, they are reasonable to prepare, and faculty around campus seem willing to commit that amount of time. In addition to issues of delivery, another change we have incorporated in our workshop is an expansion of content beyond the traditional WAC subjects to include a larger CAC purview that includes oral, written, visual, and digital communications—especially looking for subjects with overlap between them. The two-hour workshops in the past several years have expanded to include topics ranging from illuminating gender communication in the classroom to understanding communication assessment competencies to writing cohesive and articulate theses and proposals. The majority of the workshops contain some component of media and often pertain to the myriad ways in which communication technology can be incorporated into the classroom. In doing so, faculty can hone communication skills regardless of the discipline in which they teach.

The crux of the new communication workshop model is based on several key elements. The topic of the workshop must be interdisciplinary and new. One good way to examine whether the topic appeals to multiple disciplines is to outline what someone from each college within a university could gain from attending. While appeals to each department at a university may appear impossible, appealing to at least some people within each college has appeared quite plausible at Clemson University. The two-hour workshops must provide innovative content, additional sources for information if an attendee would wish to seek it, and an applied end result that can be implemented in the classroom. Additionally, workshops must be interactive, often utilizing discussion from participants. The new workshop model requires the pooling of shared information, which comes not just from the facilitator but from participants—who often sign up because a given topic fits their interest and who, consequently, have information and tips to share.

The ultimate goal is to fashion workshops that pertain to interdisciplinary communication issues in order to ensure that a large portion of the university community can be served. When implemented correctly, the two-hour workshop can be integral to the success of a CAC program, rather than being viewed as an outdated relic of previous CAC designs.

Professional Development for Graduate Students

In addition to the evolution of CAC workshop content and delivery, we have also begun to expand the base of participants to include graduate students, an underserved population within the university community despite Clemson's administrative push toward a higher priority on graduate programs. In 2002–03, the campus engaged in a year-long discussion of eight research "emphasis areas" that would guide the flow of funds and attention within the university. All faculty were under increasing pressure to win external grant funding, new graduate degrees were being proposed in most colleges, and departments were encouraged to increase graduate enrollment. In the past, the Pearce Center and CAC at Clemson had focused almost exclusively on issues surrounding the teaching of communication to undergraduates. But the new emphasis on graduate research provided a strong exigency for establishing a new partnership with the graduate school.

Meanwhile, from the graduate students' perspective, the exigency for assistance with communication had always been present, but had simply been overlooked by entities like Pearce and CAC. Graduate students, particularly those in technical and scientific fields, often receive little guidance from faculty on their writing or speaking. Yet they are expected to publish their research, create research posters, attend conferences, and—not the least of their worries—complete a thesis or dissertation. As their faculty advisors felt more pressure to write grants and work with additional students, the graduate students could expect less attention and higher expectations.

Recognizing the graduate students' current needs and anticipating that many of these students will become faculty members in the near future around the country, the Pearce Center began offering a set of professional development experiences for the students. This effort engaged CAC with a new clientele and exemplified our new approach of reaching out directly to students rather than confining our work to faculty professional development. The effort also incorporated the "sustaining set of services" (Walvoord 1996, 72) model that had been successfully tested on campus with initiatives like our plagiarism and PowerPoint series.

While the graduate student initiative goes beyond workshops, this form of delivery, however, is the entry point for participants. Graduate students from across the university are invited by the graduate school to attend workshops presented by the Pearce Center which address such topics as writing for scholarly journals, presenting at conferences, and writing thesis and dissertation proposals. They feature presentations by the workshop leader, small-group discussions on topics suggested by the leader, and whole-group discussions based on the results of the small-group discussions. These workshops are designed not only to provide an overview of strategies but also to help the students develop a few specific goals and plans to act on after the workshop.

The workshops are consistently overbooked, confirming the graduate students' desire for communications-focused professional development. They bring together students from a variety of majors in the sciences, engineering, agriculture, social sciences, and the humanities. More than half of the students are typically second-language English speakers. The students quickly recognize the opportunity for gleaning new ideas and strategies from others who, though differing greatly, are still experiencing many of the same stresses and pressures as researchers and communicators. For example, in a recent workshop several students at one table learned from others about the database-searching help offered by librarians at the university library. At another table, students engaged in a lively discussion of how to accomplish their goals despite the politics and intellectual conflict among their dissertation committee members.

The professional development initiative begins with these workshops, but does not stop there. Moving toward the "sustaining services" advocated by Walvoord, we offered interested students from the workshops the opportunity to join a Graduate Student Writing Group facilitated by faculty of the Pearce Center. Meeting every three weeks for about two hours, the writing group allows more individualized, thorough, and extended assistance for graduate students who are writing seminar papers, theses, dissertations, proposals, or articles. The meetings are facilitated by faculty but are student-directed; we attempt to balance teaching with facilitation. The participating students are asked to bring questions, concerns, and drafts to the meetings, which flow from roundtable discussion of common issues to reading and commenting and back again. At the end of the meeting, each student announces a specific writing goal that he or she promises to achieve by the next meeting.

The writing group meetings feature the sharing of ideas and strategies across disciplines, cultures, and stages of progress on writing. At a recent meeting, faculty from English who have conducted research on collaboration from a communication perspective exchanged ideas with a student from mechanical engineering who was writing a thesis proposal about a computer system designed to facilitate collaboration. On this topic and others, student and faculty participants found that they could help each other clarify their ideas because of (rather than in spite of) their disciplinary differences. Sharing also occurred across cultures, with a French student offering suggestions based on French practices of promoting organic foods to an American student studying organic food production and sales in the United States. Students who were further along in the thesis process offered suggestions to those who were just beginning. The faculty facilitators also learned from the graduate students—not only about the content of their research but also about the conventions of writing in their disciplines. All in all, the Graduate Student Writing Group provides an opportunity to reach out to a new and eager clientele, while also enriching our own understanding of communication across the disciplines.

CAC Alumni Events

One of the most successful workshops offered by the Pearce Center continues to be the CAC Alumni Event, a two-hour workshop that highlights some of the progressive and interesting communication work across the campus. Despite being offered each semester during exam week, the workshop attracts between forty and fifty attendees on a regular basis. The workshop typically highlights three examples, each typically representing a different college, of the "best CAC practices" of faculty and students in a setting that provides the presenters a chance to showcase their pedagogical work—something that continues to be valued at Clemson—to an interested audience. Recent CAC alumni events have included such communication projects as one from an abnormal psychology class where students placed painted green shoes around campus and the local community with factual information educating readers about mental disorders and promoting a local benefit walk to raise funds and awareness for mental health care. While the professor discussed the objectives of the assignment and her role, several of the students from the class shared what they had learned through the process as well. Other presentations have included service-learning projects with a strong communications emphasis, faculty members who participated in the PowerPoint workshops, PAC participants, an entomology professor's approach to integrating communication and creativity in her class, and many others. This regular workshop both creates a space for community to develop and provides continuing ideas and resources for those who are interested in integrating communication assignments and activities into their curriculum. It also provides an opportunity for those not involved with the Pearce Center to get a sense of the work and values of the CAC program at Clemson in an enjoyable, nonthreatening setting.

THE STUDIO AND THE ONLINE STUDIO

As we have seen in the preceding pages, the Pearce Center has reinvented itself to fit the changing environment at Clemson. Jay Bolter (2000) describes the ways in which our postmodern culture encourages us to revisit and rethink our artifacts in different media as remediation—not in its usual sense of being remedial, but rather in the sense of something old made new again. And our spaces, like so much of our teaching and learning, are being *remediated* to meet new demands—of undergraduate students, of overworked faculty, and of our increasingly digital culture. Recognizing, as did Louise Phelps in her 2003 WPA Conference address, the import of continual redesign and reconceptualization, we are changing spaces as we struggle to support new delivery methods, new clients, and new connections that accompany our new exigencies. The term "space" plays on multiple layers here—ambient, physical, virtual, and curricular—because it is the interplay of these multiple spaces that cultivates the context for change. Crucial to this remediation of space is seamlessness. In arguing against Kaufer and Butler's notion of design as "a seamless integration of the knowledge and goals of the designer" (1996, 33) as too complete, too neat, and too constricting of larger human functions of human activities, Phelps made a key point about reconceptualization and its role in composition and curriculum. What we have been (re)designing is a space for multiple interactions with new clients, new partners, and new technologies that foregrounds the seams of knowledge, goals and learning—the cobbling together rather than the ultimate creation. If we do not continually rebuild, we lose function over time—new media become old media, and new clients become old partners—and if design (and the structures that embody it) do not change over time, they will be abandoned or demolished. Continual redesign is a key element of technoprovocateurs[3] but is obvious only if we take note of the seams. The seams are the flexible spaces, the spaces of change.

In May 2003, Clemson University began construction on the Class of 1941 Studio for Student Communication, a 4,000-square-foot facility for students to work on communication projects in speech, writing, visual, and digital technologies. While we have been blessed with a new physical space, what has been more important for us are the ways in which the *idea* of the space and its remediation have offered us space to reconsider and remediate our existing mission. We now have two new spaces—the new physical studio and its online counterpart—that provide us the potential to fulfill and enhance the mission of the Pearce Center as it was first conceived. Now besides working with faculty, the studio provides a work environment for students as well. And when the online studio matures, we will have a space that simplifies both outreach services to K-12 schools and working with the corporate world by limiting the physical space that now separates us.

The Class of 1941 Studio for Student Communication

A reflective, collaborative approach to studio design was a key element in helping us rethink the space; we engaged over seventy-five "stakeholders" throughout the planning process, including members of the Pearce Corporate Advisory Board, faculty, administrators, IT and other staff, custodial staff, and students. In these conversations, we discovered not only the significant contributions that each had to offer but also the importance of (re)imagining our mission in light of how the space will connect us to each of these groups and how they will connect to one another once the space is in place. What follows, then, is a series of extended examples for the studio and its online counterpart, illustrating how the studio might be used; through these, we can imagine space, activity, staffing needs, scheduling issues, and curriculum.

At nine o'clock in the morning, six students appear to work on a PowerPoint presentation, due the following week, for a business class: they have to persuade a board of directors to become a silent partner in their start-up firm. They also have to complete a one-page document explaining the logic of their appeal. They seem primarily to want space, but you'd like to work with them. A first-year student is also at the door, wanting help with a classroom writing assignment; she seems to need work in invention. At quarter past nine a student comes in to talk about the Tiger Cup public-speaking competition, which has just been announced—he definitely wants to talk about what he can say. The topic focuses on Clemson, as it does every year, and you also wonder what could be said. At half past nine a portfolio mentor group shows up—they are to review their digital portfolios, adding something that they have completed this term. A Pearce faculty workshop leader appears and needs to know how to make the projection equipment work. At ten of ten faculty start streaming through the studio to get to the conference area, and the students are distracted.

Welcome to the new Class of 1941 Studio.

The Online Studio

Connected to, but not quite mirroring, the physical space is the Online Studio. We have begun planning and implementing it using a three-stage model, which we believe offers an example of how we can remediate a more traditional Online Writing Lab (OWL) into an increasingly dynamic space. Accompanying the description of each stage below are examples of how we expect the space to be used; in fact, it was these kinds of scenarios that helped us plan the space. In the first stage, we offer an electronic warehouse of communications information.

> A Clemson student needs help composing a PowerPoint presentation and looks online for pointers. The search results in two or three digitized handouts from Clemson instructors on giving PowerPoint presentations in the disciplines. Another student, working on her electronic portfolio, needs advice on how to reflect on her growth as a writer in looking at three projects: a first-year writing assignment, a poem that she wrote for a PAC project in a psychology class, and a biology lab report. The results from the search of the electronic file cabinet reveal a short handout on writing reflective memos, an article on reflection, and a PowerPoint presentation from a Pearce workshop on how to repurpose documents for the portfolio.

Second, we will construct an asynchronous network of conversations about writing and communications in and across disciplines.

> Another student, Jamal, has been placed on a team with three other Pearce clients who are also working on digital portfolios. They have a group computer space to deposit video and textual documents for review. They use the online center's listserv and discussion board spaces as well as the project management space to maintain a six-week project management calendar. The team schedules meetings with Pearce specialists to talk about reflection, choosing documents that represent a well-balanced college experience, and discussing the strengths and weaknesses of each.

Third, we invite participants to discuss issues in real time with other communicators and with specially trained consultants who can receive, view, and comment on multimedia and other projects in real time.

> Seeking immediate help with a presentation, Bill, a student based in Texas, wanders into the Pearce Center Multi-user domain Object Oriented (MOO). There he encounters scenarios that allow him to brainstorm topics, create PowerPoint slides, and share text and video with a Pearce consultant. That consultant leads Bill to a MOO room where others are working on similar projects. Students take turns sharing information and providing feedback. During the presentations, a high school English class comes online to see how high school writing differs from college writing.

Our hope, then, is to help students—and faculty—to design a facility with multimodal language that can be presented and represented visually, verbally, and virtually across time.

Lessons Learned

We have learned numerous things in the planning, the building, and the foreseeable opening of these studios. One category of learning might be titled "the politics of location, physical and curricular." If the best learning is not in the course container but rather in spaces like this studio, we will have to find new ways of defining this curricular work, of identifying spaces where it can occur, and of funding it—particularly in schools dominated by Full Time Equivalencies (FTEs) as the way of distributing resources. It may be, as Barbara Walvoord has argued, that such work in particular requires us to make alliances with other units on campus (and off), and it may also be that cross-curricular projects like studios, CAC portfolios, service learning, and ethics across the curriculum will provide focal points for such alliances. We count on the intersection of physical and curricular spaces, on our new activities, on our students, and on our colleagues to help us understand the patterns of remediation here.

THE FUTURE OF CAC AT CLEMSON UNIVERSITY

In her 1989 *College Composition and Communication* article, Susan McLeod anticipates a third stage of WAC in the academy, especially citing the modernist need for WAC to stabilize in light of a number of supposed WAC programs around the country that were neither cognitively or rhetorically based in the way that we traditionally understand WAC programs (342). She argues for WAC "as a permanent fixture in higher education" so that administrators in our institutions do not think of a WAC program as "merely additive—more term papers, more courses, more proficiency tests—but one that is closely tied with thinking and learning, one that will bring about changes in teaching as well as in student writing" (342–43). And McLeod is right about programs that effect positive change on a number of levels: administration, faculty, and students. What is perhaps ironic is that as the Pearce Center moves into the next phase of WAC, we have found strength in a postmodern malleability rather than in permanency: the evolution of WAC into CAC; partnering with other programs and people on as well as off campus, thus decentralizing the administration of pieces within the program, pieces that are distinct, paratactic, and interrelated; seeing old things in a new way; using spaces both virtual and physical in new ways to reach larger and different populations within our mission; and being fluid enough to suit the current climate of the university without losing its distinct history and identity within the institution. If anything, the CAC program is less stable and identifiable now than it might have been over the past two decades; however, it is this same fluidity and unpredictability that best positions it for continued growth and success at Clemson University for years to come.

12

MIRROR, MIRROR ON THE WEB

Visual Depiction, Identity, and the Writing Program

Carolyn Handa

A depiction is never just an illustration. . . . [I]t is the site for the construction and depiction of social difference.

—Gordon Fyfe and John Law

There will be time, there will be time
To prepare a face to meet the faces that you meet[.]

—T. S. Eliot

Information technology is identity technology.

—Sherry Turkle

And so. It's always that fairy-tale thing with the mirror. You gaze at the shiny surface. It caters to your ego, whispering that *YOU* are the center of the universe, the fairest of all. The most handsome. It reflects your very best self. That is, until one day it tells you something you've secretly feared: one day you are no longer the fairest. You have been supplanted. Or so you think. You are a composition teacher. You see a different pedagogy smiling out from that darn mirror. Or so you think. You see your fair self being blocked out, overshadowed, cast into oblivion by a change in regime, a pedagogical approach that threatens to discard you and your epistemology as easily as yesterday's antiquated fashions. And the person responsible for that new image you see?—the WPA. Or so you think.

The ideas in this chapter began with two problems interspersed by one question. The first problem: a range of unexpectedly adverse reactions to a writing program's newly constructed mission statement, goals, objectives, and outcomes. My question in response: "Why are these programmatic definitions being resisted?" As the former WPA, I was bewildered by such reactions since a committee with representatives from major departmental constituencies had collaboratively constructed our writing program's pedagogical ethos. At first I wanted to write off all the fuss as a conservative resistance to change. After all, the program had never before been described or mapped out in this way, so wanting to preserve the past was a natural tendency. But I realized that such a dismissive reaction to this discord would never lead to any further understanding, much less to any constructive problem solving or programmatic direction.

Admittedly, one of the more difficult situations for WPAs to occupy is the position of "other" or "outsider"—perhaps even "dictator"—that is invariably foisted upon most administrators, even us congenial WPAs. I am accustomed to being one of the faculty, a member of a collaborative group of peers working to sustain and strengthen a department or program. In fact, I question whether being a WPA necessarily entails being distanced as the person "in charge" rather than being accepted as a spokesperson for a group.[1] But WPAs new to the business might find themselves ostracized without their own doing. This distancing constitutes the second problem that gave rise to this chapter's ideas.

After repeatedly reviewing our program's Web site, I gradually began to wonder if the two problems could and should be traced to the medium used to display these goals: the World Wide Web. Not only the medium, I thought, but also the primary characteristic of this medium, visuality, might be a major factor contributing to the discord. Online documents are hybrid, multimodal texts, equal parts words and images, as visual as they are textual. World Wide Web documents are "visual" in ways that traditional texts are not: online digital texts are invariably marked by graphic elements and images. This multimodality differs just enough from codex texts so that it more easily triggers a variety of readings, some that could bounce up against inherited cultural practices. So the Web site as object, instead of the instructors, could hold the key to solving the puzzling problem. Gunther Kress does say that "[a] particular kind of object gives insight into complex social practices and into their individual ramification" (2000, 190). Our online construction had bifurcated, reflecting not only the program but assuming the characteristics of a visual reflection of self. In other words, "Depictions mark the point where a process of production gives way to a range of effects" (Fyfe and Law 1988, 1). Our product did just that.

As the process of creation gives way to effects, and as language and images merge in the visual space of an online Web document attempting to depict a writing program's identity, something strange takes place. Depiction is—like reflection—never a simple, straightforward act: "Depiction, picturing and seeing are ubiquitous features of the process by which most human beings come to know the world as it really *is* for them. The point is not that social life is guaranteed by some shared visual culture, neither is it that visual ideologies are imposed on individuals. Rather, it is that *social change is at once a change in the regime of representation*" (Fyfe and Law 1988, 2; original emphasis). Depictions, especially when they mirror change, offer a different sense of self that could be as shocking as seeing oneself bald.

Looking into a mirror is rarely a psychologically simple act. Whether or not we see the "truth" can be debatable. The silvery reflection is problematic, literally and figuratively mercurial, sometimes showing only the strengths we want to see, sometimes drawing on subconscious insecurities, fears, and suspicions. Sometimes when we view depictions not intended to be reflections of the self, they become transformed in the mind's eye nevertheless: the images work unintentionally and subconsciously like a mirror. So an additional problem of depictions (especially obvious for those on the World Wide Web) is that, like any artwork or text, they leave their creators to live in the world independently and to endure others' interpretations.

Mixed reactions to a set of writing program goals, objectives, and outcomes depicted in the specific context of a technological medium present an interesting opportunity for analyzing the range of rhetorical skills needed to "read" and understand such a multimodal text. Approaching this problem of resistance from the angle of identity negotiation theory, multiliteracies, visual culture theory, and definitions of power provides a way to locate the source of the problem; then to analyze why it might occur in any writing program shifting pedagogical focus and administrative styles; then attempting, as a result of this change, to embrace the discord between competing pedagogies, the previous and the incoming. Underestimating the full range of rhetorical skills, both verbal and visual, needed for today's multimodal texts obviously affects the reading. A multimethodological, postmodern approach drawing on visual rhetoric and visual culture theories may help to isolate the problem and reveal why it occurred.

The visual portrayal of a writing program's identity, I argue, often falls victim to being misperceived or misinterpreted by one particular group being portrayed visually: the program's instructors. Representations on the World Wide Web, displayed on a monitor's vertical position (instead of as horizontal, less personally charged codex pages) can be interpreted as a reflection of power if the representations are seen as mirror reflections of self. What viewers cannot actually perceive is the construction process, an interactive dialogue resulting in much debate, then final consensus about programmatic focus. The construction process of a democratic, collaboratively created group identity, however, may be impossible to convey—as Fyfe and Law suggest above. Implementing and supporting such an identity, moreover, is especially difficult in a departmental culture where members have been acculturated and programmatically socialized by a previous pedagogy and unaccustomed to a group ethos constructed via a democratic, process-constructed identity, instead of being faced with an institutionally imposed, hierarchically delineated class structure and a previous culture devoted to finding fault and highlighting shortcomings.[2]

As Fyfe and Law explain, the embedded dynamic I never anticipated in my new WPA naiveté is that

> [a] depiction is never just an illustration. It is the material representation, the apparently stabilised product of a process of work. And it is the site for the construction and depiction of social difference. To understand a visualisation is thus to inquire into its provenance and into the social work that it does. It is to note its principles of exclusion and inclusion, to detect the roles that it makes available, to understand the way in which they are distributed, and to decode the hierarchies and differences that it naturalises. (1988, 1)

While I saw a neutral illustration, my colleagues sensed that the program's site depicted a difference between them and me, a difference that emerged simply by virtue of their belief that it existed. So to begin understanding the depth and complexity of the reaction to our programmatic depiction, I based my analysis, in part, on Fyfe and Law's definition. I also drew on identity negotiation theory to help think about ways to overcome the social differences embedded in the visualization.

In his book about identity negotiations in writers' workshops, Robert Brooke explains that students' writing improved when they understood the different roles available to them as writers, not simply the role of student-writing-to-please-the-teacher. Brooke's analysis led me to think about identity negotiation in terms of WPAs and faculty teaching in their programs and to use identity negotiation as a way of analyzing and understanding the problems that arose.

Brooke explains "identity negotiations" as a term that "highlights the development of the self within a complex arena of competing social forces" (1991, 12). Brooke locates the main stress as

> a tension between social and internal understandings of the self. In any given context, a person's bearing, past, and behaviors imply that the person is a given sort of individual, but this implied identity may or may not correspond to the person's internally felt self. The problem of identity formation, thus, is how to deal with this ever-present distance between implied and felt identity. (1991, 12)

In the case of our pages, the distance between the implied and felt identities was too great for viewers to process without more help from me, the administrator, in bridging the gap. One way of anticipating potential problems or resolving them before they occurred could have been to identify the gap as best as possible before presenting an identity that could be misinterpreted as an exercise of power. The problem was that the instructors had been conditioned to see hierarchy even if no hierarchy was intended. They were accustomed to seeing the WPA as someone exercising traditional types of power as control instead of recognizing collaborative committee work as a sign that our program was on its way to becoming a collaborative web of equal colleagues. The problem is also that I brought to the hierarchically formed culture a competing or alternative cultural notion: equality rather than power exercised from above, a program perceived as collaborative rather than dictatorial.

PROVENANCE

Before the year 2002, the Expository Writing Program at my previous university had no program description, arguably no internal identity its instructors could assume, and absolutely no *online* presence or public, social face to present to its own students, the department, the university, and other writing programs across the country. What it did possess as a "unifying feature" was an assessment tool unsatisfactory to many of its instructors: a semi-holistically graded final exam for all sections of first-semester composition. Even now, I have file drawer after file drawer full of previous tests, students' exams, norming papers, and breakdowns of final class grades given by instructors in a given term. This assessment tool was epistemologically antithetical to the one I hoped would become the foundation for our revised program. It was punitive in that a WPA could use it to reprimand instructors for grading outside of a prescribed "norm," and it gave us no information whatsoever about how our program was in fact both reaching and teaching our students.

The first step toward revamping this tool and thus the entire program began with visits of assessment consultants from other university writing programs. During the academic years 2001–03, in our first-stage effort to provide internal program coherence and social visibility, a subcommittee of the Expository Writing Committee in the English Department began drafting a mission statement, goals, objectives, outcomes, and an assessment rubric based on our desired outcomes for both classes in our first-year writing sequence. We designed a set of statements intended specifically for posting on the Web as one of the university's accreditation agencies mandated. In fact, any hard copy of these statements at this point in time must be run off from the Web. That this programmatic statement was conceived of, designed, and intended for Web viewing affects the way it "lives" in the world and the way we need to think about the reactions to it.

In addition, traditional ways of viewing assessment complicated the already current-traditional, hierarchical foundations on which the program had rested. As Brian Huot explains, assessment's roots lie in progressive social action, a move "to disrupt existing social order and class systems (Hanson 1993)" (2002, 7), but this process has, in our educational system, come to represent the opposite:

> [A]s we all know, assessment has rarely delivered on this promise. Instead, assessment has been used as an interested social mechanism for reinscribing current power relations and class systems. (2002, 7)

Composition studies itself "exacerbated" assessment's negative, hierarchical reputation, Huot argues, by inadvertently relinquishing theoretical control of testing designs. Doing so allowed a sort of vacuum to open, with businesses rushing to fill the void—businesses lacking the same pedagogical values and viewpoints as teachers in the field:

> One of the results of composition's avoidance of assessment issues has been that major procedures for assessment like holistic scoring were developed by testing companies based upon theoretical and epistemological positions that do not reflect current knowledge of literacy and its teaching. . . . Constructing an agenda for writing assessment as social action means connecting assessment to teaching. . . . Instead of envisioning assessment as a way to enforce certain culturally positioned standards and refuse entrance to certain people and groups of people, we need to use our assessment to aid the learning environment for both teachers and students. (2002, 7–8)

No wonder our program's faculty read their webbed identity within the revised program assessment as yet another means of imposed, top-down gatekeeping. Previous assessment practices had caused instructors to worry about measuring up individually to a punitive set of standards. Assessment measuring a program's success rather than an individual instructor's pedagogical failing had not previously existed in this program.

THE VISUALIZATION'S SOCIAL WORK

Our visual documents bore the social work of representing a clear programmatic focus that included a range of workable pedagogies to our accrediting body, the university, other writing programs, the English Department, all instructors who teach composition for us, and most of all the community of our current and potential students. In other words, we wanted to make clear the overall writing program culture supporting each and every individual class. An identifiable, coherent writing program mission statement, goals, objectives, outcomes, and rubric for each of our first-year writing courses, we felt, would reveal to prospective students, their parents, and their high school teachers what they could expect from university-level writing courses. Presenting what we felt was a clear picture of our writing program's culture, we hoped to demystify our program and the two classes: students could view these Web pages and understand what they should learn and what level of work they could expect. Unfortunately, many students entering the university often feel that first-year courses will simply repeat the writing instruction they received in high school. Many therefore attempt to test out of first-year classes, not understanding what cognitive skills such university-level classes entail. And so these students often fail the department's proficiency tests. If our visualization did its social work, perhaps entering students would understand that testing out of first-year composition would require more than a narrative or a superficial five-paragraph essay.

The program's visualization also needed to do the social work of helping instructors new to teaching at our institution understand and conceptualize where the program expected first-year writing classes to aim. In addition, we hoped to give instructors who had been teaching for years in the previous rather formless program a better sense of programmatic coherence plus a view of the range of teaching activities possible with clear programmatic goals and outcomes.

The programmatic visualization, furthermore, would show members of the university community what they could expect of those students who had completed our first-year courses.

Finally, the visualization would show the state board of higher education and our accrediting agency the complete epistemological foundation undergirding the outcomes we used to assess our program.

Learning to write well at the college level is a complex endeavor. Building upon what students learned in high school, the first year writing sequence at SIUE is designed to help students in that complex endeavor of becoming college writers by providing quality instruction in a theoretically grounded program. In that regard, we maintain six goals that should be met in English 101, the first course in that sequence. Students who participate actively in their own education, invest in the writing process, and engage in dialogue about their writing can expect to meet the following goals with some measure of success.

This document is designed to communicate those goals to students, parents, faculty, administrators, and others interested in the first year writing program at SIUE. While we have tried to make these goals accessible to the general reader, terms such as "rhetorical strategies" and "discourse community" have rich and complex meanings to professional writing teachers, meanings that cannot necessarily be fully articulated to the general public in this brief document.

Underneath each goal, we offer objectives—or strategies—that individual teachers may use to facilitate students in reaching these goals. Instructors may employ additional pedagogically sound objectives as they see fit.

In addition, each goal is designed to foster one or more of SIUE's College of Arts & Sciences (CAS) "Desired Characteristics and Capabilities of Graduates." These desired characteristics reflect the college's and university's commitment to the intrinsic value of a well-rounded undergraduate education.

Figure 1

In retrospect I can see that we intended this document both to acculturate and socialize all groups intended as its audience. But for some instructors, socialization can be interpreted as an insidious attempt at mind control rather than a map of available options.

PRINCIPLES OF EXCLUSION AND INCLUSION

We intended no exclusion. We aimed, rather, at including groups from the most immediate—our students—to the more distant—state accrediting agencies and the Council of Writing Program Administrators. But the move from a hierarchy to a collaborative community could neither automatically eradicate long-existent feelings of exclusion and a reading of our visual documents as gatekeeping tools nor keep instructors from interpreting the visualization as forcing them to comply with unwanted change. In addition, our visual document could have contained exclusionary elements that we never consciously intended, but that appeared obvious once the document took shape. Our document could have reflected, and did, epistemological practices that often set composition instructors apart from the other fields represented in a traditional English department, in particular many literature faculty. The pages also catered to those who understand the problems of assessment versus those who had never attended the assessment workshops offered by our outside consultants. It most certainly excluded those who use the composition courses to train English majors, as opposed to those who don't. Instructors who keep abreast of current composition practices were also partly the readers for these pages as opposed to those who had taught the first-year sequence in exactly the same way for decades. Finally, the pages clearly embraced those who welcome program change versus those who do not or will not.

DETECTING ROLES THE VISUALIZATION MAKES AVAILABLE

A webbed version of our mission, goals, objectives, and outcomes—in the context of this program previously lacking a strong identity, let alone a webbed depiction—shows us something important about the complex identities and social practices existing with a writing program: that viewers could not envision the various roles available to them—actually the variety of pedagogies included—and the freedom instructors have to construct a composition course growing from their own strengths but moving toward programmatic outcomes. The goals and objectives so carefully crafted by committee, therefore, somehow became distorted reflections when perceived by this group—images of imagined inadequacies in a program that now seemed to threaten these instructors' job security, teaching abilities, and essentially their pedagogies. The revised program as portrayed on the Web asks only that instructors heed the goals of each class and work toward the stated outcomes. And although I grit my teeth when saying this, instructors can even draw on literature. As long as they realize the writing courses are not introductions to literary study and research, and as long as they do not become sidetracked by close readings of texts for the purpose of literary analysis, even a literary path toward course outcomes is possible.

Not being able to envision the roles available, instructors imagined only one, a role antithetical to whatever others they had assumed before.

Goal #1: Students will gain an understanding of rhetorical strategies and processes of analyzing and composing a variety of print, visual, and digital media.

Related Objectives:

- Work with texts and learn to interpret, incorporate, and evaluate them
- Explore the multiple facets (ideological, social, cultural, political, economic, historical) of issues and use writing to construct informed, critical positions about these topics
- Use various technological tools to explore texts
- Encourage the use of multi-sensory engagement in [sic?] texts [and in writing assignments?]

This goal and its related objectives are designed to foster the development of the following "Desired Characteristics and Capabilities of Graduates":

- communication
- critical thinking
- problem solving and framing
- knowledge
- citizenship
- life-long learning

Goal #2: Students will gain a meta-awareness of their own development as writers

Related Objectives:

- Engage in peer-reviewing activities
- Participate in self-assessment activities, i.e. evaluate individual's own writing assignments based upon assignment criteria

This goal fosters this CAS "Desired Characteristic":

- self-development

Figure 2

Two mundane parallel situations occurred to me as I was trying to explain the complex challenges to identity caused by seeing one's self clothed in strange pedagogical garb. The first is a pair of identical twins I once knew. One or the other would invariably tell her sister she hated the outfit which that sibling was wearing and wished that this sibling would never wear it again. Part of the reason for the disapproval arose from seeing the other as a mirror of the self. The disapproving twin insisted the other change her clothing because identity was so closely involved: "I don't like the way 'you' look" translated as "I don't like the way 'I' look."

The situation is especially easy to understand in the case of twins: each sees herself when she looks at her twin, sees herself dressed in a way she has not chosen. What the twins had trouble recognizing was that the other's appearance presented only one way of dressing out of a myriad of choices. Likewise, what my department's instructors could not see was that the programmatic reflection they perceived had room for many identities.

I am also reminded of a TV program that occasionally mesmerizes me. The program is called *What Not to Wear.* The point of this program is to transform an unfashionably clad, often dowdy-looking person into someone trained to use clothing to highlight strengths. A mirror plays a big part in every transformation: the hosts use the mirror to convince the chosen subjects how unflattering and often inappropriate their current wear is for their ages, body types, and professions. During the course of the program, the two hosts present sketches of styles that are more flattering, more contemporary, and more professional. Once the hosts convince the "subject" to try on items resembling those in the sketches and to remain open-minded while "trying anything," these subjects begin to see themselves differently in the mirror and actually like their newly garbed selves. They have moved from preferring an unflattering self-reflection to one that emphasizes its strengths and presents a more pleasing social self.

Of importance in this different attitude toward the self reflected back from the mirror is the guidance the hosts provide and the way they tailor their suggestions for each individual. Perhaps, then, in making a truly radical programmatic change, a WPA needs to do similar, more individual work with a program's instructors—showing how that person can try on various pedagogical roles the program is now making available, showing how these roles can be more flattering, pedagogically contemporary as well as satisfying, and socially professional.

Even the mere mention of attention to technology, for instance, has encountered an especially strong resistance from instructors who claim that difficulties scheduling composition classes in computer classrooms makes the goal of attention to technology unreasonable. Instead of seeing our online text as an affirmation of the work we all do and feeling encouraged to aim for incorporating technology in writing classes, many interpreted the mention of technology as intimidating, a picture of personal shortcomings and flaws, a mandate to use technology "or else."

UNDERSTANDING THE WAYS IN WHICH ROLES ARE DISTRIBUTED

WPAs may need to help program instructors understand how a different administrative style would distribute roles differently from previous styles. Moving from one epistemological position to another, in this case, from one grounded in current-traditional rhetorical philosophy to social epistemology is difficult because universities and departments have traditionally rested on current-traditional distributions of roles. In a university and department perpetuating such a hierarchical structure, instructors nonetheless may approach their own teaching as collaborative processes, and may believe their students should work together to arrive at a level of knowledge more sophisticated than one could attain working alone; when working within a broader university context, however, they revert to current-traditional ways of thinking.

Sharon Crowley's definition of current-traditional pedagogy is rather enlightening when applied to a WPA's administrative "style" instead of an instructor's classroom pedagogy. In the following passage, I have used strikethroughs on Crowley's original words, and then have substituted the terms "administrative style," "writing program," or "instructors" for the words "pedagogy," "discourse," and "students":

> Current-traditional ~~pedagogy~~ [administrative style] is conservative in the ordinary sense of that term insofar as it resists changes in its rules and preserves established verbal traditions and institutional lines of authority. Current-traditionalism preserves traditional social and academic hierarchies insofar as ~~students~~ [instructors] are taught to observe without question rules of ~~discourse~~ [the writing program] that were constructed long before they entered the ~~academy~~ [profession or department] and to submit their native ~~grapholects~~ [identities] to ~~grammar and usage~~ [programmatic] rules devised by a would-be elitist ~~class~~ [administration]. Current-traditional ~~pedagogy~~ [administrative style] is ~~teacher~~ [administrator]-centered: the ~~teacher~~ [administrator] dispenses information about the rules of ~~discourse~~ [the writing program] and evaluates the ~~students'~~ [instructors'] efforts in accordance with those rules. ~~Students~~ [Instructors] themselves are constructed in current-traditional ~~rhetoric~~ [administrative style] as potentially unruly novices whose work needs to be continually examined and disciplined. (1998, 218)

Well, no wonder I encountered such resistance. If I read my newly "edited" definition, I can see clearly what the instructors in my program "saw" when they looked at the document we produced:

> Current-traditional administrative style is conservative in the ordinary sense of that term insofar as it resists changes in its rules and preserves established verbal traditions and institutional lines of authority. Current-traditionalism preserves traditional social and academic hierarchies insofar as instructors are taught to observe without question rules of the writing program that were constructed long before they entered the profession or department and to submit their native identities to programmatic rules devised by a would-be elitist administration. Current-traditional administrative style is administrator-centered: the administrator dispenses information about the rules of the writing program and evaluates the instructors' efforts in accordance with those rules. Instructors themselves are constructed in current-traditional administrative style as potentially unruly novices whose work needs to be continually examined and disciplined.

No matter that we constructed the document collaboratively: viewers embedded in a program founded on a current-traditional administrative style, especially as reflected in the holistic common final with its implications for teaching skills and working within a program's "rules," could not adjust to a different style just because I told them to.

Somehow I need to demonstrate to these instructors, and help them understand, that the roles available to them were not ones I had mandated from on high but were rather varied ones that I considered to be distributed on an equal plane, one not ever being "better" than another. In a hierarchically organized program, the roles available automatically stack up so that some have more status than others, an obvious organization along lines of social classes. Tenured full professors occupy the top position and part-time staff and graduate students occupy the bottom rung of the departmental ladder. Those who have experienced hierarchically distributed roles, however, find themselves hard-pressed to recognize, then understand, that roles need not always be set up hierarchically. In a dialectic, collaborative environment, roles are equal—resting on the same plane rather than stacked vertically. The voices of those occupying all roles are equally important.

A dialectical program built upon a social-epistemic philosophy places language and dialogue, not an administrator's rules, at the program's heart. It builds upon James Berlin's view of social-epistemic rhetoric as "a political act involving a dialectical interaction engaging the material, the social, and the individual writer, with language as the agency of mediation." A social-epistemic administrative style privileges dialectical engagement, believing that a writing program, like a rhetoric, is "an historically specific social formation that must perforce change over time." Believing in change would, according to Berlin, "mak[e] possible reflexiveness and revision as the inherently ideological nature of rhetoric [and I would add, a writing program] is continually acknowledged" (1988, 488). For a writing program operating from a social-epistemic ideology,

> [T]he real is located in a relationship that involves the dialectical interaction of the observer, the discourse community (social group) in which the observer is functioning, and the material conditions of existence. . . . Knowledge . . . is an historically bound social fabrication rather than an eternal and invariable phenomenon located in some uncomplicated repository—in the material object or in the subject or in the social realm, . . . and the subject is itself a social construct that emerges through the linguistically circumscribed interaction of the individual, the community, and the material world. . . . (488–489)

Easier said than done, perhaps, but maybe easier once I understood what competing epistemologies lay beneath the identities peering forth from the mirror of program definitions.

DECODE THE HIERARCHIES AND DIFFERENCES IT NATURALIZES

Such a nonhierarchically focused program does not mean, of course, that hierarchies would cease to exist for its administrator and instructors. By working with the desired characteristics of students graduating from the College of Arts and Sciences, we do not mean to suggest that we are overlooking the differences between our program and that college or the place we as a program occupy within the hierarchy of the college. A WPA would need to point out that the writing program is still embedded in these overarching hierarchies within and beyond the university. Indeed, while the program itself would be aimed at flattening hierarchical differences, the program and its instructors as a whole still need to be conscious of the outlying hierarchies. Despite the fact that such differences would, hopefully, gradually disappear from the program, some still will exist: (1) the university will always demand program accountability and (2) the state will always hold the university accountable.

In explaining the influence of the visual on our notions of "structures of meaning and interpretation and on the epistemic and institutional frameworks that attempt to organize them" (1998, 15), Irit Rogoff presents the field of visual culture. Analyzing the situations of writing programs in these terms, namely, focusing "on the centrality of vision and the visual world in producing meanings, establishing and maintaining aesthetic values, gender stereotypes and power relations within culture" can help us to see our situation as simply "an arena in which cultural meanings get constituted" (14), not an unchangeable situation, and not a situation bound eternally by tradition.

A writing program—that is, its instructors and its administrator—are situated in a world where educational administration is still hierarchically oriented. This vertical line running from the state to the university, the college, the writing program, and its administrator as well as instructors marks a difference between classes that has actually been naturalized: we take for granted that we must report to "higher" authorities. But these power relations are ones simply produced by the educational culture; they are not necessarily natural.

> It is this questioning of the ways in which we inhabit and thereby constantly make and remake our own culture that informs the arena of visual culture. . . . [T]he field is made up of at least three different components. First, there are the images that come into being and are claimed by various, and often contested histories. Second, there are the viewing apparatuses that we have at our disposal that are guided by cultural models such as narrative or technology. Third, there are the subjectivities of identification or desire or abjection from which we view and by which we inform what we view. . . . I am obviously focusing here on the reception rather than the production of images and objects or environments. . . . (Rogoff 1998, 18)

Rogoff stresses that as a field of knowledge, visual culture helps us to analyze our cultural situations: "To be able to assemble a group of materials and a variety of methodological analyses around an issue that is determined out of cultural and political realities rather than out of traditions of learned arguments, seems an important step forward in the project of reformulating knowledge to deal responsibly with the lived conditions of highly contested realities, such as we face at the turn of this century in the West" (23).

ANALYZE THE WAYS IN WHICH AUTHORSHIP IS CONSTRUCTED OR CONCEALED

Authorship was constructed collaboratively and indicated clearly on the pages: committee members are named. However, some instructors who viewed the site seemed to feel that single authorship (i.e., mine) was being somehow concealed, if I judge by questions about the pages that began with "Why do *YOU* want. . . . " As I explained above, moving from considering the pages as traditionally singly authored to the actual collaboratively authored ones they were can be difficult, depending upon the degree to which instructors' psyches are embedded with current-traditional notions of administration. The chart below depicts the visual disjunction between what the committee portrayed and what appeared to some readers:

What the Program's Site Displays:	What Those Viewing It See:
• Collaboratively Constructed Document	• Singly Authored Document
• Processual Program Focus	• Static Program Focus
• Program Focus as a Developing Map	• Program Focus as Repressive Dogma
• Suggestions for New Methodologies	• Disapproval of Previous Methodologies
• Assessment of Program's Effectiveness	• Assessment as Evaluation of Instructors
• Multifaceted Pedagogy	• Unilateral Pedagogy
• WPA as Facilitator, Guide, Dialogist	• WPA as Autocrat

Rogoff makes the point above that analyzing the ways visuality has shaped a culture actually shifts focus to the viewer, to the way a document is received rather than on itself and its production "in substituting the historical specificity of that being studied with the historical specificity of he/she/they doing the studying."

> In order to effect such a shift without falling prey to endless anecdotal and autobiographical ruminating which stipulates experience as a basis for knowledge, we attempt to read each culture through other, often hostile and competitive, cultural narratives. This process of continuous translation and negotiation is often exhausting in its denial of a fixed and firm position, but it does allow us to shift the burden of specificity from the materials to the reader and prevents us from the dangers of complete dislocation. Perhaps it might even help us to understand that at the very moment in which historical specificity can provide liberation and political strength to some of the dispossessed, it also imprisons others within an old binary structure that no longer reflects the conditions and realities of their current existence. (1998, 24)

The competing cultures that would produce the visual discrepancy I have been discussing come from focusing on the document rather than on the viewer, on supposed administrative motives rather than on the individual instructor and, actually, the liberties afforded each instructor.

In ENG 102, students will continue to build upon the skills and knowledge developed in ENG 101, as outlined in the ENG 101 Goals & Objectives statement. Each ENG 102 goal is also designed to foster one or more of SIUE's College of Arts & Sciences (CAS) "Desired Characteristics and Capabilities of Graduates." These desired characteristics reflect the college's and university's commitment to the intrinsic value of a well-rounded undergraduate education.

Goal #1: Students will gain an understanding of elements of formal argumentation.

Related Objectives:

- Examine accepted methods of academic argumentation
- Read critically a variety of argumentative texts in order to discuss claims and issues from those readings
- Evaluate academic arguments for logical effectiveness, validity, and soundness
- Explore the ways in which argumentation is used in the discourse of various disciplines
- Examine and analyze peers' written arguments for the effective use of structures of academic argument, avoidance of logical fallacies and other errors in reasoning, and the ethical use of sources

This goal and its related objectives are designed to foster the development of the following "Desired Characteristics and Capabilities of Graduates":

- critical thinking
- problem solving and framing
- knowledge

Figure 3

PERCEIVE THE WAYS IN WHICH THE SENSE OF AUDIENCE IS REALIZED

As we created the content for our pages and discussed ways in which that content could be conveyed, we understood that our documents would have multiple audiences: the program's current instructors and its students, the parents of these students, new graduate TAs, and future instructors new to our program. We also hoped for an audience in the university community so that we could show colleges and departments across campus what we were trying to accomplish in our writing classes. Finally, we wanted to show our accreditation agencies that we considered our assessment to be systemic—that is, based on our program's fundamental beliefs, rather than superficially added on and conducted apart from the way we taught our classes. However, instructors viewing the site had so much trouble distinguishing between a current-traditional and social-epistemic structure that they forgot about multiple audiences and instead imagined themselves as the sole audience.

As the chair of the committee, I expected a certain amount of resistance to our now-focused writing program from more distant groups like our administration, and/or our state accrediting agency, or the Illinois Board of Higher Education (IBHE). Naively, I expected the pages as a picture of program identity to work to empower its instructors, especially a program that had been in need of clarification and leadership by a composition professional. I thought that having a "clear" picture of what we were working toward in our writing classes plus shifting assessment to programmatic assessment (away from a competitive and punitive common final) would lay the groundwork for our instructors perceiving themselves and the program as a stronger, more mature endeavor. But instead we encountered a great unwillingness to identify with the program as presented and an inability to understand that the program and its assessment tool were not focusing on individual instructors and individual students as we examined the program in order to strengthen it.

In all seriousness, I now realize our site needed instructions for "reading" it, or understanding its visuality. A critical examination of visual documents includes the ability to perceive the social context surrounding the creation of a document rather than having the "document" work as a reflection of one's own cultural background and baggage. In a very insightful essay discussing the Vietnam Veterans Memorial and the controversy surrounding its construction, Marita Sturken makes several astute observations about the ways we tend to "see." Her analysis might be applied in this situation, one that is albeit smaller in scale and importance. Seeing the visual represented as an architecturally constructed space can help us realize a difference between space as constrictively state mandated or space as liminal.[3]

Sturken analyzes the Vietnam Veterans Memorial by using the concept of a screen, "a surface that is projected upon; it is also an object that hides something from view, that shelters or protects" (1998, 163).

The screen and the mirror both allow projections as they are viewed. In the memorial's case, some of its first viewers "read" the architectural construction in coded ways that projected, then revealed, their particular cultural biases:

> The criticism leveled at the memorial's design [i.e., horizontal, polished black granite cut into the earth] showed precisely how it was being "read" by its opponents, and their readings compellingly reveal codes of remembrance of war memorials [i.e., vertical white stone erected for distant viewing]. Many saw its black walls as evoking shame, sorrow, and dishonor and others perceived its refusal to rise above the earth as indicative of defeat. Thus, a racially coded reading of the color black as shameful was combined with a reading of a feminized earth connoting a lack of power. Precisely because of its deviation from traditional commemorative codes—the design was read as a political statement. (1998, 167)

In much the same way that viewers described above projected their own codes onto the Vietnam Veterans Memorial, viewers of our program's goals and outcomes projected their only understanding of administration onto the site as they read it and interpreted the documents as a political statement of power from a program administrator.

Unfortunately, traditional notions of power will always complicate the ways audiences read such a programmatic document. While we did envision the audience as multiple and complex, we believed most would be grateful for the direction and mapping we provided and thought that the cultural contexts of the site should be obvious to all viewers. We never fully understood the degree to which some would see it representing traditional lines of power: repressive rather than dialogic and interactive. Cheris Kramarae and her colleagues remind us that "most classical definitions of power treat it as static rather than processual" (1984, 11). But they believe, and I agree, that we can conceptualize power in other interactive ways more consistent with a social-epistemic philosophy:

> Interest in presenting power as interactive and all discourse as hierarchical has lead Foucault, among others, to set forth an an[a]lysis of power as internal to all relationships, not "held" or exercised by individuals but, rather, developed through interaction in a multiplicity of relationships. Power, in his analysis, is not a limitation of freedom, not a possession, not a control that can be stored or a system of domination exercised by an individual or group over another individual or group. Rather, power comes from below as well as above, in a shifting relationship of force and resistance. It is not merely

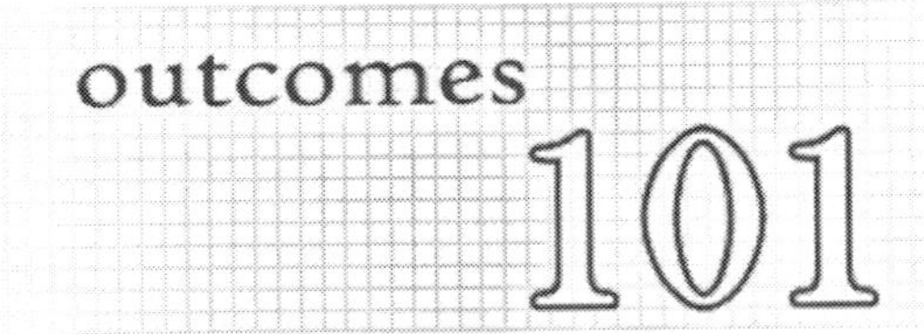

The following outcomes for ENG 101 reflect the governing assumptions of the English Composition Program as well as the ENG 101 Goals & Objectives set forth by the program.

It is important to note that as students move beyond English 101, "their writing abilities do not merely improve. Rather, students' abilities not only diversify along disciplinary and professional lines but also move into whole new levels where expected outcomes expand, multiply, and diverge" (Writing Program Administrators Outcomes Statement). It is our desire that students continue developing as writers long after they leave English 101, that they continue to be life-long writers in their academic, civic, and professional lives. English 101 is simply the starting point.

Invention

- Purpose of the essay is clear and appropriate to the assignment.
- Introduction engages the reader and creates interest.
- Essay maintains interest by the creative choices made in content selection.

Arrangement

- Organization is effective in developing and supporting a thesis.
- Introduction includes an "essay map" (forecasting statement) and/or a clearly stated thesis.
- Discussion paragraphs present a coherent, logical case in support of the thesis, with appropriate rhetorical strategies, examples, definitions, and explanations.
- Essay concludes smoothly and powerfully.

Style

- Language, content, and persona are appropriate to subject, audience, and purpose.
- Essay exhibits sophisticated control of language and syntactic structures.

Conventions

- Essay uses Edited American English and includes features of other dialects only when they serve particular rhetorical purposes.

Figure 4

> negative or repressive, but also positive and implicit in the constitution of discourse and knowledge. (Kramarae, Schulz, and O'Barr 1984, 12)

Power can be dialogic, "processual" rather than "static," an invitation rather than a decree. To keep from ending up feeling battered and paralyzed by positions that others may project upon them, WPAs may need to hold serious discussions with their faculty members over questions of writing program identity and differing concepts of power.

This discord was also exacerbated by the appearance of the Web pages themselves: in many ways they resemble PowerPoint slides, bullets and all. Edward Tufte argues that "PowerPoint is entirely *presenter-oriented*, and *not content-oriented, not audience-oriented*" (2003, 4; original emphasis). So in our case, our visual presentation on the World Wide Web may have distorted the way one of our audiences received the information. Not analyzing the rhetoric behind the presentation software, I neglected to figure out that

> [t]he metaphor behind the PP cognitive style is *the software corporation itself*. That is, a big bureaucracy engaged in *computer programming* (deeply hierarchical, nested, highly structured, relentlessly sequential, one-short-line-at-a-time) and in *marketing* (fast pace, misdirection, advocacy not analysis, slogan thinking, branding, exaggerated claims, marketplace ethics). (Tufte 2003, 11)

Tufte continues to stress the way PowerPoint emphasizes power: "The pushy PP style imposes itself on the audience and, at times, seeks to set up a dominance relationship between speaker and audience. The speaker, after all, is making *power points with bullets to followers*. Such aggressive, stereotyped, over-managed presentations—the Great Leader up on the pedestal—are characteristic of hegemonic systems" (2003, 11). Web presentations may differ enough from PowerPoint presentations to leave open a possibility for dialogue rather than monologue. Nevertheless, I unwittingly invited an audience to interpret our visualization as the dictate of a new hegemonic system.

I am not arguing, ultimately, that visual, multi-mediated texts in particular trigger the problems discussed above while codex texts do not. My point is rather that considering the visuality of our document helped me approach the problem from angles not commonly used to study the work and the problems WPAs encounter. Considering identity negotiation, visual culture, and the parallels between administrative styles and pedagogical epistemologies helped me to understand the problems better. Emphasizing the visuality of our program's Web site and perceiving the ways it would be received by an audience accustomed to traditional notions of power, then analyzing our presentation within arenas of visuality helped unearth possible—and now quite understandable—motives for the mixed reactions to what we intended as a simple picture of the program. Surrounded by current-traditional cultural baggage, our simple picture morphed into a complex mirror, a screen for projecting various and sundry self-concepts. Tim Peeples lists the various metaphors used to conceive of writing program administration, metaphors ranging from management and collaborative research all the way through to plate tectonics, plate twirling, marketing, and film directing (2002, 116). Peeples asks, "Why do we take these metaphorical journeys? For many reasons. . . . [T]hey give us new eyes for seeing the work we do, and in so doing, often expose parts of our work to which we have become blind" (116). Peeples's own metaphoric language alluding to blindness, seeing, and framing actually points to the importance of vision—in all the various permutations of that word—as continually of importance to WPAs.

> Each new [metaphoric] conception also re-frames our work, defamiliarizing its landscapes so we can become more aware of them. Additionally, each new conception takes steps towards a theory of writing program administrations and opens doors to theorizing new or revised administrative practices. (116)

In our postmodern world, anticipating a document's reception is difficult. Our document, without our intent, turned into a mirror. And as Margaret Atwood so aptly and wryly observes, "mirrors are crafty" (1976). Indeed, it seemed to me that every possible meaning of the word "crafty" colored the way our document was viewed. Some saw it as a deceitful, tricky edict, sly in its presentation of our program, and cunning in the way it appeared to undermine instructor freedom. The committee constructing it, however, believed the document to be crafty in that it was put together with special skill, much discussion, and an analytic dexterity that incorporated outcomes describing programmatic freedom rather than constriction.

So considering notions of the visual may help WPAs find direction after serious bouts of discord. But then again, who can say? Ours is, as the new saw goes, a postmodern world.

NOTES

INTRODUCTION (MCGEE AND HANDA)

1. Earlier versions of this schematic include only the verbal elements; see "The Culture of Postmodernism," (1985, 123–24). Interestingly, the revised version, which appears in 1987's *The Postmodern Turn*, includes two visuals: a vertical double-headed arrow above the "Modernist" column, and a horizontal double-headed arrow above the "Postmodernist" column (91–92). Faigley reprints a select part of the earlier schematic in his text.
2. This discussion started on February 24, 2000, on the WPA listserv when a frustrated WPA posed the following question: "What happens if people trained in R & C can no longer stomach coordinating their school's writing program?" Other WPAs contributed their posts, discussing the local problems that lead them to feel physically, mentally, and emotionally exhausted and/or silenced by their particular situations. While we do not mean to suggest that all WPAs in all locations feel exhausted and silenced, many WPAs at some point in their tenure do experience extreme frustration.
3. See Gunner (1994, 2002).
4. Rita Malenczyk discusses the problems of WPAs misreading audience and the consequences that occur. Her essay also begins to develop a rhetorical theory of writing program administration.
5. See Gunner (1994, 2002).

CHAPTER 1 (HOLDSTEIN)

Thanks to Carolyn Handa for her inspiration.

1. The author, at the time of writing this essay, was one of the C-Es.
2. Anonymous, interview on December 8, 2003.

CHAPTER 3 (DESMET)

1. In an essay that reinforces Nancy Welch's critique, Joseph Janangelo argues that critical pedagogy, while it purports to liberate both teachers and students, actually calls upon teachers to accept their job as a selfless, all-consuming, religious calling. Although Janangelo targets liberatory pedagogy specifically, I think that the tendency toward a religious vocabulary is more widespread in educational circles, and, in fact, the relationship between religion and education is important to the history of university teaching, if not specifically to literacy practices or to the teaching of writing. On this subject, see Martha Nussbaum, *Cultivating Humanity* (1997).
2. As Trimbur wryly notes, "In fact, Michel Foucault's account of how discipline works sounds remarkably like a description of a WPA doing course scheduling at the beginning of a term," partitioning academic space to accommodate the requisite number of bodies, so that "'each individual has its own place; and each place its individual'" (Foucault 143; cited by Trimbur 143).
3. For a rather extreme example, see Vaughan (1993). From a behaviorist perspective, Margaret Vaughan discusses ways in which supervisors and consultants can help teachers address and reform unproductive behaviors, although she does note that resistance to change is a persistent and fairly widespread problem.
4. In characterizing the writing program as a bricolage, I define the term "program" against Sharon Crowley's understanding of the politics of writing instruction as

colonization of institutional "turf" that has been constructed independent of curricular belief or ideology, through the first-year writing requirement (Crowley 1998, 232–35). For a good description of the kind of program in which I teach and that I describe here—housed in the English Department of a large state university, led by a succession of short-term administrators who follow on the heels of a very long-term shepherd, designed to serve over six thousand students who take one or more required classes in first-year composition, and staffed largely by a somewhat volatile community of TAs and lecturers—see Farris (1996, 35–53).

5. David Kenyon, in a recent piece from the *Chronicle of Higher Education* (2003), describes the long-standing incoherence of English studies generally as a discipline ("What People Just Don't Understand About Academic Fields").
6. A succinct account of the debate can be found in Sharon Crowley, "Let Me Get This Straight" (1994).
7. A faith in the progress of composition theory can inform even apparently neutral bibliographical sources, such as the *Guide to Writing Programs* put together by Tori Haring-Smith and others in 1985, which included in its survey only "nontraditional," and so presumably "innovative," programs (ix).
8. I should note that North investigates the relation between composition research and practice rather than the dynamics of writing instruction or programmatic ideology. Nevertheless, his argument is relevant to mine. North generally sees "paradigm hope" as a conservative force. For him, composition research that is fueled by paradigm hope "disciplines" teachers and limits pedagogical practice precisely because it has accepted responsibility for systematically generating change in the practice of writing instruction (North 1996, 203). To extend North's argument, if proper research can identify the "best" way to teach writing, to stray from the programmatic path is not only disobedience, but "heresy."
9. I would not want to ignore the importance of the historical studies of composition teachers and programs that have emerged in the last twenty years, but I still think that for the most part, prominent figures and programs stand as synecdoches for a field that, because of inadequate evidence, resists thick description.
10. Rose and Weiser (2002) make a persuasive argument for program research and the establishment of program archives as an important part of reviewing and reforming any given program's structure and practices.
11. My argument here builds on an earlier essay in which I used feminist jurisprudence, and specifically Cornell's earlier work, to define power dynamics within the writing classroom ("Equivalent Students and Equitable Classrooms," Desmet 1998).
12. The first position may be represented by Robin West (1993), the second by Iris Marion Young (1990).

CHAPTER 4 (MCGEE)

1. I do not mean to suggest that administering a writing program is fraught only with negative emotions; in fact, much WPA work is professionally and personally fulfilling and intellectually engaging. Often, however, WPAs discuss the negative emotions involved with their jobs. I believe that by examining these emotions and their sources, WPAs can begin to find local means of deconstructing the sources of negative emotions, which in turn may lead to increased job satisfaction.
2. Because WPAs are in supervisory positions over faculty teaching in the writing program, they could be seen to "have power" at the expense of others. However, much WPA scholarship argues against this kind of power and for a collaborative notion of administration. See Gunner 1994 for a useful discussion of decentered administration.
3. Chapter 5 ("The Interest Is Embodied in the Map in Signs and Myths") and chapter 7 ("The Interest the Map Serves Can Be Your Own") of Wood's 1992 book are most relevant to this discussion.

4. I would like to be able to report that this map has proven rhetorically persuasive to the university to view the WPA as a program director of the same status as other program directors, but that hasn't happened yet. However, we are making progress because different people within the university are beginning to recognize the writing program and the WPA as points on the larger (metaphorical) institutional map.
5. Given the scope of this essay, I cannot fully unpack the intricacies of the Porter et al. discussion of institutional critique (2000).
6. Arguing that institutional critique is not, in fact, a way to change institutions, Marc Bousquet (2002) posits management science as the optimal method for making institutional change happen. Peggy O'Neill (2002) and Joseph Harris (2002) provide useful counterpoints to Bousquet's argument. Janet Atwill (2002) also offers a helpful explanation of institutional critique's usefulness.

CHAPTER 5 (EDGINGTON ET AL.)

1. This move is not unlike the one accomplished by the City University of New York and discussed by Barbara Gleason (2000).
2. In 2001 we changed the required score on the ACT verbal to twenty-one. Reading and math were already at twenty-one, and we were confident that a writing sample was the most accurate way to place students in writing courses.
3. For a good summary of the implementation and use of portfolios in Kentucky see Steve Smith's 2002 essay "Why Use Portfolios? One Teacher's Response."
4. Terri Lowe and Brian Huot reported on the first three years of the program in a *Kentucky English Bulletin* article in 1997. As we write this essay, Anthony Edgington, Brian Huot, Vicki Hester, Michael Neal, and Peggy O'Neill are working on two book chapters that report on the next five years and the conclusions of our experiment in using high school portfolios for placement at U of L.
5. Of course, we also need to acknowledge here that other variables, especially costs, would need to be accounted for. Again, this is why we feel it is important for WPAs to continually evaluate and remain knowledgeable about mainstreaming and the political climate at the university.

CHAPTER 7 (PALMQUIST)

1. For selected scholarship on the uses of word processing in composing and instructional settings see Bridwell, Nancarrow, and Ross (1984), Collier (1983), Haas (1989, 1990), Haas and Hayes (1986), Hawisher (1986, 1988, 1989), Kaufer and Neuwirth (1995), LeBlanc (1988), Sudol (1985), Sullivan (1989), and Susser (1998). For selected scholarship on the use of style and grammar analysis tools in writing instruction see Cohen and Lanham (1984), Dobrin (1986), Kiefer (1987), Kiefer and Smith (1983, 1984), Kiefer, Reid, and Smith (1989), McDaniel (1985), and Smith and Kiefer (1982). For more information about scholarship on computer-aided instruction see Burns (1983, 1984a), Duin (1987), Langston (1986), Schwartz (1982), and Wresch (1982). For selected scholarship on network-based communication (e.g., e-mail, chat, newsgroups and electronic discussion lists, and Multi-user domains Object Oriented (MOO)s/Multi-User Domain (MUD)s/Multi-User Shared Hallucination (MUSH)s) see Batson (1988, 1993), Coogan (1995), Cooper and Selfe (1990), Hawisher (1992), Hawisher and Moran (1993), Kinkead (1987, 1988), Mabrito (1992), Moran (1995), Peyton (1989), Sirc and Reynolds (1990), Spooner and Yancey (1996), and Webb (1997). For selected scholarship on hypertext see Bolter (1991, 1993), Charney (1992), Dewitt (1996), Johnson-Eilola (1993), Joyce (1992), Kaplan and Moulthrop (1990), Moulthrop (1989, 1991), Moulthrop and Kaplan (1991), Slatin (1988, 1990), Smith (1991), Sorapure, Inglesby, and Yatchisin (1998), and Thompson, English, and Doherty (1998).

2. For a selection of scholarship on teaching in computer-supported classrooms see Balester (1992), Barker and Kemp (1990), Bruce, Peyton, and Batson (1993), Dobrin (1987), Eldred (1991), Harralson (1992), Neuwirth et al. (1993), Palmquist et al. (1998), Schwartz (1987), and Selfe (1987a, 1987b, 1989). See Hartman et al. (1991) and Palmquist et al. (1998) for discussions of using information technology to support instruction in traditional classrooms. See Bradshaw (1997), Day et al. (1996), Feenberg (1999), Gillette (1999), and Shoemake (1996) for discussions of teaching writing in online contexts. For a discussion of hybrid writing classes see Day (2000), Peterson (2001), Ross (2000), Smelser (2002), and Yagelski and Graybill (1998).

CHAPTER 11 (BILLINGS ET AL.)

1. For further discussion of the future of WAC/WID, see also McLeod, Miraglia, Soven, and Thaiss (2001) *WAC for the New Millennium* and the online discussion "Forum on CAC: Principles That Should Guide WAC/CAC Program Development in the Coming Decade," with Anne Herrington, Donna LeCourt, Susan McLeod, David Russell, and Art Young.
2. For recent articles on which this discussion of PAC is based, see Art Young's "Writing Across and Against the Curriculum" (2003) and the special issue on PAC of *The Journal of Language and Learning Across the Disciplines* (June 2003), which includes Young's "Introduction: A Venture into the Counter-Intuitive" and "Poetry Across the Curriculum: Four Disciplinary Perspectives" with Patricia Connor-Greene, Jerry Waldvogel, and Catherine Paul.
3. Eric Crump's term for agents of change in redefining academic literacy. (1995)

CHAPTER 12 (HANDA)

1. Susan Popham, Michael Neal, Ellen Schendel, and Brian Huot discuss the problem of hierarchy and writing program administration in "Breaking Hierarchies: Using Reflective Practice to Re-Construct the Role of the Writing Program Administrator" (2002). They argue that reflecting "helps eliminate many old structures of hierarchy and power" (20).
2. Jeanne Gunner has explored the subject of leadership style in relation to WPAs in "Collaborative Administration" (2002). I agree completely with Gunner when she says that anyone taking on the role of a WPA inherits the leadership style of the preceding administrator and that this style is usually hierarchical—that is, one conceiving of the WPA as a person in charge of subordinates.
3. See bell hooks for a short discussion of the politics of space and of space as liminal rather than confining (1995, 149).

REFERENCES

Adams, Peter Dow. 1993. Basic Writing Reconsidered. *Journal of Basic Writing* 12: 22–36.

Albaugh, Patti R. 1997. The Role of Skepticism in Preparing Teachers for the Use of Technology. Presented at Education for the Community: A Town and Global Discussion, Westerville, OH.

Anderson, Douglas. 1995. *Strands of System: The Philosophy of Charles Peirce.* West Lafayette, IN: Purdue University Press.

Atwill, Janet. 2002. Rhetoric and Institutional Critique: Uncertainty in the Postmodern Academy. *JAC* 22: 640–45.

Atwood, Margaret. 1976. Tricks with Mirrors. In *Selected Poems,* 183–86. New York: Simon and Schuster.

Balester, Valerie. 1992. Sharing Authority: Collaborative Teaching in a Computer-Based Writing Course. *Computers and Composition* 9: 25–40.

Barker, Thomas T., and Fred O. Kemp. 1990. Network Theory: A Postmodern Pedagogy for the Writing Classroom. In *Computers and Community: Teaching Composition in the Twenty-First Century,* edited by Carolyn Handa, 1–27. Portsmouth, NH: Boynton/Cook.

Bartholomae, David. 1985. Inventing the University. In *When a Writer Can't Write: Studies in Writer's Block and Other Composing-Process Problems,* edited by Mike Rose, 134–165. New York: the Guilford Press.

Batson, Trent. 1988. The Enfi Project: An Update. *Teaching English to Deaf and Second Language Students* 6 (2): 5–8.

———. 1993. The Origins of Enfi. In *Network-Based Classrooms: Promises and Realities,* edited by Bertram C. Bruce, Joy K. Peyton and Trent Batson, 87–112. New York: Cambridge University Press.

Beidler, Peter. 1991. The WPA Evaluation: A Recent Case Study. *WPA: Writing Program Administration* 14 (3): 69–72.

Berlin, James A. 1982. Contemporary Composition: The Major Pedagogical Theories. *College English* 33: 765–77. Reprinted in Villanueva 1997, 233–48.

———. 1987. *Rhetoric and Reality: Writing Instruction in American Colleges, 1900–1985.* Carbondale and Edwardsville, IL: Southern Illinois University Press.

———. 1988. Rhetoric and Ideology in the Writing Class. *College English* 50 (5): 477–94.

Berthoff, Ann E. 1981. *The Making of Meaning.* Portsmouth, NH: Boynton/Cook.

———. 1989. *The Sense of Learning.* Portsmouth, NH: Boynton/Cook.

———. 2000. *The Mysterious Barricades: Language and Its Limits.* Toronto: University of Toronto University Press.

Blakesley, David. 2002. Directed Self-Placement in the University. *WPA: Writing Program Administration* 25 (3): 9–39.

Bloom, Lynne Z., Donald A. Daiker, and Edward M. White, eds. 1996. *Composition in the Twenty-First Century: Crisis and Change.* Carbondale and Edwardsville, IL: Southern Illinois University Press.

Bolter, Jay D. 1991. *Writing Space: The Computer, Hypertext, and the History of Writing.* Hillsdale, NJ: Lawrence Erlbaum Associates.

———. 1993. Alone and Together in the Electronic Bazaar. *Computers and Composition* 10: 5–18.

Bolter, Jay D., and Richard Grusin. 1999. *Remediation: Understanding New Media.* Cambridge, MA: MIT Press.

Bousquet, Marc. 2002. Composition as Management Science: Toward a University without a WPA. *JAC* 22 (3): 493–526.

Bradshaw, Allen. 1997. Designing a Virtual Classroom for Distance Learning Students through the Internet. Presented at the Annual International Conference of the Chair Academy, Reno, NV.

Brady, Laura. 2004. A Case for Writing Program Evaluation. *WPA: Writing Program Administration* 28 (1/2): 79–94

Brereton, John C., ed. 1995. *The Origins of Composition Studies in the American College, 1875–1925.* Pittsburgh: University of Pittsburgh Press.

Bridwell, Lillian S., Paula Reed Nancarrow, and Donald Ross. 1984. The Writing Process and the Writing Machine: Current Research on Word Processors Relevant to the Teaching of Composition. In *New Directions in Composition Research,* edited by Richard Beach and Lillian Bridwell, 381–97. New York: The Guilford Press.

Broad, Bob. 2003. *What We Really Value: Beyond Rubrics in Teaching and Assessing Writing.* Logan, UT: Utah State University Press.

Brooke, Robert E. 1991. *Writing and Sense of Self: Identity Negotiation in Writing Workshops.* Urbana, IL: National Council of Teachers of English.

Brown, Stuart C. and Theresa Enos. 2002. *The Writing Program Administrator's Resource: A Guide for Reflective Institutional Practice.* Mahwah, NJ: Lawrence Erlbaum.

Bruce, Bertram C., Joy Kreeft Peyton, and Trent Batson. 1993. *Network-Based Classrooms: Promises and Realities.* New York: Cambridge University Press.

Burke, Kenneth. 1961. *The Rhetoric of Religion.* Boston: Beacon Press.

Burns, Hugh. 1983. Computer-Assisted Prewriting Activities: Harmonics for Invention. *Pipeline* 8 (1): 7–10.

———. 1984a. Recollections of First-Generation Computer-Assisted Prewriting. In Wresch 1984, 15–33.

———. 1984b. The Challenge for Computer-Assisted Rhetoric. *Computers and the Humanities* 18: 173–81.

Cain, Mary Ann, and George Kalamaras. 1999. (Re)Presenting the Work of Writing Program Administrators. *WPA: Writing Program Administration* 23 (1–2):45–58.

Charney, Davida. 1992. The Impact of Hypertext on Processes of Reading and Writing. In *Literacy and Computers,* edited by Susan J. Hilligoss and Cynthia L Selfe. New York: MLA.

Chase, Geoffrey. 1988. Accommodation, Resistance, and the Politics of Writing. *College Composition and Communication* 39: 13–22.

Clegg, Sue, John Konrad, and Jon Tan. 2000. Preparing Academic Staff to Use ICTs in Support of Student Learning." *The International Journal for Academic Development* 5 (2): 138–48.

Cohen, Michael E., and Richard A. Lanham. 1984. Homer: Teaching Style with a Microcomputer. In Wresch 1984, 83–90.

Colapietro, Vincent M. 1989. *Peirce's Approach to the Self: A Semiotic Perspective on Human Subjectivity.* Albany: State University of New York Press.

Collier, Richard M. 1983. The Word Processor and Revision Strategies. *College Composition and Communication* 34: 149–55.

Coogan, David. 1995. E-Mail Tutoring, a New Way to Do New Work. *Computers and Composition* 12 (2): 171–81.

Cooper, Marilyn, and Cynthia Selfe. 1990. Computer Conferences and Learning: Authority, Resistance, and Internally Persuasive Discourse. *College English* 52: 847–869.

Corder, Jim W. 1985. Argument as Emergence, Rhetoric as Love. *Rhetoric Review* 4 (1):16–32.

Cornell, Drucilla. 1993. Sex-Discrimination Law and Equivalent Rights. In *Transformations: Recollective Imagination and Sexual Difference,* 147–55. London: Routledge. Originally published in *Dissent* (1991) 38: 400–05.

———. 1999. *Beyond Accommodation: Ethical Feminism, Deconstruction, and the Law.* New edition. Lanham, MA: Rowman and Littlefield.

———. 2000. *Just Cause: Freedom, Identity, and Rights.* Lanham, MA: Rowman and Littlefield.

Cornell, Drucilla, Michael Rosenfield, and David Gray Carlson. 1992. *Deconstruction and the Possibility of Justice.* New York: Routledge.

Council of Writing Program Administrators. 1998. Evaluating the Intellectual Work of Writing Administration. *WPA: Writing Program Administration,* 22 (1): 85–104.

———. 2003. *The Portland Resolution: Guidelines for Writing Program Administrator Positions* Available from www.ilstu.edu/~ddhesse/wpa/positions/portlandres.htm (accessed 21 October).

Cox, Margaret J., Kate Cox, and Christina Preston. 1999. What Factors Support or Prevent Teachers from Using ICT in Their Classrooms. Presented at the British Educational Research Association Annual Conference, University of Sussex, Brighton.

Crawford, Caroline M., and Ruth Gannon-Cook. 2002. Faculty Attitudes Towards Distance Education: Enhancing the Support and Rewards System for Innovative Integration of Technology within Coursework. Presented at the 13th International Conference of the Society for Information Technology & Teacher Education, Nashville, TN.

Cronbach, Lee J. 1988. Five Perspectives on Validation Argument. In *Test Validity,* edited by Harold Wainer, 3–17. Hillsdale, NJ: Lawrence Erlbaum.

Crowley, Sharon. 1994. Let Me Get This Straight. In Vitanza, ed. 1994, 1–19.

———. 1998. *Composition in the University: Historical and Polemical Essays.* Pittsburgh, PA: University of Pittsburgh Press.

Crump, Eric. 1995. Writing Centers as Technoprovocateurs. *CCCC95 Online.* Available from http:/www.missouri.edu/~cccc95/abstracts/crump2.html (accessed March 14, 1999).

Cuban, Larry. 2001. *Oversold and Underused: Computers in the Classroom.* Cambridge, MA: Harvard University Press.

Davidson, Donald. 1984. *Inquiries into Truth and Interpretation.* Oxford: Clarendon-Oxford University Press.

Day, Michael. 2000. Teachers at the Crossroads: Evaluating Teaching in Electronic Environments. *Computers and Composition* 17 (1): 31–40.

Day, Michael, Cynthia Haynes, Jan Rune Holmevik, Sharon Cogdill, Judith Kirkpatrick, Leslie Harris, Avigial Oren, Jane Lasarenko, and Claudine Keenan. 1996. Pedagogies in Virtual Spaces: Writing Classes in the MOO. *Kairos* 1 (2).

Derrida, Jacques. 1978. Structure, Sign, and Play in the Discourse of the Human Sciences. In *Writing and Difference,* translated by Alan Bass, 278–293. Chicago: University of Chicago Press.

———. 1992. Force of Law: The 'Mystical Foundation of Authority.' In Cornell, Rosenfield, and Carlson 1992, 3–67.

Desmet, Christy. 1998. Equivalent Students, Equitable Classrooms. In *Feminism and Composition Studies: In Other Words,* edited by Susan C. Jarratt and Lynn Worsham, 153–71. New York: Modern Language Association.

Dewey, John. 1916/1944. *Democracy and Education.* New York: The Free Press. Reprint, 1944.

Dewitt, Scott L. 1996. The Current Nature of Hypertext Research in Computers and Composition Studies: An Historical Perspective. *Computers and Composition* 13 (1): 69–84.

Dickson, Marcia. 1993. Directing without Power: Adventures in Constructing a Model of Feminist Writing Program Administration. In *Writing Ourselves into the Story: Unheard Voices from Composition Studies,* edited by Sheryl I. Fontaine and Susan Hunter, 140–153. Carbondale and Edwardsville, IL: Southern Illinois University Press.

Dobrin, David N. 1986. Style Analyzers Once More. *Computers and Composition* 3 (3): 22–32.

———. 1987. Minicomputers for a Microcomputer Lab? *Computers and Composition* 5 (1): 7–16.

Dooley, Kim E. 1999. Towards a Holistic Model for the Diffusion of Educational Technologies: An Integrative Review of Educational Innovation Studies. *Journal of Educational Technology & Society* 2 (4). ifets.ieee.org/periodical/vol_4_99/kim_dooley.html.

Duin, Ann Hill. 1987. Computer Exercises to Encourage Rethinking and Revision. *Computers and Composition* 4 (2): 66–105.

Durrington, Vance A., Judi Repman, and Thomas W. Valente. 2000. Using Social Network Analysis to Examine the Time of Adoption of Computer-Related Services among University Faculty. *Journal of Research on Computing in Education* 33 (1): 16–27.

Ebest, Sally Barr. 2002. When Graduate Students Resist. *WPA: Journal of the Council of Writing Program Administrators* 26 (1–2): 27–43.

Eldred, Janet M. 1991. Pedagogy in the Computer-Networked Classroom. *Computers and Composition* 8 (2): 47–61.

Eliot, T.S. 1970. *Collected Poems 1909–1962.* New York: Harcourt.

Enoch, Jessica. 2002. Resisting the Script of Indian Education: Zitkala Sa and the Carlisle Indian School." *College English* 65 (2):117–141.

Evans, Robert. 1993. The Human Face of Reform. *Educational Leadership* 51 (1): 19–23.

Ewell, Peter. 1999. Assessment of Higher Education Quality: Promise and Politics. In *Assessment in Higher Education: Issues of Access, Quality, Student Development, and Public Policy*, edited by Samuel Messick, 147–56. Mahwah, NJ: Lawrence Erlbaum.

Faigley, Lester. 1992. *Fragments of Rationality: Postmodernity and the Subject of Composition.* Pittsburgh: University of Pittsburgh Press.

Farris, Christine. 1996. *Subject to Change: New Composition Instructors' Theory and Practice.* Creskill, N.J.: Hampton Press.

Feenberg, Andrews. 1999. No Frills in the Virtual Classroom. *Academe* 85 (5): 26–31.

Fish, Stanley. 2000. Nice Work If You Can Get Them to Do It. *ADE Bulletin* 126:15–17.

———. 2004. Make 'Em Cry. *The Chronicle of Higher Education.* 50(26): C1, C4. March 5.

Forum on CAC: Principles that Should Guide WAC/CAC Program Development in the Coming Decade. 2000. *academic.writing.* Available from wac.colostate.edu/aw/forums/winter2000 (Accessed March 1, 2003).

Foucault, Michel. 1979. *Discipline and Punish: The Birth of the Prison.* Translated by Alan Sheridan. New York: Vintage.

———. 1984. Panopticism. In *The Foucault Reader*, edited by Paul Rabinow, 206–13. New York: Pantheon Books.

Fyfe, Gordon, and John Law. 1988. *Picturing Power: Visual Depiction and Social Relations, Sociological Review Monograph 35.* London: Routledge.

George, Diana, ed. 1999. *Kitchen Cooks, Plate Twirlers, Troubadours: Writing Program Administrators Tell Their Stories.* Portsmouth, NH: Boynton/Cook

Giddens, Anthony. 1971. *Capitalism and Modern Social Theory: An Analysis of the Writings of Marx, Durkheim and Max Weber.* Cambridge, UK: Cambridge University Press.

Gillette, David. 1999. Pedagogy, Architecture, and the Virtual Classroom. *Technical Communication Quarterly* 8 (1): 21–36.

Giroux, Henry. 1983. *Theory and Resistance in Education.* South Hadley, Mass.: Bergin and Garvey.

———. 1988. *Schooling and the Struggle for Public Life: Critical Pedagogy in the Modern Age.* Minneapolis: University of Minnesota Press.

Gleason, Barbara. 2000. Evaluating Writing Programs in Real Time: The Politics of Remediation. *College Composition and Communication* 51: 560–85.

Goodburn, Amy and Carrie Shively Leverenz. 1998. Feminist Writing Program Administration: Resisting the Bureaucrat Within. In *Feminism and Composition Studies: In Other Words*, edited by Susan C. Jarrett and Lynn Worsham, 276–290. New York: The Modern Language Association.

Greg, Rhonda , and Nancy Thompson. 1996. Repositioning Remediation. *College Composition and Communication* 47: 62–84.

Groves, Melissa M., and Paula C. Zemel. 2000. Instructional Technology Adoption in Higher Education: An Action Research Case Study. *International Journal of Instructional Media* 27 (1): 57–65.

Gunner, Jeanne. 1994. Decentering the WPA. *WPA: Writing Program Administration* 18 (1–2): 8–15.

———. 2002. Collaborative Administration. In Brown and Enos 2002, 253–262.

———. 2002b. Ideology, Theory, and the Genre of Writing Programs. In Rose and Weiser 2002, 7–18.

Haas, Christina. 1989. How the Writing Medium Shapes the Writing Process: Effects of Word Processing on Planning. *Research in the Teaching of English* 23 (2): 181–207.

———. 1990. Composing in Technological Contexts: A Study of Note-Making. *Written Communication* 7 (4): 512–47.

Haas, Christina, and John R. Hayes. 1986. What Did I Just Say? Reading Problems in Writing with the Machine. *Research in the Teaching of English* 20 (1): 22–35.

Hairston, Maxine. 1982. The Winds of Change: Thomas Kuhn and the Revolution in the Teaching of Writing. *College Composition and Communication* 33: 76–88.

Hanson, F. Allen. 1993. *Testing Testing: The Social Consequences of the Examined Life.* Berkeley: University of California Press.

Haring-Smith, Tori, Nathaniel Hawkins, and Elizabeth Morrison. 1985. *A Guide to Writing Programs: Writing Centers, Peer Tutoring Programs, and Writing-Across-the-Curriculum.* Glenview, IL; London: Scott, Foresman and Company.

Harkin, Patricia and John Schilb, eds. 1991. *Contending with Words: Composition and Rhetoric in a Postmodern Age.* New York: Modern Language Association.

Harralson, David. 1992. We've Barely Started—and We've Already Done It Wrong: How Not to Start a Computer-Assisted Writing Classroom. *Computers and Composition* 9 (3): 71–77.

Harrington, Susanmarie, Steve Fox, and Tere Molinder-Hogue. 1998. Power, Partnership, and Negotiations: The Limits of Collaboration. *WPA: The Journal of the Council of Writing Program Administrators* 21 (2/3): 52–64.

Harrington, Susanmarie, Steve Fox, Anne Williams, and Wanda Worley. Living and Working in the New University: A Collage in Five Voices. In *Reimagining the Instructorate,* edited by Michael Murphy. Portsmouth, NH: Heinemann-Boynton/Cook, under submission.

Harris, Joseph. 2002. Behind Blue Eyes: A Response to Marc Bousquet. *JAC* 22 (4): 891–98.

Hartman, Karen, Christine M. Neuwirth, Sara Kiesler, Lee Sproull, Cynthia Cochran, Michael Palmquist, and David Zubrow. 1991. Patterns of Social Interaction and Learning to Write: Some Effects of Network Technologies. *Written Communication* 8 (1): 79–113.

Hassan, Ihab. 1985. The Culture of Postmodernism. *Theory, Culture & Society* 2 (3): 119–131.

———. 1987. *The Postmodern Turn: Essays in Postmodern Theory and Culture.* Columbus, OH: Ohio State University Press.

Haswell, Richard, and Susan McLeod. 1997. WAC Assessment and Internal Audiences: A Dialogue. In *Assessing Writing across the Curriculum: Diverse Approaches and Practices,* edited by Kathleen B. Yancey and Brian Huot, 217–36. Greenwich, CT: Ablex.

Hawisher, Gail E. 1986. Studies in Word Processing. *Computers and Composition* 4 (1): 6–31.

———. 1987. The Effects of Word Processing on the Revision Strategies of College Freshmen. *Research in the Teaching of English* 21 (2): 145–59.

———. 1988. Research Update: Writing and Word Processing. *Computers and Composition* 5 (2): 7–28.

———. 1989. Computers and Writing: Where's the Research? *English Journal* 78 (1): 89–91.

———. 1992. Electronic Meetings of the Minds: Research, Electronic Conferences, and Composition Studies. In Hawisher and LeBlanc 1992, 81–101.

Hawisher, Gail E., and Paul LeBlanc, eds. 1992. *Re-Imagining Computers and Composition: Teaching and Research in the Virtual Age.* Portsmouth, NH: Boynton/Cook.

Hawisher, Gail E., and Charles Moran. 1993. Electronic Mail and the Writing Instructor. *College English* 55 (6): 627–43.

Haynes, Cynthia, and Jan Rune Holmevik. 1998. *High Wired: On the Design, Use, and Theory of Educational MOOs.* Ann Arbor, MI: The University of Michigan Press.

Herling, Thomas J. 1994. Resistance to the Adoption of Computer Communication Technology by Communication Faculty. Presented at the 77th Annual Meeting of the Association for Education in Journalism and Mass Communication, Atlanta, GA.

Herrington, Anne, and Marcia Curtis. 2000. *Persons in Process: Four Stories of Writing and Personal Development in College.* Urbana, IL: National Council of Teachers of English.

Hesse, Doug. 2002. Understanding Larger Discourses in Higher Education: Practical Advice for WPAs. In Ward and Carpenter 2002, 299–314.

Hindman, Jane. 2000. Fostering Liberatory Teaching: A Proposal for Revising Instructional Assessment Practices. *WPA: Writing Program Administration* 23 (3):11–31.

Holt, Mara. 1999. On Coming to Voice. In George 1999, 26–43.

Holt, Mara, and Leon Anderson. 1998. The Way We Work Now. *Profession 98*: 131–42.

hooks, bell. 1995. Black Vernacular: Architecture as Cultural Practice. In *Art on My Mind: Visual Politics,* 145–51. New York: The New Press.

Howard, Rebecca. Email message to Duane Roen. June 29, 2002.

Huot, Brian. 2002. *(Re)Articulating Writing Assessment for Teaching and Learning.* Logan, UT: Utah State University Press.

Irmscher, William F. 1987. Finding a Comfortable Identity. *College Composition and Communication* 28: 81–87.

Janangelo, Joseph. 1993. To Serve, with Love: Liberation Theory and the Mystification of Teaching. In Kahaney, Perry, and Janangelo 1993, 131–50.

Johnson-Eilola, Johndan. 1993. Control and the Cyborg: Writing and Being Written in Hypertext. *Journal of Advanced Composition* 13 (2): 381–99.

———. 2002. Fucking in the Wreckage: After Postmodernism. *JAC* 22 (2): 433–438.

Jones, Robert, and Joseph J. Comprone. 1993. Where Do We Go Next in Writing Across the Curriculum? *College Composition and Communication* 44 (1): 59–68.

Jordan-Henley, Jennifer, and Barry M. Maid. 1995. Tutoring in Cyberspace: Student Impact and College/University Collaboration. *Computers and Composition* 12 (2): 211–18.

———. 1995. MOOving Along the Information Superhighway: Writing Centers in Cyberspace. *Writing Lab Newsletter* 19 (6): 1–6.

Joyce, Michael. 1992. New Teaching: Toward a Pedagogy for a New Cosmology. *Computers and Composition* 9 (2): 7–16.

Kahaney, Phyllis, Linda A. M. Perry, and Joseph Janangelo, eds. 1993. *Theoretical and Critical Perspectives on Teacher Change.* Norwood, N.J.: Ablex.

Kaplan, Nancy, and Stuart Moulthrop. 1990. Other Ways of Seeing. *Computers and Composition* 7 (3): 89–102.

Kaufer, David S., and Brian B. Butler. 1996. *Rhetoric and the Arts of Design.* Mahwah, NJ: Lawrence Erlbaum.

Kaufer, David S., and Christine M. Neuwirth. 1995. Supporting Online Team Editing: Using Technology to Shape Performance and to Monitor Individual and Group Action. *Computers and Composition* 12 (1): 113–24.

Keifer, Kate E. 1987. Revising on a Word Processor: What's Happened, What's Ahead. *ADE Bulletin* 87: 24–27.

Keifer, Kate E., Stephen Reid, and Charles R. Smith. 1989. Style-Analysis Programs: Teachers Using the Tools. In *Computers in English and the Language Arts: The Challenge of Teacher Education,* edited by Cynthia L Selfe, Dawn Rodriguez and William R. Oates, 213–25. Urbana, IL: National Council of Teachers of English.

Keifer, Kate E., and Charles R. Smith. 1983 . Textual Analysis with Computers: Tests of Bell Laboratories' Computer Software. *Research in the Teaching of English* 17 (3): 201–14.

———. 1984. Improving Students' Revising and Editing: The Writer's Workbench System. In Wresch 1984, 65–82.

Kent, Thomas. 1993. Language Philosophy, Writing, and Reading: A Conversation with Donald Davidson. *JAC* 13:1–20.

Kenyon, David. 2003. What People Just Don't Understand about Academic Fields. *Chronicle of Higher Education.* July 9. chronicle.com/weekly/v49/i44/44b00401.htm.

Kinkead, Joyce. 1987. Computer Conversations: E-Mail and Writing Instruction. *College Composition and Communication* 38 (3): 337–41.

———. 1988. The Electronic Writing Tutor. *Writing Lab Newsletter* 13 (4): 4–5.

Kramarae, Cheris, Muriel Schulz, and William M. O'Barr. 1984. Toward an Understanding of Language and Power. In *Language and Power*, edited by Cheris Kramarae, Muriel Schulz and William M. O'Barr, 9–22. Beverly Hills, CA: Sage Publications.

Kress, Gunther. 2000. Multimodality. In *Multiliteracies: Literacy Learning and the Design of Social Features*, edited by Bill Cope and Mary Kalantzis, 182–202. London: Routledge.

Langston, M. Diane. 1986. The Old Paradigm in Computer Aids to Invention: A Critical Review. *Rhetoric Society Quarterly* 16 (4): 261–84.

Latour, Bruno. 1993. *We Have Never Been Modern.* Translated by Catherine Porter. Cambridge, MA: Harvard University Press.

LeBlanc, Paul. 1988. How to Get the Words Just Right: A Reappraisal of Word Processing and Revision. *Computers and Composition* 5 (3): 29–44.

Lee, HeeKap. 2001. Teachers' Perceptions of Technology: Four Categories of Concerns. Presented at the 24th National Convention of the Association for Educational Communications and Technology, Atlanta, GA.

Lowe, Teresa J., and Brian Huot. 1997. Using KIRIS Writing Portfolios to Place Students in First-Year Composition Courses at the University of Louisville. *Kentucky English Bulletin* 46 (2): 46–64.

Mabrito, Mark. 1992. Real-Time Computer Network Collaboration: Case Studies of Business Writing Students. *Journal of Business and Technical Communication* 6 (3): 316–36.

Malenczyk, Rita. 2002. Administration as Emergence: Toward a Rhetorical Theory of Writing Program Administration. In Rose and Weiser 2002, 78–89.

McDaniel, Ellen. 1985. A Bibliography of Text-Analysis and Writing-Instruction Software. *Computers and Composition* 2 (3): 8–9.

McLeod, Susan H. 1989. Writing Across the Curriculum: The Second Stage and Beyond. *College Composition and Communication* 40 (3): 337–343.

———. 1991. Requesting a Consultant-Evaluation Visit. *WPA: Writing Program Administration* 14 (3): 73–77.

McLeod, Susan H., Eric Miraglia, Margot Soven, and Christopher Thaiss, eds. 2001. *WAC for the New Millennium.* Urbana, IL: National Council of Teachers of English.

Messick, Samuel. 1989. Meaning and Value in Test Validation: The Science and Ethics of Assessment. *Educational Researcher* 18 (2): 5–11.

Micciche, Laura. 2002. More Than a Feeling: Disappointment and WPA Work. *College English* 64 (4): 432–58.

Miller, Richard. 1999. Critique's the Easy Part: Choice and the Scale of Relative Oppression. In George 1999, 3–13.

Miller, Susan. 1991. *Textual Carnivals: The Politics of Composition.* Carbondale and Edwardsville, IL: Southern Illinois University Press.

Mirtz, Ruth M. and Roxanne M. Cullen. 2002. Beyond Postmodernism: Leadership Theories and Writing Program Administration. In Rose and Weiser 2002, 90–102.

Mirzoeff, Nicholas, ed. 1998. *The Visual Culture Reader.* London: Routledge.

Moran, Charles. 1995. Notes toward a Rhetoric of E-Mail. *Computers and Composition* 12 (1): 15–21.

Moss, Pamela A. 1992. Shifting Conceptions of Validity in Educational Measurement: Implications for Performative Assessment. *Review of Educational Research* 62: 229–58.

———. 1994. Can There Be Validity without Reliability? *Educational Researcher* 23 (2): 5–12.

Moulthrop, Stuart. 1989. In the Zones: Hypertext and the Politics of Interpretation. *Writing on the Edge* 1 (1): 18–27.

———. 1991. The Politics of Hypertext. In *Evolving Perspectives on Computers and Composition Studies: Questions for the 1990s*, edited by Gail E. Hawisher and Cynthia L Selfe, 253–71. Urbana, IL and Houghton, MI: National Council of Teachers of English and Computers and Composition.

Moulthrop, Stuart, and Nancy Kaplan. 1991. Something to Imagine: Literature, Composition, and Interactive Fiction. *Computers and Composition* 9 (1): 7–23.

Mumtaz, S. 2000. Factors Affecting Teachers' Use of Information and Communications Technology: A Review of the Literature. *Journal of Information Technology for Teacher Education* 9 (3): 319–41.

Myers-Breslin, Linda, ed. 1999. *Administrative Problem Solving for Writing Programs and Writing Centers.* Urbana, IL: National Council of Teachers of English.

Neuwirth, Christine M., Michael Palmquist, Cynthia Cochran, Terilyn Gillespie, Karen Hartman, and Thomas Hajduk. 1993. Why Write—Together—Concurrently on a Computer Network? In *Network-Based Classrooms: Promises and Realities*, edited by Bertram C. Bruce, Joy K. Peyton and Trent Batson, 181–209. New York: Cambridge University Press.

Noblitt, James S. 1997. Top-Down Meets Bottom-Up. *Educom Review* 32 (3): 38–43.

North, Stephen M. 1996. The Death of Paradigm Hope, the End of Paradigm Guilt, and the Future of (Research in) Composition. In Bloom, Daiker, and White 1996, 194–207.

Nussbaum, Martha. 1997. *Cultivating Humanity: A Classical Defense of Reform in Liberal Education.* Cambridge, Mass.: Harvard University Press.

O'Neill, Peggy. 2002. Unpacking Assumptions, Providing Context: A Response to Marc Bousquet. *JAC* 22 (4): 906–16.

Olson, Gary, and Joseph Moxley. 1989. Directing Freshman Composition and the Limits of Authority. *College Composition and Communication* 40 (1): 51–59.

Palmquist, Michael, Kate E. Keifer, James Hartvigsen, and Barbara Godlew. 1998. *Transitions: Teaching Writing in Computer-Supported and Traditional Classrooms.* Greenwich, CT: Ablex Publishing.

Peeples, Tim. 1999. "Seeing" the WPA with/through Postmodern Mapping. In Rose and Weiser 1999, 153–167.

Peirce, C. S. [1868] 1931–58. On a New List of Categories. *Collected Papers of Charles Sanders Peirce*, edited by Charles Hartshorne and Paul Weiss, 1:545–559. 6 Vols. Cambridge: Harvard University Press.

———. 1869. Grounds of Validity of the Laws of Logic: Further Consequences of Four Incapacities. *Journal of Speculative Philosophy* 2:193–208.

———. 1877. The Fixation of Belief. *Popular Science Monthly* 12:1–15.

———. 1878. How to Make Our Ideas Clear. *Popular Science Monthly* 12:286–302.

Persichitte, Kay A., Donald D. Tharp, and Edward P. Caffarella. 1999. Contingent Innovation-Decisions, Infrastructure, and Information Technologies. *Educational Technology & Society* 2 (1).

Peterson, Patricia Webb. 2001. The Debate About Online Learning: Key Issues for Writing Teachers. *Computers and Composition* 18 (4): 359–70.

Peyton, Joy K. 1989. Computer Networks for Real-Time Written Interaction in the Writing Classroom: An Annotated Bibliography. *Computers and Composition* 6 (3): 105–22.

Phelps, Louise Wetherbee. 2002. Turtles All the Way Down: Educating Academic Leaders. In Brown and Enos 2002, 3–39.

———. 2003. Administration as a Design Art. Presented at Annual Conference of Writing Program Administrators, at Grand Rapids, MI.

Popham, Susan, Michael Neal, Ellen Schendel, and Brian Huot. 2002. Breaking Hierarchies: Using Reflective Practice to Re-Construct the Role of the Writing Program Administrator. In Rose and Weiser 2002, 29–41.

Porter, James E. 1992. *Audience and Rhetoric: An Archaeological Composition of the Discourse Community*. Englewood Cliffs, NJ: Prentice Hall.

Porter, James E., Patricia Sullivan, Stuart Blythe, Jeffrey T. Grabill, and Libby Miles. 2000. Institutional Critique: A Rhetorical Methodology for Change. *College Composition and Communication* 51 (4): 610–42.

Reigeluth, Charles, and Robert Garfinkle, eds. 1994. *Systemic Change in Education*. Englewood Cliffs, NJ: Educational Technology Publications.

Rhodes, Keith. 2000. Marketing Composition for the 21st Century. *WPA: Writing Program Administration* 23(3):51–69.

Rickard, Wendy. 1999. Technology, Education, and the Changing Nature of Resistance: Observations from the Educom Medal Award Winners. *Educom Review* 34 (1): 42–45.

Rogers, Everett M. *Diffusion of Innovations*. 1995. 4th ed. New York: The Free Press.

Rogoff, Irit. 1998. Studying Visual Culture. In Mirzoeff 1998, 14–26.

Rose, Shirley K 1999. Preserving Our Histories of Institutional Change: Enabling Research in the Writing Program Archives. In Rose and Weiser 1999, 107–18.

Rose, Shirley K. and Irwin Weiser. 2002. The WPA as Researcher and Archivist. In Brown and Enos 2002, 275–90.

Rose, Shirley K, and Irwin Weiser, eds. 1999. *The Writing Program Administrator as Researcher*. Portsmouth, NH: Heinemann-Boynton/Cook.

———. 2002. *The Writing Program Administrator as Theorist: Making Knowledge Work*. Portsmouth, NH: Heinemann-Boynton/Cook.

Ross, Jeffrey. 2000. My Eng 102 Class Has Gone to Hec: Creating the Hybrid Electronic Course. Paper presented at the Central Arizona College Special Task Force for On-line Courses.

Royer, Daniel, and Roger Gilles. 1998. Directed Self-Placement: An Attitude of Orientation. *College Composition and Communication* 50 (1): 54–70.

Russell, David R. 1991. *Writing in the Academic Disciplines, 1870–1990: A Curricular History*. Carbondale and Edwardsville, IL: Southern Illinois University Press.

Schilb, John. 1994. Future Historio-graphies of Rhetoric and the Present Age of Anxiety. In Vitanza 1994, 128–38.

Schön, Donald. 1982. *The Reflective Practitioner: How Professionals Think in Action*. New York: Basic Books.

Schwartz, Helen J. 1982. Monsters and Mentors: Computer Applications for Humanistic Education. *College English* 44 (2): 141–52.

———. 1987. Planning and Running a Computer Lab for Writing: A Survival Manual. *ADE Bulletin* 86: 43–47.

Scott, Joan. 2001. Deconstructing Equality versus Difference: Or, the Uses of Poststructuralist Theory for Feminism. In *Theorizing Feminism: Parallel Trends in the Humanities and Social Sciences*, edited by Anne C. Herrmann and Abigail J. Stewart 2001, 254–70. Boulder, CO: Westview Press.

Selfe, Cynthia L. 1987a. Creating a Computer-Supported Writing Lab: Sharing Stories and Creating Vision. *Computers and Composition* 4 (2): 44–65.

———. 1987b. Creating a Computer Lab That Composition Teachers Can Live With. *Collegiate Microcomputer* 5 (2): 149–58.

———. 1989. *Creating a Computer-Supported Writing Facility: A Blueprint for Action*. Houghton, MI: Computers and Composition.

Shaughnessy, Mina P. 1977. *Errors and Expectations*. New York: Oxford University Press.

Shepard, Lorrie. 1993. Evaluating Test Validity. *Review of Research in Education* 19: 405–50.

Shoemake, Barbara. 1996. *Cyberspace Class: Rewards and Punishments.* Bloomington, IN: ERIC Clearinghouse on Reading, Education, and Communication.

Sim, Stuart, ed. 2001. *The Routledge Companion to Postmodernism.* London: Routledge.

Sirc, Geoff, and Thomas Reynolds. 1990. The Face of Collaboration in the Networked Writing Classroom. *Computers and Composition* 7 (3): 53–70.

Slatin, John M. 1988. Hypertext and the Teaching of Writing. In *Text, Context, and Hypertext: Writing with and for the Computer,* edited by Edward Barrett, 111–29. Cambridge, MA: MIT Press.

———. 1990. Reading Hypertext: Order and Coherence in a New Medium. *College English* 52 (8): 870–83.

Smelser, Lynne M. 2002. Making Connections in Our Classrooms: Online and Off. Presented at the Conference on College Composition and Communication, Chicago, IL.

Smith, Catherine F. 1991. Reconceiving Hypertext. In *Evolving Perspectives on Computers and Composition Studies: Questions for the 1990s,* edited by Gail E. Hawisher and Cynthia L Selfe, 224–52. Urbana, IL and Houghton, MI: National Council of Teachers of English and Computers and Composition.

Smith, Charles R., and Kate E. Keifer. 1982. Computer-Assisted Editing in Expository Writing. Presented at the 2nd Annual Role of Computer in Education Conference, Glenview, IL and Palatine, IL.

Smith, Steven P. 2002. Why Use Porfolios?: One Teacher's Response. In *Practice in Context: Situating the Work of Writing Teachers,* edited by Cindy Moore and Peggy O'Neill, 274–84. Urbana, IL: National Council of Teachers of English.

Smith, William L. 1993. Assessing the Reliability and Adequacy of Using Holistic Scoring of Essays as a College Composition Placement Technique. In *Validating Holistic Scoring for Writing Assessment: Theoretical and Empirical Foundations,* edited by Michael M. Williamson and Brian Huot, 142–205. Cresskill, NJ: Hampton.

Soliday, Mary. 1996. From the Margins to the Mainstream: Reconceiving Remediation. *College Composition and Communication* 47: 85–100.

Sorapure, Madeleine, Pamela Inglesby, and George Yatchisin. 1998. Web Literacy: Challenges and Opportunities for Research in a New Medium. *Computers and Composition* 15 (3): 409–24.

Spooner, Michael, and Kathleen Blake Yancey. 1996. Postings on a Genre of Email. *College Composition and Communication* 47 (2): 252–78.

Sternglass, Marilyn. 1997. *Time to Know Them: A Longitudinal Study of Writing and Learning at the College Level.* Mahwah, NJ: Lawrence Erlbaum.

Stocker, Bradford R. 1999. The Choice Not to Use Computers: A Case Study of Community College Faculty Who Do Not Use Computers in Teaching. Ph.D. Diss., Florida International University.

Strickland, Donna. 2001. Taking Dictation: The Emergence of Writing Programs and the Cultural Contradictions of Composition Teaching. *College English* 63 (4): 457–479.

Sturken, Marita. 1998. The Wall, the Screen, and the Image: The Vietnam Veterans Memorial. In Mirzoeff 1998, 163–78.

Sudol, Ronald A. 1985. Applied Word Processing: Notes on Authority, Responsibility, and Revision in a Workshop Model. *College Composition and Communication* 36 (3): 331–35.

Sullivan, Patricia. 1989. Human-Computer Interaction Perspectives on Word-Processing Issues. *Computers and Composition* 6 (3): 11–33.

Surry, Daniel W., and Susan M. Land. 2000. Strategies for Motivating Higher Education Faculty to Use Technology. *Innovations in Education and Training International* 37 (2): 145–53.

Susser, Bernard. 1998. The Mysterious Disappearance of Word Processing. *Computers and Composition* 15 (3): 347–71.

Szabo, Michael and Sonia A. Sobon. 2003. A Case Study of Instructional Reform Based on Innovation Diffusion Theory through Instructional Technology. *Canadian Journal of Learning and Technology* 29 (2): 59–78. www.cjlt.ca/content/vol29.2/cjlt29-2_art-3.html.

Tate, Gary, and Edward P. J. Corbett, eds. 1988. *The Writing Teacher's Sourcebook.* Second edition. New York: Oxford University Press.

Thompson, Sandye, Joel A. English, and Mick Doherty. 1998. The Impossible Dream: An InterMOO with Michael Joyce and Mark Bernstein. *Kairos* 3 (1).

Trimbur, John. 1996. Writing Instruction and the Politics of Professionalization. In Bloom, Daiker, and White 1996, 133–45.

Tufte, Edward R. 2003. *The Cognitive Style of Power Point.* Cheshire, CT: Graphics Press LLC.

Turkle, Sherry. 2004. How Computers Change the Way We Think. *The Chronicle of Higher Education*: 26–28. January 30.

Vaughan, Margaret E. 1993. Why Teachers Change: An Analysis of Consequences and Rules. In Kahaney, Perry, and Janangelo 1993, 113–27.

Villanueva, Victor, Jr. 1997. *Cross-Talk in Comp Theory: A Reader.* Urbana: National Council of Teachers of English.

Vitanza, Victor, ed. 1994. *Writing Histories of Rhetoric.* Carbondale and Edwardsville, IL: Southern Illinois University Press.

Walvoord, Barbara E. 1996. The Future of WAC. *College English* 58 (1): 58–79.

Ward, Irene, and William J. Carpenter, eds. 2002. *The Allyn and Bacon Sourcebook for Writing Program Administrators.* New York: Longman.

Webb, Patricia R. 1997. Narratives of Self in Networked Communications. *Computers and Composition* 14 (1): 73–90.

Weiser, Irwin and Shirley K Rose. 2002. Theorizing Writing Program Theorizing. In Rose and Weiser 2002, 183–195. Portsmouth, NH: Boynton/Cook.

Welch, Nancy. 1993. Resisting the Faith: Conversion, Resistance, and the Training of Teachers. *College English* 55: 387–401.

West, Robin. 1993. *Narrative, Authority, and the Law.* Ann Arbor: University of Michigan Press.

White, Edward M. 1995. The Rhetorical Problem of Program Evaluation and the WPA. In *Resitutating Writing: Constructing and Administering Writing Programs,* edited by Joseph Janangelo and Kristine Hansen, 132–150. Portsmouth, NH: Boynton/Cook.

———. 1998. Re: Politicians, Testing, and Academic Freedom. E-mail posting to WPA-L. 6 October.

———. 2002. Use It or Lose It: Power and the WPA. In Ward and Carpenter 2002, 106–13.

Williams, Raymond. 1973. *The Country and the City.* London: Chatto and Windus.

Wood, Denis. 1992. *The Power of Maps.* New York: The Guilford Press.

Wresch, William. 1982. Computers in English Class: Finally Beyond Grammar and Drills. *College English* 44 (5): 483–90.

———, ed. *The Computer in Composition Instruction: A Writer's Tool Kit.* Urbana, IL: National Council of Teachers of English.

Yagelski, Robert P., and Jeffrey T. Graybill. 1998. Computer-Mediated Communication in the Undergraduate Writing Classroom: A Study of the Relationship of Online Discourse and Classroom Discourse in Two Writing Classes. *Computers and Composition* 15 (1): 11–40.

Yancey, Kathleen Blake. 1998. *Reflection in the Writing Classroom.* Logan, UT: Utah State University Press.

Young, Art. 2003. Introduction: A Venture into the Counter-Intuitive. *The Journal of Language and Learning Across the Disciplines* 6 (2): 4–13.

———. 2003b. Writing Across and Against the Curriculum. *College Composition and Communication* 54 (3): 472–485.

Young, Art, Patricia Connor-Greene, Jerry Waldvogel, and Catherine Paul. 2003. Poetry Across the Curriculum: Four Disciplinary Perspectives. *The Journal of Language and Learning Across the Disciplines* 6 (2): 14–44.

Young, Iris Marion. 1990. *Deconstruction and the Possibility of Justice.* Princeton: Princeton University Press.

CONTRIBUTORS

SHARON JAMES MCGEE is Assistant Professor in the Department of English Language and Literature at Southern Illinois University Edwardsville. She helps direct the Expository Writing Program and also teaches in the graduate Teaching of Writing specialization.

CAROLYN HANDA, Professor of English and Director of the Writing Program at The University of Alabama, has been interested in visual and digital rhetoric for nearly a decade. She is the author of *Visual Rhetoric in a Digital World: A Critical Sourcebook* plus other studies of composition, technology, and pedagogy.

ANDREW BILLINGS, TEDDI FISHMAN, MORGAN GRESHAM, ANGIE JUSTICE, MICHAEL NEAL, BARBARA RAMIREZ, SUMMER SMITH TAYLOR, MELISSA TIDWELL POWELL, DONNA WINCHELL, KATHLEEN B. YANCEY, and ART YOUNG are all associated with Clemson University's R. Roy and Marnie Pearce Center for Professional Communication, which houses the University's communication-across-the-curriculum (CAC) program. These eleven members of the Pearce Team meet regularly to plan, administer, and assess the Center's new and continuing initiatives. Art Young founded Clemson's CAC program in 1989 and Kathleen B. Yancey has directed the Pearce Center since 2000. In 2006, she will join the English faculty at Florida State University.

MICHAEL J. CRIPPS is Assistant Professor of English at York College of The City University of New York, where he co-coordinates the WAC Program. His work on academic hypertext has appeared in *Computers & Composition Online* and *Enculturation.* He is currently studying graduate students who work in interdisciplinary writing programs.

CHRISTY DESMET is Associate Professor of English at the University of Georgia, where she directs the First-year Composition Program. She is co-founder of *Borrowers and Lenders: The Journal of Shakespeare and Appropriation* and one of the original developers of <emma>: The Electronic Markup and Management Application.

ANTHONY EDGINGTON is an Assistant Professor at the University of Toledo, where he also serves as Associate Director of the Composition Program. His research focuses on writing assessment, teacher response, and reflection. He has published articles in *Teaching English in the Two Year College* and the *Journal of Teaching Writing.*

JEANNE GUNNER is Associate Provost for Academic Programs and Professor of English and Comparative Literature at Chapman University. Her research interests include writing program ideology and history. With Donna Strickland, she is editing a volume on critical issues in WPA work.

SUSANMARIE HARRINGTON is Professor of English and Director of Writing at Indiana University Purdue University Indianapolis. Her research has addressed issues in writing assessment, technology, and program development. Most recently, with Keith Rhodes, Rita Malenczyk, and Ruth Fischer, she co-edited *The Outcomes Book: Consensus and Debate in the Wake of the WPA Outcomes Statement.*

DEBORAH H. HOLDSTEIN, the editor of *College Composition and Communication*, publishes widely in composition and rhetoric, film, and literary studies. An early adopter of technology, she has written extensively about technology and the humanities. At Governors State University for twenty years, Holdstein now chairs the English Department at Northern Illinois University.

BRIAN HUOT is Professor of English and Writing Program Coordinator at Kent State University. Currently the editor of the *Journal of Writing Assessment*, his work on the teaching and assessing of writing and the administration of writing programs has appeared in a monograph and in journals and anthologies.

FRED KEMP is an Associate Professor of Rhetoric at Texas Tech University. He has written and spoken extensively about computer-based instruction and administrative systems, and over the last twenty years has designed and programmed a number of network-based instructional-support implementations, including Texas Tech's first-year composition courseware, TOPIC.

RICHARD E. MILLER, Chair of the Rutgers English Department and Executive Director of the Plangere Writing Center, is the author of *As If Learning Mattered: Reforming Higher Education* and of *Writing at the End of the World.* He and Kurt Spellmeyer co-edit *The New Humanities Reader*, now in its second edition.

MIKE PALMQUIST is Professor of English and University Distinguished Teaching Scholar at Colorado State University. His scholarly interests include writing across the curriculum, the effects of computer and network technologies on writing instruction, and the use of hypertext/hypermedia in instructional settings.

KEITH RHODES served as a composition administrator at Northwest Missouri State University and at Missouri Western State University. His publications mostly interrogated the conventions and institutional status of first-year composition, culminating in co-editing *The Outcomes Book.* He has returned to his former career as a commercial trial lawyer.

MARCY TUCKER is an Assistant Professor of Writing at the University of Central Arkansas, where she currently teaches first-year writing and composition theory courses. Her scholarship focuses on issues of gender, class, and discourse.

KAREN WARE is currently ABD at the University of Louisville. Her research interests include visual rhetoric and writing instruction for at-risk students. Her administrative experience includes work as an Assistant Director of Composition at the University of Louisville and Writing Coordinator for the Governor's Scholars Program.

INDEX